The Nobel Prize in Literature

A Study of the Criteria behind the Choices

The Nobel Prize in Literature

A Study of the Criteria behind the Choices

KJELL ESPMARK

G.K. Hall & Co.

Boston, Massachusetts

Det litterära Nobelpriset: Principer och värderingar bakom besluten was first
published in Sweden in 1986 as part of a series celebrating the bicentenary of
the Swedish Academy.

The English translation, *The Nobel Prize in Literature,* was funded by the
Swedish Academy and was prepared by G.K. Hall & Co. on the basis of a
translation provided by Robin Fulton and Kjell Espmark.

First published 1991
by G.K. Hall & Co.
70 Lincoln Street
Boston, Massachusetts 02111

10 9 8 7 6 5 4 3 2 1

Library of Congress Cataloging-in-Publication Data

Espmark, Kjell, 1930–
    [Litterära Nobelpriset. English]
    The nobel prize in literature : a study of the criteria behind the
choices / Kjell Espmark.
      p. cm.
    Translation of : Det litterära Nobelpriset.
    Includes bibliographical references and index.
    ISBN 0-8161-1842-6
    1. Literature – Competitions – History. 2. Nobel prizes – History.
3. Svenska akademien – History. I. Title.
PN171.P75L5413   1991
807.9 – dc20   90-45089
                                                   CIP

The paper used in this publication meets the minimum requirements of
American National Standard for Information Sciences – Permanence of
Paper for Printed Library Materials. ANSI Z39.48-1984.   ∞™
MANUFACTURED IN THE UNITED STATES OF AMERICA

CONTENTS

INTRODUCTION

When the poet Carl Gustav Leopold gave his speech accepting membership in the newly established Swedish Academy in 1786, he addressed himself to the "legislative arbiters of Sweden's letters" who would perhaps one day become the arbiters of European letters. A little over a century later, in December 1896, the academy learned of a commission whose challenge would be of exactly that order.

In 1895 Alfred Nobel, a Swedish industrialist, bequeathed the greater part of his estate for the establishment of the Nobel Prizes. He specified that the interest from the invested capital should be annually distributed as prizes to those who in the course of the previous year had been of the greatest benefit to mankind; one-fifth of the total amount was intended for "the person who shall have produced in the field of literature the most outstanding work of an idealistic tendency," that person to be determined "by the Academy in Stockholm." It was Nobel's "express wish that in awarding the prizes no consideration whatever shall be given to the nationality of the candidates, but that the most worthy shall receive the prize, whether he be a Scandinavian or not."

Two of the members spoke strongly against accepting Alfred Nobel's legacy. One feared that the obligation would detract from the academy's proper concerns and turn it into "a cosmopolitan tribunal of literature." The other shared these misgivings and added that the pressure of international opinion "would affect the nerves of the academy much more powerfully than the criticism of its distribution of 6,000 crowns among Swedish authors." The two sceptics could have added that the Swedish Academy, which excluded the leading Swedish writers and the most distinguished literary scholars of the day, simply lacked the competence to manage the sensitive undertaking. The academy was in the doldrums at that point and in fact for many years to come would be ill equipped for the proposed task. This did not prevent its permanent secretary, Carl David af Wirsén, from making strenuous efforts to ensure that the academy accepted it. Refusal, he argued, would mean the loss of the legacy as far as literary rewards were concerned, "and thus the great figures of Continental literature would be deprived of the chance of enjoying the exceptional recognition and the exceptional privileges that Nobel intended as rewards for prolonged and illustrious literary activity." He conjured up the weighty reproach that would be directed at the academy, then and in the future, for "its failure, on the grounds of its own convenience, to acquire an influential position in world literature." To the objection that the task would be foreign to the purposes of the academy, he answered that it would be novel and more far-reaching, indeed, but scarcely foreign: "Without proper knowledge of the best in the literature of other countries, the academy can and may not proceed to judge the literature of its own country, and the prizes in question are intended for the very best authors, as a rule, that is, for men with whose work the academy ought in any case to be familiar."[1] This effective argument, which won a qualified majority for Wirsén's point of view, showed not only "an honorable breadth of mind" and "sympathy for Nobel's intentions" (Anders Österling). For Wirsén and those who shared his views the task of rewarding the best literature of an "idealistic" nature offered, as we shall see, not only unsuspected opportunities in the field of the politics of culture, but also (as he wrote in a letter of 1897) "the enormous power and prestige that the Nobel will bequeat to the Eighteen [members of the academy]."

Wirsén's mixed motives would eventually give way to the less hazardous intentions of later administrators of the fund. But he expressed the feelings shared by all the members of the successive Nobel prize committees in a poem he recited at the first Nobel banquet on 10 December 1901; it began:

> Unwished the task, unsought for, bearing now
> so weightily on Swedish backs; it seems
> we tremble taking obligation's vow:
> henceforth a world will deem how Sweden deems.

The hesitation he expressed was overcome by the chance to celebrate not only the results of medical research ("Hygiea's discoveries") but also "the healing that the art of poetry brings," thus emphasizing the idealistic notion of the function of literature that was so evident in the early history of the prize.

That sense of responsibility among those who choose the recipients of the Nobel Prizes was first articulated by Wirsén but would be expressed many times through the years to come; in 1914 historian Harald Hjärne, who was chairman of the Nobel Committee for a decade, would call it the "weighty task." This book is a study of the attempts made to live up to that responsibility and make decisions that on the one hand try to realize Nobel's intentions and on the other hand express the views and sensibilities of the eighteen members themselves.

Published discussion of the Nobel Prize in Literature is already fairly extensive, quite apart from the abundant press coverage that has created its own genre with its special conventions and recurring rhetorical stances. The best-informed accounts are Anders Österling's "The Literary Prize" from the anthology *Nobel: The Man and His Prizes* (1972), and Lars Gyllensten's compact presentation, *The Nobel Prize in Literature* (1978). In the unpublished last part of Henrik Schück's history of the academy, there is a detailed study – no fewer than 132 pages – of the first decade of the Nobel Prize in Literature, up to the death of Wirsén. The annals of the separate prizes up to 1970 can be read in the introductions by Gunnar Ahlström and Kjell Strömberg – based on inside information whose extent is at times surprising – to the volumes in the series *Nobel Prize Library*. Shorter accounts can also be found, of course, in the biographies of authors who have received the prize. Some reference works provide encyclopedia-style coverage – that is, each prize winner is given a few pages of biography and description.

This book does not focus on the works of individual authors and the fate of those works in the annals of the Nobel Foundation, still less on *la chronique scandaleuse* that surrounds the different prizes. Instead, I have studied the patterns of evaluation behind the Nobel Prize in Literature. By examining, above all, the verdicts of the Nobel Committee we can discern certain guiding principles, both ideological and aesthetic, behind many of the choices – and the rejections – that posterity has come to question. At the same time we can see how each period had its own characteristics. Criticism of the Swedish Academy's choice of prize winners over the past nine decades has generally treated that period as a whole. But a closer examination allows us to differentiate the separate phases in the history of the literature prize with a view toward the norms applied in making value judgments. If the picture is not altogether flattering for the arbiters of the first four decades, the Österling epoch, from the late 1940s onward, should appear in a much better light.

The history of the Nobel Prize in Literature offers a unique opportunity for study of literary reception: almost nine decades of critical activity – with its evaluative criteria being thoroughly and constantly revised – by highly intelligent, sensitive, and widely read individuals involved in a continuing discussion of the literature of their age, with the object of selecting its most outstanding work. The special nature of the situation is heightened by the creative tension between the critical norms of the individual judges and the more or less obligatory demand by Nobel that the works recognized by the prizes be "of an idealistic tendency." Indeed, the history of the literature prize is in some ways a series of attempts to interpret an imprecisely worded will.

Certain important aspects of its provisions are clarified in the statutes of the Nobel Foundation, royally decreed in 1900 on the basis of proposals from the committees of the awarding bodies. As well as specifying that "the Academy in Stockholm" is to be taken to mean the Swedish Academy, paragraph 2 defines "literature" as "not only belles-lettres, but also other writings which, by virtue of their form and style, possess literary value," and specifies that works appearing "during the preceding year" can include "older works only if their significance has not become apparent until recently." Paragraph 4 carries an essential rider: "A prize may be equally divided between two works each of which may be considered to merit a prize."[2] The possibility is raised of making a posthumous award "if . . . a prize-winner dies before he has received the prize." Paragraph 5 stipulates that the amount of the prize "shall be reserved until the following year" if none of the works under consideration is found "to be of such outstanding importance as is manifestly intended by the will." There are also rules for frequency–prize giving at least once in every five-year period–financial management, and so on, which are of limited interest to an investigation of the criteria behind the choice of recipients.[3] The statutes specify that the Nobel Committee shall have between three and five members, whose task will be "to give their opinion in the matter of the award of prizes."[4] A candidate must be nominated in writing by a person competent to make such nominations before 1 February of each year. A special regulation gives the right of nomination to members of the Swedish Academy and of other academies, institutions, and societies that are similar to it in constitution and purpose, and to teachers of aesthetics, literature, and history at universities. An emendation of 1949 specifies the category of teachers: "professors of literature and of philology at universities and university colleges." The right to nominate is at the same time extended to previous prize winners and to "presidents of those societies of authors that are representative of the literary production in their respective countries." The statutes also provide for the Nobel Institute, which has a substantial library containing mainly modern literature, a librarian and staff, "and, if necessary, officials and assistants with a literary training."[5] In practice this last category refers to the specialists who are to be more or less regularly connected with the Swedish Academy's Nobel Institute.

A crucial point in the will–that prize-winning works of literature would have an "idealistic tendency"–appeared in a new light a couple of decades ago through the discovery of a letter received by the Danish literary critic Georg Brandes. Brandes had asked Nobel's close friend Gustaf Mittag-Leffler about the meaning of the term and received the answer that Nobel "was an Anarchist: by idealistic he meant that which adopts a polemical or critical attitude to Religion, Royalty, Marriage, Social Order generally."[6] Such an intention would stand the Nobel Prize practice of decades on its head. A number of prizes would seem to have been quite mistakenly awarded, and those to Sinclair Lewis, Halldór Laxness, and the French writers who engaged themselves in the Dreyfus affair more to the point;[7] more recently, revolutionaries like Pablo Neruda and Gabriel García Márquez were certainly well qualified on this score. Above all, though, many candidates would appear to have been rejected on false premises. This information, however, comes to us at third hand, with the slant of a man critical of the Swedish Academy; it must be taken with a good deal of reserve. I would share Knut Ahnlund's judgment: "This interpretation needs on the whole to be modified because far too much evidence tells a different story from the one suggested by Brandes. But no doubt there is *something* in it." There is no denying that Wirsén's age was loyal to the throne, the altar, and the current social order – attributes hard to reconcile with the outlook of a testator who, in the words of Österling, adopted the "utopian idealism" and the "religiously colored spirit of revolt" of Shelley, and who was also a radical anticleric.[8] Knut Ahnlund concluded: "When he spoke, therefore, of an 'idealistic tendency' he undoubtedly gave more scope to rebellious and independent dispositions than his interpreters understood – to the extent that they wanted to understand the matter."[9]

The reports delivered to the academy by the Nobel Committee – never used for such a purpose until now – are my primary source.[10] From as early as 1901, the chairman of the committee – who has usually also been the academy's permanent secretary – has articulated the working group's opinions of the nominees.[11] (Since the 1970s these group reports have been replaced by each committee member's individual assessment, an arrangement that better reflects the attitudes and criteria and to a greater extent transfers the actual decision to the academy itself.) This source material has been supplemented by documents supporting the nominations, comments from specialists outside the immediate circle (their services started to be requested as early as 1902), correspondence between academy members, memoirs, and the voluminous amount of material to be found in newspapers. Finally, I would add personal experience of the academy's work with the Nobel Prize from 1982 onwards.

It should be said at once that giving a complete picture of all of these interconnections would be an enormous undertaking. What is really needed is an analytical consideration of the general criteria and aesthetic assumptions of each of the academy members, as manifested by their interplay within the circle and by their roles in a process as diffuse as it is comprehensive. Such a field of study could be tackled seriously only when research into the relevant individuals has been completed. The aim of this book must be significantly more modest: it sketches the larger context, with a special focus on prevailing tendencies and on identifying the different periods in the history of the prize. The bulk of the picture remains to be filled in. I hope that the patterns I make visible here will nonetheless increase understanding of a renowned but often misinterpreted area of Swedish culture.

The limited extent of this study is reflected in the fact that the documentation is basically confined to the principal source, the reports of the Nobel Committee, while a tighter rein has been held on the use of the extensive correspondence between the academy members and of the enormous press coverage. As source material, the committee's reports need careful handling. First, its opinions cannot automatically be taken as those of the Swedish Academy as a whole. On the contrary, we shall encounter several instances when the academy in pleno sided differently from its committee. Secondly, the summing-up process conducted by the committee chairman cannot with certainty be taken as an accurate reflection of the views of the whole committee. Wirsén wrote what he considered the opinion of the group; as members began asking to see what he had expressed on their behalf, he gradually began to include dissenting views in his reports. Harald Hjärne continued that practice, and later chairmen have shown greater sensitivity still in their reporting of shifting opinions. Nevertheless, the chairman has to try to do justice to the general feeling; if he does not, attention is aroused and members may make individual statements that can thus indicate how unrepresentative the report may be. Similarly, the committee's opinion cannot diverge from the opinion of the academy without the nomination being rejected. A good measure of how well the reports succeed in accommodating the views of the academy members can be found in the rich exchange of their letters, which, to a surprising degree, confirm the conclusions found in the committee reports. Read with reasonable common sense – and compared with other sources – the reports of the Nobel Committee can thus contribute greatly to our picture of the criteria that from time to time have governed the academy's choice of prize winners.

One troublesome circumstance is the strict secrecy that allows me to study all of the material but not to quote nominations, reports, letters, and discussions from any time in the past fifty years. To be able to see everything yet to wear a muzzle is for a researcher a predicament as fascinating as it is trying. One immediate advantage is that nothing need be said against one's better judgment. That is, one is not forced to rely on guesswork, suppositions, and uncertain hearsay. Moreover, one can keep an eye on the evidence and pick out from generally available material precisely those lines of approach, those combinations of facts and arguments, that are pertinent, avoiding the many false clues. As for quotation, it often happens that an important comment in a report – a passage whose significance is evident only in that context – also appears in a speech addressed to the prize winner in question, a newspaper review, or an interview. In many cases vital information can also be found in correspondence that is housed in public libraries, where it is not classified as confidential; in such correspondence I found documents in which several permanent secretaries spoke quite unreservedly about the criteria followed by themselves and by the academy in the recent past. At other times the odd piece of confidential information that the trusted Kjell Strömberg has leaked in his introductions to the Nobel volumes can prove to be an important fragment in the overall puzzle.

This book also includes certain statements of principle that in themselves are confidential, but that in fact are well known from other sources; in such cases I have thought it important to secure a more correct wording than can normally be obtained from, say, a newspaper interview. Without violating the regulations about confidentiality, then, one can say surprisingly much about matters that have been stamped "confidential." But the ability to give a comprehensive account is, in the final analysis, limited; as far as the last half-century is concerned, my account must be primarily concerned with tendencies and general patterns.

Finally, the fact that this book has been commissioned by the Swedish Academy does not mean that I have had to work to any directive. On the contrary, I have been free to reconstruct whatever connections I have been able to distinguish. This book is not, I may add, any kind of apologia for the way in which the Nobel Committee and the Swedish Academy carry out their work. If on various occasions I try to answer criticism of the committee and the academy, I do so with regard to historical context, for in too many cases such criticism is unhistorical and sometimes indeed quite anachronistic. In writing this study, I have regarded myself not as a counsel for the defense but as a literary historian.

CHAPTER 1

"A Lofty and Sound Idealism"

A suitable caption for the first decade of the history of the Nobel Prize in Literature can be found in Carl David af Wirsén's reading of the phrase "of an idealistic tendency" in Nobel's will: the prize winner's works ought to be of "a lofty and sound idealism," characterized "by a true nobility not simply of presentation but of conception and of philosophy of life." This formula, embodied in the 1905 report of the Nobel Committee, is an important indication that the prize was understood to be not just a *literary* reward.[1] Esaias Tegnér, Jr., developed the idea in a separate report in the same year. Prize-winning works should exhibit more than "literary talents" such as "narrative gifts." He described the "qualifications to which the regulations of the Nobel Prize refer" as "such properties as lead humanity forward in an idealistic direction, widen the horizons of humanity beyond the average reach, and enable humanity to be better and nobler than before."[2] During this early period the objective in considering a candidate – such as Paul Bourget – was to determine whether he was worthy on account of idealism "both in content and in style" (1909).

The balancing of "idealistic" spirit and "literary talents" was evident in the heated discussion in 1908, when the choice was between Selma Lagerlöf and Algernon Swinburne (the dilemma being eventually resolved by giving the prize to Rudolph Eucken, whom few wanted). Following Tegnér's explication of 1905, a committee member criticized "the unfortunately widespread misconception that the Nobel Prize concerns *purely literary* merits." Wirsén retorted that the Nobel Prize "is after all a literary prize, so that literary merits must then be taken into account"; some sort of prize for virtue "was never Nobel's intention." But in saying so Wirsén in no way denied his previous emphasis on idealism "of conception and of philosophy of life." For the sake of his argument, he attributed what seemed "offensive and objectionable" in his candidate Swinburne to an earlier lapsed phase and stressed those "literary merits" that he felt gave Swinburne a lead over Lagerlöf. Tegnér, as a supporter of the latter, admitted that Swinburne, "in spite of regrettable deviations," could claim the advantage if the Nobel award were "a *purely literary prize,*" but that he had not made so great a contribution "to the good of humankind" as Lagerlöf: "To my mind no one ought to entertain a doubt that Lagerlöf's books, with their pure, loving spirit that, in combination with a blossoming poetry and a brimming wealth of imagination, so strongly characterizes them, should offer assistance and advancement to humanity in the striving toward the ideal, on a scale far beyond that of the work of the now proposed British poet."

Comparing the idealism of the message with the idealism of the form was a recurrent dilemma. In the particular case of Lagerlöf, Wirsén suffered from certain idiosyncracies that led him to stress literary merit while the opposing group's high admiration led them to emphasize idealistic aspiration. It is abundantly clear, however, that during this period the Nobel Prize in Literature was not primarily a literary prize; the literary quality of a work was weighed against its contribution to humanity's struggle "toward the ideal."

When the Nobel Committee and the Swedish Academy sought candidates of "the noblest artistic and ethical idealism" (words of Antonio Fogazzaro in 1910), the will was being interpreted in the light of the conservative idealistic currents of the nineteenth century, as represented by the leading Swedish philosopher Christopher Jacob Boström, and also in the light of the earlier idealist aesthetics of the nineteenth century, as embodied in F. T. Vischer's monumental compendium *Aesthetik* (1846-57). Wirsén's lifework is in fact framed by his homage to Boström, at whose funeral in 1866 the young poet presented a eulogy that concluded: "And the youth of the North pledge at your grave today bravely to strive, to strive for light and justice, for the everlasting truth sanctified by you throughout your life of holy ardor." Even in his last year, in 1912, Wirsén wrote that Boström "remains the most outstanding and most independent of Swedish thinkers." In the same year in which he read his tribute at the philosopher's grave he defended a thesis partly dedicated to Vischer, his other great authority–in his own words, "the greatest aesthetician of our days."

The "striving" that Wirsén spoke of in his eulogy was something to which the dedicated disciple would devote himself, both as leading critic in *Posttidningen* and *Vårt Land* and as permanent secretary to the Swedish Academy for almost three decades. In both positions he was the implacable opponent of the new directions in Swedish and Scandinavian literature, first of the authors of the modern breakthrough in the 1880s–Georg Brandes, Henrik Ibsen, August Strindberg, and others–then of the romantically oriented authors of the 1890s, most notably, Selma Lagerlöf and Verner von Heidenstam. In a strange way Wirsén came to fight against both wings of the literary civil war that ensued between authors of the 1880s and 1890s.

The Swedish Academy became a vital bastion in this struggle. Wirsén was not only the leading proponent of conservatism but he conducted an election policy that broadened support for his ideas. In a letter of 1889 he declared his ambition to "maintain the Swedish Academy as a bulwark of literary moderation and conservatism in the midst of the strange upheaval now taking place." The academy that at the turn of the century accepted the commission to distribute the Nobel Prize in Literature was in fundamental aspects a reflection of an election policy based on this provincial strategy. Boströmism had a strong foothold within the academy, though it is still difficult to gauge how extensive this influence was. At all events, it is clear that Boströmian conservative idealism had an overwhelming influence, ensured by Wirsén through his election policy. In 1901 only one poet of significance, Carl Snoilsky, was a member of the academy. Eventually, two less awkward 1890s authors were allowed in, Erik Axel Karlfeldt in 1904 and Per Hallström in 1908. Otherwise, throughout the Wirsén epoch, modern Swedish literature in its entirety, from Strindberg to Selma Lagerlöf, was kept outside, including the founder of modern Swedish literary scholarship, as well as the sworn enemy of idealistic aesthetics, Henrik Schück. Schück was formally elected to the academy in 1906, but Wirsén managed to block his election by securing King Oscar's veto.

This does not mean that idealism was an unproblematic issue within the Nobel Committee itself. In a letter of 28 January 1903 to a member of the academy, Wirsén complained that there was opposition on the committee to his "attempts to emphasize that through our choices we must attach great importance to the ideal, the pure, and the elevated in the views and productions of the author." His fellow committee members at that time no doubt shared this idealistic conviction as such; but a practice that had recently rejected Tolstoy and Ibsen and was turning against Selma Lagerlöf was not likely to win a consensus even among those who shared common principles.

In spite of everything, however, Wirsén succeeded in creating an academy that could align all the forces of conservative idealism and classically inspired aesthetics behind Nobel's demand for literature of an idealistic tendency. In his account of the matter, Schück was naturally aware of these guiding principles, but in writing of all the manipulation surrounding individual candidates he tended to accentuate the conspirator in Wirsén more than the militant idealist. The element of intrigue in Wirsén's activity is certainly not to be denied – in fact, it is often striking – but what is more important is how this conservative idealist and his like-minded colleagues in the academy widened their struggle against the 1880s worldview and turn-of-the-century aesthetics from Sweden and Scandinavia to an international arena. Wirsén's early conservative criticism of Brandes and Ibsen was authorized by the words of the testator and substantiated by the six-figure prizes. The Nobel Prize as an institution became a weapon whose range extended beyond Scandinavian borders. An irony of history allowed an academy purposefully created to act as a bulwark in a provincial struggle against the ideas and language of a new age to assume the responsibility of administering *the* great international literary prize.

What does the phrase "a lofty and sound idealism" imply? Of primary importance was an idealistic view of the nature of reality, particularly the Christian conception of reality. In the report from 1911 we can read: "Time and space are forms of finite life, but true reality is of a spiritual kind and elevated above space and time. God is a spirit. In His spiritual world everything has its ultimate ground. No empiricism, no realism can reach the foundations of existence." Theistic conceptions of the nature of God were favored: God is both elevated above the world and empowered to intervene in its destinies. The American philosopher Borden Browne is referred to with approval in 1906: "In his view of life he is a theist and turns against both abstract deism, according to which the world is like a clock wound up once and for all and now going by itself, and against naturalism. He refutes the claim of misdirected science to be able to explain the world and relegates natural science to its proper task, the investigation of nature."[3]

A critical or negative attitude in a candidate toward Christianity was a disqualification. Giosuè Carducci's immortal songs would have made him worthy of the Nobel Prize, but his provocative "detestation of positive religion" did not impress the committee in 1902. This did not prove to be an insuperable obstacle to his winning the 1906 prize, but by that time the heathen element in his work was excused on the grounds that the ardent patriot had confused Christianity with the often secularized Catholic Church that stood in the way of Italian liberation.[4]

An agnostic outlook could also cause difficulties. That is clear from the 1902 evaluation of Herbert Spencer, who has unjustly been called a materialist – which alone would have disqualified him – and who was "in the field of science the foremost spokesman for agnosticism. ... The deepest needs of the human spirit are satisfied less by his agnostic philosophy than by that of the great idealists, whether they are pantheists like Hegel or theists like Boström." Here in full view is the real measure. The academy's conception of the nature of reality had its philosophical basis in Kant's idealism, and its view of God naturally had its primary support in the Swedish church, but within that framework Boström had special significance. Spencer's work was found unsatisfactory "to adherents of the philosophy of personality" – the master of which was Boström – according to which the ideas constitute a hierarchy of "personalities" within the divine ; it was a system elevated beyond the phenomenal world's illusions of time and space, movement and change – the whole physical universe, which is an optical illusion.

Both the philosophically idealistic and the Christian perspective attribute to humanity a personal role in which striving toward higher things and moral responsibility are important features. The work of the "religious doubter" Sully Prudhomme – dubbed thus in 1905 – is qualified in exactly this way: "He is a searching and watchful spirit who finds no rest in the temporal and who, when knowledge of the immaterial appears to him, to his sorrow, as impossible, nonetheless in the practical-ethical field, like Kant, in the undeniable and imperative fact of duty, finds a witness to humanity's supersensual mission" (1901). Underlying such an observation is not only Kant's imperative but Boström's idea that humans can choose either lower and sensual motives or higher and rational motives and can advance through ascending degrees of consciousness in the spiritual hierarchy. From this perspective, every deterministic or fatalistic viewpoint is rejected. The freedom of the will is fundamental.

An important aspect of this idealistic philosophy is its view of society. The sanctity of the state and the sovereignty of the crown are above all criticism. In several Nobel reports, an author's "glowing love of his native land" is approvingly noted. In evaluating Carducci in 1902, it was remarked that his republican sympathies, "fortunately, have not prevented him supporting the Italian monarchy, even if from time to time he makes a sally at its leading statesmen." Striking, too, is the observation that while the protagonist of Henryk Sienkiewicz's *The Deluge* at first "allowed himself to be lured into fighting against his rightful king," later, under the influence of love, he "redeems ... his lost reputation through a series of brilliant feats in the service of the legitimate social order" (1905). In the formula "fulfillment of duties under all circumstances" we can see what constituted the "nobility" that distinguished José Echegaray (1904).

A key position in the social sphere was given to the family, the home, and the virtuous life connected with them. Bjørnstjerne Bjørnson's "Laboremus" was credited with glorifying the "rightness of the ethical life in contrast to the natural power of heedless passion, and in 'Paa Storhove' (At Storhove) he paid dramatic homage to the tutelary powers of the home"; this "poet of hearth and home ... always fought against the instincts' claims of mastery over humankind."[5]

This view of society derived not only from a general conservative idealism but more specifically from Boström's views, which gained their strongest influence outside the circle of academic philosophy in this particular respect. The state, in his conception, has the nature of a person, represented by a monarch whose sovereignty comes from above and is superior to all private considerations and all parties. Individuals are merely the organs of the state, and representation of the people is no more than a way of expressing the views of the populace; decision-making powers belong to the absolute king within the framework of those laws that are binding on him. In retrospect, the Boströmian viewpoint looks like an ideal bureaucratic philosophy, one also conservative in the sense that its "extreme idealism was designed to veil social reality and thereby create a defense against radical and reformist tendencies."[6] If the Swedish Academy cut itself off from the more modern wing of Swedish literature and literary scholarship, it entered instead into an unspoken pact, under the aegis of Boström, with the world of King Oscar's civil service. Its application of Nobel's "idealist" requirement would express this widespread and deeply conservative idealism.

Corresponding to this idealistic philosophy of life and view of society, then, was the "true nobility" in literary presentation valued by the academy. The basic theoretical approach to literature was grounded in German idealistic aesthetics – from Goethe and Kant to Schelling and Hegel – as codified in Vischer's *Aesthetik*. In the Nobel Committee reports the great masters are assumed to include the ancient poets such as Homer and Aeschylus, as well as Dante, Shakespeare, and Goethe, the Swede Tegnér, and the Finnish-Swede Johan Ludvig Runeberg.

With a starting point in Hegel, Vischer defined the beautiful as the harmonious union of spiritual and sensual, the plastic form-giving in which the idea appears in totally visible guise – the art of Greek antiquity and of Goethe. Vischer resorted to the term "ideal realism"; the same label has been applied to the poetry of Runeberg.[7] Recently, the epoch between romanticism and realism has been dubbed "ideal realism," and attempts have been made to see how much it affected our own century's views of literature. The aesthetics of the first Nobel Committee provide an example of such an influence.

Wirsénian aesthetics aimed at a literature that united an idealistic conception of reality with sensual "concretion." The mark of a "great master" was that he "renders human life distinctly" (1903), but this realistic aspiration was only one element. The other was a view – shared with Goethe – of nature as a synonym for "truth" and "spirit"; a key term is "true to nature," and Runeberg's *Tales of Ensign Stål* was held up as a model of "characterization true to nature" (1909).[8]

Idealistic realism thus favored the plastic rendition of a nature that in the final analysis was conceived as spirit; on the one hand it abhorred abstraction and symbolizing, and on the other hand it was remote from "every naturalistic, photographic depiction of low, ugly reality," as we find the matter expressed in the highly appreciative evaluation of Paul Heyse in 1910. If we are reminded of neoclassical marble, that is no coincidence; in 1905 the committee excused the chilliness of one of Sienkiewicz's works by relating it to the "coolness of plasticity," which we "so often come across, for example, in Goethe."[9]

An important aspect of this alloy of idea and plastic reality was objectivity. Before all others it was Goethe who incarnated the ideal of "pure," "objective" poetry. Heyse, described as the greatest artist since Goethe, was found to be "nontendentious in Goethe's manner"; less appealing were his longer stories, which "to a greater or lesser extent deal with problems" (1910). It was the Goethean ideal that was thus set against that of Brandes and the authors of the modern breakthrough, with their desire to take up problems and instigate debate. Such a combination of objective configuration and idealistic aspiration was sanctioned by Vischer, who explicitly warned against sinking into tendentiousness.[10]

Ideal realism had, then, pronounced classical features. The classical respect for the genres was preserved, in reaction to the impure mixtures of romanticism. With a Goethean reluctance to accept such blurring of borderlines, Wirsén found that a blending of saga and reality "deprives the representation of objectivity" (1908).[11]

The elevated aesthetic values were moderation, balance, and harmony – terms of approbation and respect stemming ultimately from Winckelmann's conception of the art of ancient Greece as "noble simplicity and calm greatness." The figurehead was, once again, Goethe, but Vischer's aesthetics raised these virtues to a golden mean. In such a spirit the committee reports spoke of "that nobility, that calm moderation that one loves to see in a work of art" (1903) and sought "harmonious and finely balanced composition" (1901). As something of an English counterpart to the standard represented by Goethe we find Alfred, Lord Tennyson, whose "steadfastly maintained moderation and inner balance," as well as his "quiet grace," were noted as exemplary in the reports.

When the Nobel Committee defined a great master as one who "renders human life distinctly," it added to the demand for formal plasticity a further requirement: clarity. "Obscure" and "unclear" were recurring and strong terms of disapproval: "The poet ought to be forthright about what is on his heart if he wishes to be understood and not simply to behave as a hierophant in a small circle of the initiated" (1903).[12] Along with this classical and Tegnérian demand, the committee praised simplicity. Characteristic was a judgment of a dramatic art that "unites a strong imaginative power with a high, unaffected simplicity."[13] The last desirable quality, according to this classical type of aesthetics, was concentration. Thus, Gaspar Núñez de Arce "lacks concentration and at times is much too circumstantial" (1902). In this criterion we can glimpse both the Goethe ideal – "mastery through restraint" – and Vischer's laws of inner and outer dimension.[14]

Given this background, several of the decisions reached in the first period of the Nobel Prize in Literature appear less enigmatic. On the whole, the prize-winning authors correspond well to the above description of idealism with only minor deviations, which can be defended or excused. In 1901 discussion of the twenty-five names proposed reduced the field to two competitors, the French candidates Sully Prudhomme and Frédéric Mistral. In Prudhomme's "plastic" poetry the confiding spirit was "noble, melancholy, thoughtful," certainly not believing but at least searching, conscious of "humanity's supersensual condition"; this poetry, "whose painful spiritual probing inspires the reader to a melancholy that is deep but not tearful," at the same time revealed its author – through "the noble, exquisite, endlessly refined charm of his diction" and his "artistic mastery" – to be "one of the most outstanding poets of our age." In contrast to such an "inward-turned creative temperament" was the epic poet of Provence, Mistral, whose "sunny imagination is outward-turned," a writer who distinguished himself "by his unaffected closeness to the people and by the dew-fresh and sparkling genuineness of his inspiration," properties manifested in episodes of, "in a word, Homeric graphicness"; if he did not "penetrate to the wellsprings of the deepest stirrings of the soul," nonetheless, he was richly endowed with "the prime poetic quality . . . *genius.*" With the respective merits of the two candidates balanced "so evenly," it was found proper "to take into account the large measure of support expressed for Prudhomme by members of the French Academy, an institution that has served as the model for the Swedish Academy."[15] Awarding the author with such "a weighty recommendation" should "at least within a large part of the educated world be greeted with justified assent." This institutionally based confidence turned out to be greatly mistaken. The immediate reaction on Swedish soil was the famous address to Tolstoy, signed by forty-two leading authors, artists, and critics. Tolstoy, however, had not been proposed in 1901; in those first years the academy members made sparing use of their right to nominate candidates, and the Nobel Committee members abstained altogether as a matter of principle. The issue came to a head the next year, in 1902, when Tolstoy was one of thirty-four candidates. How could the leading candidate be rejected?

The system of evaluative norms outlined earlier in this chapter gives us the answer. The committee report stated that Tolstoy occupied "a high place" in world literature. The author of *War and Peace* was a "master in the art of epic description," even if he showed "features of a fatalistic view," overvalued chance, and undervalued "the significance of personal initiative." A "higher artistic worth" was assigned to *Anna Karenina,* a work permeated by "a deep ethical conception." On the basis of "such immortal creations" it would be "comparatively easy" to give the prize to "this great Russian author." Yet alongside these masterpieces (to which *Resurrection,* with its "moral indignation," was added) there was also *The Power of Darkness,* with its "ghastly naturalistic descriptions," and *The Kreutzer Sonata,* with its "negative asceticism." Tolstoy was discredited above all by his animosity toward culture, his "one-sidedness," and his plea for "a natural life deprived of its connection with higher culture"; particularly disqualifying was his criticism of the state and the Bible: "He has rejected the state's right to punish, indeed he has rejected the state itself and preached a theoretical anarchy; he has, although quite unversed in biblical criticism, capriciously reedited the New Testament in a half-rationalistic, half-mystic spirit; he has in all seriousness denied both individuals and nations the right of self-defense."

An author who had recently spoken of "the worthlessness, indeed the harm, of monetary awards" was not going to have thrust upon him an award that would have required the explanation that it was made "exclusively out of admiration for his purely literary works, while his religious and social-political writings appeared to be immature and misleading."[16] In his 4 February 1902 reply to the address of homage from the forty-two, Tolstoy had said he was "very glad" not to be given the Nobel Prize, being thus freed from the trouble of deciding how to deal with money, which "can bring nothing but evil."[17] That comment thus played a part in the Nobel Committee's judgment of Tolstoy's work, but it is obvious that the objections on matters of principle were decisive, particularly the principle of "a lofty and sound idealism":

> In spite of all the admiration for many of Tolstoy's creations, it may well be asked to what extent idealism can be sound in an author who in his otherwise magnificent *War and Peace* attributes to blind chance such a decisive role in the great events of world history, who in *The Kreutzer Sonata* frowns upon intimate relations between spouses, and who in countless of his works denies not only the church, but the state, even the right of property (which he himself, inconsistently, enjoys), and contests the right of individuals and peoples to self-defense (1905).[18]

The 1902 prize went instead to "the greatest living master of the art of historical writing," Theodor Mommsen, for his monumental *A History of Rome.* The "concretion" of the descriptions and the sharpness and clarity of his characterization made the learned historian "one of the greatest writers of our time." A writer of history who reproved Polybius for "having overlooked the moral powers in mankind" and for "having entertained an altogether too mechanistic worldview" could easily pass the test of "idealistic" worth.

On the basis of "the sound idealism that Nobel's will appears to call for" (1905), both naturalism and the social-critical writing of the modern breakthrough were rejected. The treatment of the very first year's prime candidate, Émile Zola, was the occasion for establishing this position. While acknowledging his "gigantic industry and a colossal gift for descriptions of reality with powerful mass-effects and lurid coloring," the committee found that "the spiritless, and often grossly cynical in his naturalism makes it difficult to recommend him for a prize that, according to the words of the testator, ought to be given to what is most distinguished by 'an idealistic tendency.' "[19] In this dismissive conclusion we see a combination of an idealistic worldview and a classical type of aesthetics, with a demand for moderation and harmony in the rendition of human life.

In 1903 a similar combination proved fatal to the chances of the foremost figure in the new literature of Scandinavia, Georg Brandes. He had "had a great influence on his age," but that influence had "not always been of a beneficent sort. ...He is often very unjust in that he disapproves of and denigrates whatever fails to agree with his own negatively sceptical, totally atheistic, and, in ethical-sexual questions, highly adventurous and lax outlook." With this disqualifying view of life and ethics, Brandes combined a manner of writing that clashed with the Olympian ideal. He could be considered on account of his "stylistic merits," but here, too, there were deficiencies: in addition to "an excessive striving for effects," the report mentioned his "insinuating sneering tone," which often "deprives ... his presentation of the calm nobility, the pure objectivity, that one would prefer to find both in works of literary history and in works of history in general."

Henrik Ibsen was passed over for similar reasons. While "all could unite in admiration of the author of *Brand, The Pretenders, Emperor and Galilean,* and other distinguished works," strong doubts had been expressed about Ibsen's "later production, whose negative and enigmatic features have repelled even those who would have willingly given the world-famous author a substantial recognition" (1902). The brief conclusion was allusive: Wirsén's audience knew his many judgments of Ibsen's later works, most recently in his volume *Critical Essays* (1901). The accusation of "negative features," which resembles the reproach against Brandes, arose, of course, from Ibsen's social criticism in plays such as *The Pillars of Society, Ghosts,* and *An Enemy of the People;* the objection to his "enigmatic features" refers to works such as *The Wild Duck, Rosmersholm,* and *The Lady from the Sea.* The secretary was "no friend of Ibsen's symbolism." In general terms, he was voicing the demand for "clarity"; more specifically, he was expressing the distrust of symbolism implicit in "ideal realism."[20]

In 1903, after the idea of a shared prize was dismissed, the winner was Bjørnstjerne Bjørnson, whose writing "placed itself at the service of pure and elevated ideas" and "united poetic and ethical soundness." On that account Bjørnson fit the norms of the Nobel Committee in exactly the manner that Ibsen did not.

A third major writer of the modern breakthrough in Scandinavia – August Strindberg – was never even formally nominated for a Nobel Prize, a reflection of conservatism among the proposers as well.[21]

Among the most representative evaluations of those first years is that of Gerhart Hauptmann, a transitional figure belonging to two epochs. The 1902 report, which repeated the dismissive judgment of Zola, widened the perspective to include Hauptmann's earlier work, which it characterized as "crass naturalism." In *Vor Sonnenaufgang* (Before Sunrise), Hauptmann had "descended into the most repulsive descriptions of drunkenness and vice, even on the verge of incest," and his *Einsame Menschen* (Lonely Lives) (strongly influenced by Ibsen's *Rosmersholm*) had an air of "appalling individualism." A political accent could be heard in *Die Weber* (The Weavers); at the premiere in Berlin, the praise was led by the prominent Social Democrats Bebel, Liebknecht, and Singer, and "part of the audience encouraged the actors on the stage to plunder the factory owner's residence." Such remarks reflect the importance of the role of the existing legal order in the "idealistic" set of norms.

The treatment of Hauptmann also shows, however, how naturalism's antipode, symbolism, was excluded by the idealistic criteria. In *Hanneles Himmelfahrt* (The Assumption of Hannele) there were, as in *Die versunkene Glocke* (The Sunken Bell), "deeply poetic details," but over the whole work "there rests something melodramatically unreal, there floats a hospital smell mixed with a damp mysticism. ... The symbolism is carried to the point of affectation." The demand for "a lofty and sound idealism" excluded on the one hand "cynical" or "crass" naturalism, and on the other, "hospital-smelling" symbolism.

This attitude toward symbolism partly explains the ungracious treatment of Maurice Maeterlinck in 1903. But the influence on Maeterlinck of "agnosticism's master, Herbert Spencer," was particularly discrediting. Even if Maeterlinck's views seemed to be changing, "agnosticism is still there in him, and even if he now gives more emphasis to man's capacity to determine his life according to moral precepts, he nonetheless sees it as altogether extraordinary that his actions can have any bearing on his future life, insofar as such a thing exists, or on the development of the world, which, unaffected by man's more or less moral behavior, goes its own mechanical way." In 1909 Wirsén, in his increasing sympathy for Maeterlinck, found him "distinctly superior to [Selma Lagerlöf] as regards the subtly spiritual," but there was still the complaint that Maeterlinck "has not elevated his views to a definitely admitted theism," which "would have had a beneficent influence on his dramatic art." Wirsén believed, though, that Maeterlinck "is not basically a denier," he "just finds that which is the ground for existence to be veiled" – adding, "he is perhaps regretful on that account." Maeterlinck also grasped "the significance of duty and right ... even if his agnosticism prevents him from granting to duty and right their fulfilling guarantee in a moral world order."

Another shift in the committee's opinion of Maeterlinck occurred on the question of free will. In 1903 the committee felt that "Maeterlinck's fatalism makes all his characters into the marionettes of dark powers." In 1909 *La Sagesse et la destinée* (Wisdom and Destiny) was judged to be a work in which fatalism is "defeated" and man's fate is located "in his own heart and in his own way of exercising his will." These changes of opinion were preparing the way for a prize.

The committee had not only philosophical and religious doubts but aesthetic ones. Maeterlinck's "generally symbolic" poetic works certainly revealed "a wealth of intimation" in their suggestive presentations "of various more occult aspects of spiritual life" and captivated the reader through "the secretive power of an *atmosphere*"; but they did not fulfill the fundamental requirement of clarity. The poetry in *Serres Chaudes* (Hothouses) was "very obscure," and the drama showed "the same lack of clarity." So much for 1903. The report of 1909, showing a deeper response to works like *L'Intruse* (The Intruder) and *Aglavaine et Sélysette,* found the latter to be "one of the finest jewels of world literature"; in the description of the lovers, drawn to each other "not by evil desire but by a powerful, heavenly, greatly spiritualized sympathy," struggling to prevent the suffering of a weaker soul, we can detect a whiff of Wirsén's own secret biography. Maeterlinck's "honest searching for the truth" and "his genius as a literary author" succeeded at last in overcoming the reservations of those who found "his worldview as a whole not quite such as would completely satisfy us" and who "entertain no special love of symbolism in art." This 1909 evaluation provided in its essentials the justification of the 1911 prize.

The prizes for the years 1904-1906 went to candidates who by and large matched the criteria well. In Frédéric Mistral the committee discerned "in abundance" those qualities that Alfred Nobel required; here was an author who "never aimed at anything low, who is distinguished by a sound and flourishingly rich artistic idealism," and who "devoted his life to one idea, to the elevation and ennoblement of the spiritual interests, the language, and the literature of his native Provence." The work of the 1904 cowinner, the Spanish playwright José Echegaray, at times could be reproached for "a certain arbitrariness, a certain predilection for the shocking and the ennervating," as well as for "occasional deficiencies in motivation," but was nonetheless "distinguished by a lofty idealism." Unlike other contemporary dramatists with their often one-sided individualism, he celebrated "obedience to ethical laws, even if compliance with them should be at the cost of the individual's wordly happiness" (1902). In the 1905 winner, Henryk Sienkiewicz, the committee found that "high nobility" stipulated by the testator. The author of *Quo Vadis?* treated "an elevated theme ... in an elevated manner." The requirements are also fulfilled by his "objectivity," apparent partly in his "simultaneously powerful and warm-hearted worldview," free of "disturbing tendencies," partly in the wealth of "plastic characterization." An interesting aspect of this choice is that it claimed to make good a certain neglect of Slavonic literature – Sienkiewicz "enjoys general admiration" not only "at the side of Tolstoy, but he is in the process of displacing [Tolstoy]." In the 1906 winner, Giosuè Carducci, there was difficulty over his "paganism" and republican sympathies, but excuses were found: Carducci's attacks were not against Christianity as such, and his "antimonarchical temper [has] softened with the years." While "his songs, from an aesthetic point of view, are to be rated unusually highly," he could also be credited with "an idealistically inclined nature" in that he "is perpetually inspired by patriotic ardor and love of freedom and has never sacrificed his beliefs for gain and has never in his poetry fallen a victim to low sensualism."

The choice of Rudyard Kipling in 1907 fit in well with the above pattern; it also provides a fuller picture of the interplay of the various criteria. From the point of view of Wirsénian norms, Kipling was, quite simply, the almost perfect candidate; paradoxically, he is also one of the few "great, canonic names" on the Nobel list, according to a recent backbiter (George Steiner) – in fact the only one as far as this first epoch is concerned.[22] How can this be possible? Let us look first at how Kipling incarnated the "idealism in conception and art" that was expressly required. His view of life was "colored by the Old Testament or perhaps, rather, a blunt, puritanical fear of God"; his ethics were idealistic "through the sense of duty fired by religious conviction"; and he was the "flag-bearer of law-abiding discipline," the singer of "industriousness and obedience." At the same time there was in Kipling "an idealism of imaginative power and feeling," evident in, among other things, the fact that he created "not merely exact copies of nature, but visions," and understood how, "immediately, with the first words, to reveal the essential in character and temperament" – in contrast to naturalism with its photographic reproduction and circumstantial documentation of reality – while simultaneously he was "devoted to concretion" and despised "empty abstractions" – in contrast to symbolism.[23] Compared to Swinburne, Kipling had one limitation: he lacked Swinburne's "refined breeding and polished beautiful style, but then he is also free of Swinburne's paganlike thirst for pleasure and his admittedly charming yet morbid languishing." None of the early prize winners met so well as Kipling the requirement of "a lofty and sound idealism."

But how can such criteria – already antiquated by the beginning of the century and in our eyes highly prejudiced – favor a writer whom posterity finds to be a master of lasting worth? The answer, of course, must be that in addition to the "idealism" of Kipling's moral and artistic views his work also has more universal qualities. As early as 1903 the committee reports referred to Kipling's inexhaustible "inventive genius," and the 1907 report found in *The Jungle Book* "a primitive, almost myth-making strength of imagination," a power of visionary observation that made the landscape pictures "seem like sudden apparitions" and the figures reveal their inner nature immediately. In such turns of phrase the reports tried to describe those qualities that have also appealed to more recent readers. In the event, these qualities, admirable in themselves, united with features that made possible a prize honoring an "idealistic tendency."

In Kipling, England's "greatest contemporary narrative gifts" were rewarded. But Wirsén wanted, the very next year, to also reward England's foremost poet, Swinburne, "one of the greatest of our age." His haste was tactical: a worthy candidate to set up against Selma Lagerlöf had to be found; the sublime Antonio Fogazzaro could not gather a majority. This consideration contributed in no small degree to the increasingly sympathetic evaluation of Swinburne, who on a first examination in 1903 had been unquestioningly deemed "an immortal bard," thanks to "the power of his inspiration" and "the melting euphony of his formally perfect writing," but had been disqualified by "lack of nobility," evident in "his impassioned and excessive atheism," his inclination "to surrender himself to the dark power of unbridled sensuality," and the absence of "the measured nobleness" that had aroused the committee's admiration for Tennyson. One found "something of learned alexandrianism, of sumptuous decadence in Swinburne's luxurious poetry. . . . Sound it most certainly is not" (1905).

By 1908, however, Swinburne had acquired three of the Nobel Committee's votes; the other two were to go to Lagerlöf. Wirsén himself had reevaluated Swinburne, giving him high marks for a series of works. The choral songs in *Atalanta in Calydon,* for example, were found to be perhaps the most beautiful "since the days of Goethe and Schiller," and the trilogy on Mary Stuart was called "one of the most significant dramatic works in the whole of literature." In Swinburne's first collection, *Poems and Ballads* (1866), the erotic element was at times "much too daring and unrefined," even if the form revealed "great beauties" and individual poems had "an altogether captivating charm." The censured poems were, however, to be regarded as the productions of a crisis period, influenced by Baudelaire's unhealthily perverse genius: "Swinburne underwent an inner crisis of a dangerous kind, during which his poetry acquired something abnormal in its dark passion, its obscurity, its strange blend of learned overripeness and voluptuousness. His desire for freedom became negative and shied away from all restraints; his distaste for all sorts of hypocrisy turned into a distaste for all positive religion." Swinburne's aggressive attacks on "religious objects" were, on closer inspection, excused as expressions of the poet's "justified dissatisfaction with ultramontanism, the one-sided adherence to medieval cult forms, and all manner of ecclesiastical persecution mania." Swinburne had also modified "in the course of his continuing development the provocative tone he had adopted." The result was apparent in his third collection, *Poems and Ballads* (1889): "The former intransigent republican now celebrates legitimate monarchy and . . . the singer whose lyre was previously tuned to pleasure now most beautifully lauds the innocence of childhood and makes the strings reverberate to the heart's purity."

This transformation of the decadent atheist into the sublime bard inspired, as may be expected, certain reservations in the committee members pledged to Lagerlöf. Tegnér found support in the Englishman's latest drama, *The Duke of Gandia,* for his criticism of "how the old Swinburne ... still displays the same penchant for the disagreeable, the same pleasure in reveling in general ugliness, that we remember and recognize from certain poems of the author's turbulent youth." Both Tegnér and a colleague found Swinburne's work incompatible with the demand for literature that would be to "the good of mankind"; the colleague also worried about the reaction to an inconsistency: "One would return repeatedly to the question of why–with such a conception of the 'ideal'–authors like Tolstoy and Ibsen had not been rewarded."

Wirsén's sympathy for Swinburne had, of course, a tactical motivation. But his further study had also led him naturally to a more subtle understanding of the English poet. And we can add that his attitude toward Swinburne probably owed much to a personal ambivalence, described by one scholar as follows: "The critic who sternly condemned, for instance, the 'immorality' of Zola and Strindberg was attracted by the sophisticated sensualism he found in the 'gardens of Eden' of Almquist and then in decadent literature generally. Wirsén felt the lure of the 'demonic,' an inclination that was nonetheless nearly always balanced by warnings and condemnations attributable to that fear of sexuality that can be detected in him at an early stage."[24]

The vigorous promotion of Swinburne over Lagerlöf resulted in a stalemate; the pale Jena philosopher Rudolf Eucken emerged as the compromise selection for 1908. The report had characterized him as "an original but hardly an epoch-making thinker," "pleasant and noble in his diction," but without "the beauty of genius" of a Plato, a Kant, or a Schelling. The committee relegated him to future consideration. When the academy finally settled on Eucken after all, Wirsén could not subscribe to the choice and demonstrated his disapproval by abstaining from the task of giving the address to the winner.

Yet the chief character is not Eucken but Lagerlöf, whom Wirsén for the last time managed to block, in the face of steadily growing opposition. From our point of view the most interesting aspects of the case are the patterns of evaluation with which Lagerlöf's writing came into conflict–and those that enabled her finally to achieve the prize. On the publication of *The Story of Gösta Berling,* Wirsén had already adopted the position of an adversary and he stuck to that position. To a certain extent his prestige was involved in his stubborn resistance. Yet Lagerlöf's writing was in fact in conflict with the aesthetic position Wirsén had adopted as his own, and we can see his response as a question of critical consistency.

Without denying her "ethical purity" and the advance in "the noble artistry of the style," the Wirsénian report of 1904 on Lagerlöf contained an important reservation: "But there are those who cannot wholly reconcile themselves to the mannerism of *The Story of Gösta Berling* or to the mode of presentation in *The Miracles of Antichrist* or to the author's inclination, even when she is describing reality, to let it merge with saga and legend; there are certainly many poetic beauties in her most recent collection of stories, *Christ Legends,* but even in this case one or another reader has been offended by the arbitrary and bizarre elements."

These strictures were repeated in the reports of the following years, in 1907 with an added complaint about "the capricious mixing of saga and reality" to be found in the Nils Holgersson stories. In 1908 Wirsén clarified his objections in an interesting manner. He viewed *The Story of Gösta Berling* as "unnatural in very many of its depictions" and *The Miracles of Antichrist* as altogether lacking in "simple natural truth." Lagerlöf was in these works in conflict with the classical type of idealism whereby the concept of "nature" had the meaning fixed in the period around 1800. When Wirsén found in this author "something exaggerated and artificial," he was explicitly falling back on the "poets of antiquity," as well as on Tegnér and Runeberg. But perhaps more serious was another crime against this aesthetic view, more specifically, Lagerlöf's failure to observe the separation of genres: "Reality and saga are sometimes mixed in her writing in a manner that deprives her presentation of objectivity." The Nils Holgersson stories contributed to this criticism. They were criticized not only on account of "mistakes"–which had been pointed out by specialists–that "destroy the illusion" but also because "the elements of saga do not give a sagalike impression, and the elements of reality do not give a realistic impression, but both types are stirred together in a confused manner that allows neither to prevail." For this blend–exactly what makes Lagerlöf relevant once more, in the age of magical realism–she was condemned from the standpoint of an aestheticism with roots in German neoclassicism.

The arguments of Wirsén's opponents, however, at last prevailed. Tegnér eloquently developed his idea that with every page she had written Lagerlöf "served the good, the ideal, the human." Another committee member drew attention to "her uncommon ability to conjure visions" and added a national consideration: "It could well be time for the world to be reminded that Nobel's fatherland also has a literature."

The Wirsén epoch contains two further riddles with regard to Anglo-Saxon writers.[25] Why were Thomas Hardy and Henry James pushed aside? That George Meredith was rejected–as early as 1902–had to do with the demand for "nature" and "measure." His novels were undoubtedly original, but "often artificial and febrile." In England the author had already been blamed for his taste for "strong and unusual effects. . . . To non-English readers his creations appear mostly to be exaggerated or to carry a taste of affectation." In the same year W. B. Yeats was turned down. The committee noted his "particular and remarkable poetic individuality," but his manner of presentation was nonetheless found to be "often obscure"; we recognize the ever-present distaste for symbolic poetry. Even less surprising is the dismissive attitude towards George Bernard Shaw in 1911. He was critiqued in detail and with a degree of appreciation – even if *Mrs. Warren's Profession* appeared "downright disturbing because of its subject matter." As a dramatist "not particularly strong in invention, but reasonably so in sentiment and not so seldom in characterization," Shaw was often "vivacious," but "also very frequently unreasonable." The conclusion was that "in his strength he is much too brutal, not nearly artistic enough to be recommended for the Nobel Prize."

The principle behind the judgment meted out to Hardy in 1910 is more interesting. His works, it was said, "are likely to attract particular attention on account of the solid merits of the style and the unusual power of the landscape descriptions." On the other hand, exception was taken to "the lack of character in his heroines, who seem to lack all religious and ethical firmness." The committee also noted his sometimes tiring degree of detail and a "liking for sensational, disturbing, even upsetting effects," in conflict with his "calm and well-judged presentation . . . the nobly shaped and clear prose," which was Hardy's forte. What in the end disqualified him, though, was his bitter determinism and his "strange aversion to God, who in his conception lacks any sense of justice or mercy and allows chance its way with the children of men." The report concurred with the words of the admirer Burton: "Hardy's deterministically colored works are basically unaesthetic for they do not provide that soothing recreation that beautiful art ought to offer the spirit, and one loses interest in creatures who are ruled by a blind caprice. Rebelliousness against the ruler of all is, besides, if one considers the matter, not just impiety, but folly." What makes the committee reject Hardy – in spite of admiration for his "unprecedented merits, especially in the depiction of landscape" – was the fact that he had a view of the scope of the will and the government of the universe that was at odds with what the committee regarded as compatible with an "idealistic tendency." There was also the idea of art's "soothing" function; Hardy could never earn the sympathy of those "who seek in literature for something comforting and liberating."

The epilogue to this series of attempts to bring German idealistic philosophy and aesthetics to bear on the literature of the early twentieth century is the sentence passed on Henry James in 1911, Wirsén's last year as secretary. James was regarded by many as "the greatest among American novelists and story writers in our time." The committee admitted that he had "a good, often fine style, and his technique is often splendid," even if his writings were for the most part "conversation and situation novels." There were objections, however, on principle. One was a demand for "motivation,"[26] which was "fundamentally weak" in *The Portrait of a Lady* "because one never understands how it can be possible for the heroine,

Isabel Archer, endowed with all perfections, to be so imperceptive as to reject the excellent Lord Warburton and give her hand to such an egoistic dilettante as Mr. Osmond." A related objection was that *The Wings of the Dove* was built on "an at once improbable and odious subject." The ultimate criticism, however, was that James "too often lacks ... concentration." Thus, in *The Portrait of a Lady,* "the meticulous analyses of thought and feeling, drawn out in the minutest detail," are found "tiring." In general the author "spins out quite excessively the depiction of small matters that do not have much bearing on the action. ... Broad and circumstantial treatment may be allowed to an author with the genius of a Walter Scott; in Henry James, for all his elegance, it has a wearying effect."

Summing up this first period of the Nobel Prize in Literature, Henrik Schück assessed the impact of the prize on *literature.* His judgment was severe: "It would no doubt have been wiser if the academy had abstained from this task, which as far as literature is concerned is more or less worthless." In his "lust for power" Wirsén apparently hoped "to direct European literature into those channels that he considered the proper ones." But on that point his expectations were frustrated: "Literary development went its own way quite regardless of the Nobel Prizes." Otherwise, Wirsén was, even in the eyes of the strongly critical Schück, "in many essentials ... fully up to the task. ... In his capacity for work, his interests, his reading, he was superior to all his colleagues in the academy, and his taste, too – when not misled by his strong antipathies and sympathies – was undeniably that of the true poet. But the prizes he distributed made neither himself nor the academy popular, for *de gustibus semper disputatum est.*"[27]

With his generous words on "the true poet's" taste, Schück sidestepped the central problem of the prize policy in Wirsén's epoch. It was not until 1920, in an individual memo attached to that year's committee report, that he could maintain that the academy "had interpreted the word *idealistic* much too narrowly" and in a manner that would have excluded "masses of the great works of world literature." Here, of course, is the crucial point. The meager results of this early period are to be explained by the fact that according to Wirsén's literary strategy, Nobel's will was to be interpreted in the light of idealistic philosophy, particularly in its Boströmian version, and in the light of the idealistic aesthetics codified by Vischer in the mid-nineteenth century. It has been said of Wirsén that he "represented a tendency that had already outlived itself by the time he espoused it. ... He was the Don Quixote of Swedish romantic idealism."[28] A historical coincidence allowed Wirsén's anachronistic campaign to be conducted in the field of international literature.

CHAPTER 2

Literary Neutralism

The next period of the Nobel Prize in Literature began with a careful reorientation. After awarding the mildly seraphic writers Paul Heyse and Maurice Maeterlinck, the choice in 1912 was Gerhart Hauptmann – in spite of his past associations with both naturalism and symbolism – and in 1913 the European orientation was abandoned with the selection of the Indian writer Rabindranath Tagore.

Behind these tentative new moves we can see a younger element at work in the academy, as early as 1912. As noted, Hauptmann was rejected in 1903. Numbered in the majority on the committee who placed him first in 1912 was Erik Axel Karlfeldt, who, elected in 1904, had not been a party to the 1903 discussion of Hauptmann. Karlfeldt became permanent secretary of the academy in 1912, in which capacity, and thanks to his popularity, he "rescued" the academy, according to Schück, after the decline of the Wirsén period.[1] It is interesting to see the transformation of the negative labels attached to Hauptmann's work – "crass naturalism" and "hospital-smelling" symbolism. In 1912 his drama ranged from the "markedly realistic" to "Traumdichtung," from "an extremely remarkable drama" that enthralled "with a peculiar power" (*Die Weber*) to writing "filled with the finest poetry," whose like is difficult to find in world literature (*Hanneles Himmelfahrt*).

In the 1913 choice the signs of thaw were even clearer – though not in the report itself, with its plea for the French literary scholar Émile Faguet, valued above all as a master of "a moralist genre" with roots in Montaigne, Pascal, and La Rochefoucauld. The argument proceeded in the spirit of the Wirsén period, that is, by setting up Faguet against his predecessors, the "champions of negativism" Hippolyte Taine and Ernest Renan. Faguet admittedly "started out from positivism" but narrowed it to "an intention to hold strictly to induction from the given reality." On the other hand, he did not, like Taine, attribute "to origin and environment some fatalistically determining power" but regarded personality "preferably from the viewpoint of moral responsibility." In accordance with a process we have already observed, "le

Sainte-Beuve de notre époque" was qualified for a prize on the basis of his "idealistic tendency": "It has increasingly become evident that his conception of reality does not limit itself to the purely tangible occurrences, but, as befits a thinker more familiar than the majority of influential positivists with the views of Plato and Kant, it includes the innate capacity of the human spirit to maintain its moral consistency and persistence. His psychological . . . writings have thereby gained a higher dimension, which has carried him over to a firm and complete view of life whose content is idealistic." This evaluation of Faguet illustrates how representative Wirsén had been; the evaluations he voiced can be found again in the mouths of others.

Rabindranath Tagore was discussed in the context of his newly published *Gitanjali;* the author's role as translator was said to make the English version "equivalent to an original work." The sympathetic evaluation of Tagore reveals a discreet stress on aspects that were compatible with the criteria developed in the previous decade. Tagore's religion was designated "a kind of aesthetic theism. . . . His belief is not of the pantheistic and in reality abstract sort that is usually taken to be characteristic of India's higher culture." And his mystical outlook could be fitted into the Nobel mold: the poet "appears as if listening to the voices of nature in a warm faith in elevated ideals of secret origin." The committee, however, went no further than expressing "its interest in the future development of this remarkable Indian poet." The document was signed on behalf of the committee by the historian Harald Hjärne, whose chairmanship was to last for almost a decade.

Signs of a new sensibility, however, are to be seen not in the Nobel Committee report but in an individual memo from one who was involved in the Nobel deliberations of the academy for the first time, and outside the committee: Wirsén's successor as a member of the academy, Verner von Heidenstam. While expressing confidence in the committee's "impartiality and objectivity," he could not agree to support its candidate and could not "help thinking that we really ought to give the prize to literary authors"; on that year's list he found one poet "who towers over others." With a sound intuition he recalled the touchstone Goethe:

> Just as a selection of Goethe's poems could well convince us of Goethe's greatness, even if we were unfamiliar with his other writings, so we can say quite definitely of these poems by Tagore, which we have had in our hands this summer, that through them we have come to know one of the very greatest poets of our age. I read them with strong emotion, and I can say that in the course of decades I have not met their like in poetic literature. The hours they gave me were special, as if I had been allowed to drink from a fresh and clear spring. The loving and intense religious sense that permeates all his thoughts and feelings, the purity of heart, and the noble and unaffected elevation of the style – all amount to a total impression of deep and rare spiritual beauty. There is nothing disputable and disturbing, nothing vain, worldly, or petty, and if it can ever be said of a poet that he

possesses the qualities that make him deserving of a Nobel Prize, then it must be Tagore. No one else now alive can in that respect, so far as I know, compete with him.[2]

Those remarkable lines must be assigned a decisive significance for that year's choice. A point of view that was unusual for its time and would not play a leading role in the Nobel discussions until six decades later may have had an impact: "For the first time, and perhaps also for the last time in the foreseeable future, we would have the chance to discover a great name before it has already spent years haunting the newspaper columns." Heidenstam ended by pointing out that a chance had presented itself to fulfill the will's original intention of rewarding a book published during the previous year.

The thrust of Heidenstam's argument was not without its tactical motives. In a letter revealing that the proposal originated with the addressee, Per Hallström, Heidenstam had written: "What you say about the Indian does not sound so bad. It is necessary in some way to break the routine." In clarification, Heidenstam added, with regard to another proposal made in 1913, "The danger with Spitteler could well be just that it would not entail such a break." The Nobel Committee had "been a kind of Foreign Office," which had allowed the prize to be shared out "country by country. . . . "On the first occasion, for instance, it was the French Academy."[3] The policy implied in Heidenstam's memo would mean a departure from this diplomatic approach. The correspondence between Heidenstam and Hallström about the possibility of a "break" with previous practice also suggests something of the 1890s generation's wish to tidy up after the archenemy Wirsén. But the wish was not limited to provincial considerations. Heidenstam's eloquent plea for Tagore resulted – and without such a viewpoint being spelled out – in the first break from the European cultural hegemony.

The outbreak of World War I, however, checked all such outward-reaching initiatives and gave rise to a new attitude toward the whole Nobel enterprise. The new dominant ideology, formulated by Harald Hjärne in 1914, could be called "literary neutralism." It was expressly based on an impartiality that not even criticism of the choice of winners could discredit. The committee had found that Nobel's purpose was above all to prevent any kind of nationalist partiality, which had by no means hindered an unbiased distribution of the prize, so long as the "overriding requirement" of choosing "truly outstanding recipients" could be met. This was the first of the committee's declarations of the political integrity of the institution of the Nobel Prize.

"Without ever doubting that literature is high above the political disturbance of the age," the academy would have been justified in rewarding "the most personally worthy" works, irrespective of the "profane unrest."

"The circumstances of the fatherland," however, compelled a certain consideration:

> The Swedish Academy, as one of the institutions entrusted with the distribution of the Nobel Prize, is sufficiently representative to be regarded abroad as an organ of determining opinions in our country, perhaps to a higher degree than the daily press, whose conduct already now in the early stages of the war is subject to a suspicious examination from many influential quarters. It is not possible for us to give any public explanations that could forestall such interpretations of our behavior in the matter that may be unfavorable to Sweden. Yet without a doubt it would be desirable if through our manner of fulfilling our task we could – without infringing upon our accepted duties – give as little opening as possible to politicized discussion, which in these turbulent times would be more than usually objectionable.

An additional factor, then, had to be allowed for in the evaluation of candidates: the possibility that a particular choice might give rise to "new outbursts of bitterness that, through some not unexpected misunderstanding of the academy's purpose and position, could be directed at our country."

Along with these patriotic considerations the committee also kept asking the question of loyalty to Nobel's intentions. It was felt that the academy ought as far as possible to avoid – "even unwittingly" – giving encouragement to international antagonisms and to bear in mind that the aim of the prize "is closely associated, especially in other countries, with the founder's ideal of world peace"; it must be "considered unfortunate if a prize intended to encourage the best efforts on behalf of mankind as a whole should be misinterpreted as favoring some particular nation."[4]

But it is not just a wish for neutrality that appears in this interesting report. Awareness of a more active role is apparent, too: "A conscientious administration of the Swedish Academy's international task" induced it, "as far as it is able, to exercise a restraining and counterbalancing influence on the excesses" that nationalism in contemporary literature and "the competition for power in general" could so easily generate. Sharing the prize between two recipients was discussed, though not with the intention of achieving political balance. Any thought, for instance, of a German-French "quota" is not discernible. On a lower, national level, however, certain arguments in the "counterbalancing" spirit remained.

This policy of literary neutralism should also be seen in the light of Hjärne's general idea of the cultural development of Western countries. In his eyes, Western culture was unified by its classical and Christian inheritance. In every vigorous people "the general culture" has "a strength much more extensive than its own particular achievement." The 1914 report is marked by the awareness that this general culture was being weakened by manifestations of nationalism: "Very few nowadays are those authors who succeed in elevating and ennobling their nationally concrete and characteristic impulses to clear and living expressions of true human visions in a manner reminiscent of, if hardly on the grand scale of, the still unclouded geniuses of the past classical ages."

This perspective valued "the literature of common humanity," an orientation that, in the short view, served a policy of literary neutralism and, in the longer view, served the historically conditioned unity of Western culture. The literary situation in 1914, however, inspired pessimism that was also retrospective. We can scarcely, said Hjärne, "conceal from ourselves and others the fact that so far we have not succeeded . . . in honoring any master of the indisputably highest order." This comment was not directed at the academy's criteria; rather, Hjärne was questioning whether contemporary literature was up to the mark: "Nor are the prospects bright, at least not for the reasonably foreseeable future, for any hope that we may be in a position to maintain the standard that we have so far sought to uphold through our distribution of the prizes. The number of authors whose reputations are of the widest is almost used up, and it will take much time for new world reputations to be established and confirmed."

The first manifestation of this neutral policy was the unanimously proposed choice for 1914: the Swiss writer Carl Spitteler.[5] In his main work, *Der Olympische Frühling* (Olympian Spring), Spitteler had not only created a mythology that expressed "an independent view of the development of the world and human life," in language that was "both masterly in a classical sense and national in a Swiss sense." He also appeared to be a voice of neutrality – on grounds wider than those of Swiss nationality and diction: "The author raises himself, as concerns both form and content, above the contradictions of the age, holds himself, so to say, neutral in the face of all its vain and bitter strife."

Nonetheless, like the other Nobel institutions, the academy decided not to give the award for 1914. Thus Spitteler lost, in the short run, his neutral position. Already in the 1915 report it was noted that "his political behavior . . . gave rise to the greatest offense in Germany and Austria. There can be no doubt that the choice of Spitteler, while the war continues, would in those countries cause the utmost embarrassment and instigate manifold misinterpretations." Spitteler was not alone in having compromised himself. Many of those whose names were put forward, as well as many actual winners, "especially the Frenchmen Bergson, Faguet, Bazin, and Bourget, have with overwhelming zeal participated in the ongoing bellicose polemics." It was felt that the choice of Romain Rolland could lead to embarrassing reactions of "a possibly even higher degree," for he had "through his comments on the war earned himself reprobation not only in Germany but also in his native France." Likewise, the Belgian poet Émile Verhaeren had "aired his feelings in bitter accusations against the Germans and their warfare." Such activities might not have influenced "the judgment of the literary writings of these authors," but it was another question whether it was "suitable to give the Swedish Nobel Prize to such men, who are more or less compromised by their having taken sides." The academy could well regard its task as "high above everything to do with war and politics" and carry it out "on behalf of all mankind" on purely literary grounds, doing so being much easier as candidates were found who approached the Nobel ideal. But if the benefits did not outweigh the "fury" the choice could stir up, then it seemed "not unjustified" to heed the responsibility that the academy "as a Swedish institution could incur through arousing, even unwittingly, popular feelings abroad against our country."

It would be to go too far, the report concluded, if out of consideration for neutrality the academy "were deliberately and through knowing neglect of the merits of the author in question to avoid giving the year's Nobel Prize to any of the subjects of the belligerent nations." But in the academy it had often been found desirable that "the separate countries could be considered as near as possible on an equal footing"; the choices up until that time could be said "to have turned out likewise." The principle of rotation established in the course of the first decade, however, was given a special application, in line with the policy of neutrality: "Now especially seems a favorable opportunity to not ignore the less populous nations." For the 1915 prize, this meant awarding Spanish literature; the candidate proposed by Hjärne and the majority on the committee was Benito Pérez Galdós, who, in his broad epic works *Episodios nacionales* and *Novelas contemporaneas,* had shown himself to be "a truly significant and in his own country highly regarded author of a manly, noble, and high-minded spirit." An essential part of Hjärne's plea was devoted to the question of whether Pérez Galdós showed any disqualifying "tendency."[6] The reproaches of "chauvinism" from the French side were shown to be unjustified, and the accusations of "partiality" for certain historical figures was said "to have been successfully refuted. . . . He presents himself as the supporter not of a party but of general patriotism." Faced with the tension between liberals and clerics in contemporary Spain, he strived "to do justice to both. . . . Any enmity toward Christianity or the church is not to be seen, at least not by those outside the circle of extreme Spanish clericalism." Yet Pérez Galdós also did not belong "to those who in an abstract manner 'raise problems for debate.' " He sought to illuminate the conflicts "through a multitude of sharply drawn and strangely complicated personal fates." In view of Hjärne's reservations about contemporary literature's pronounced nationalism in the expressions of the universally human, it is of particular interest that in depicting Spanish figures Pérez Galdós was said to give them "something typical, which makes them more comprehensible to those readers not familiar with Spanish characteristics." Hjärne combined the earlier era's demand for nontendentious objectivity with the new requirement of universal relevance in a manner well suited to the declared policy of neutrality. The treatment of the matter in the committee illustrates at the same time the limitations of Hjärne's evaluation; Hallström, who welcomed the candidacy of Pérez Galdós "with great sympathy," felt compelled to write an individual memo in order to demonstrate how Pérez Galdós's writing was also highly striking "from an aesthetic point of view."

The recommendation of the committee in 1915 included two names. Spitteler ought to be given the 1914 prize that was "reserved"in 1914. It was found that the benefits would outweigh the anger it was assumed would follow. Pérez Galdós had a majority in his favor for the 1915 prize, whereas a minority preferred Romain Rolland. As we know, however, the academy decided not to make any award that year, and the money from 1914 was added to the capital.

Rolland, proposed by Schück, was subjected to stern criticism in Hjärne's report. Hjärne found the great work *Jean-Christophe* to be, in spite of its many merits, on the whole "somewhat formless." The depiction of the main character "suffers excessively from a fantastic and misleading cult of genius," and the idealism confessed was "an emotional scepticism and sophistry." Hjärne also expressed an interesting idiosyncracy vis-à-vis the genre itself, the "artist's novel." Since all art was "a kind of reflection of life," so a piece of writing about art and artists was "a reflection of a reflection," wherein the author, instead of "immediately" entering upon "the life he wants in the final analysis to describe," devotes himself to "a kind of generalized and floating self-reflection" and, instead of "the trial of strength between living personalities," conveys "a lusterless interior play of shadows." This criterion dismissed much contemporary writing that was focused on the problems of the artist.

The 1916 report recommended, as before, that the 1915 prize be given to Pérez Galdós (with two committee members in favor of Rolland) and that the prize for 1916 be shared between the Danes Karl Gjellerup and Jakob Knudsen (with a minority in favor of the whole prize going to Gjellerup). The academy opposed the committee on both counts and gave the 1915 prize to Rolland, "as a tribute to the lofty idealism of his literary production and to the sympathy and love of truth with which he has described different types of human beings," and at the same time gave the 1916 prize to Heidenstam "in recognition of his significance as the leading representative of a new era in our literature."

The decision of the academy, however, diverged only partly from Hjärne's point of view and, in fact, was in accordance with the policy of neutrality outlined by him. In judging Rolland, the academy simply had another way of looking at his idealism and a different evaluation of his depiction of human character. The academy was still supporting the choice of an author whose significance was more than national and whose fiction included both Germany and France without committing itself to either – and of a pacifist who in his Swiss exile had been subjected to criticism from both sides. The bitterness that he had aroused "not only in Germany but also in his native France" could equally well be cited in support of his impartiality. The prize to Rolland in fact fit in not so badly with the policy laid down in 1914.

Heidenstam's prize also reflected that policy. As Österling suggested, rejecting both of the committee's Danish candidates was a temporary measure while the academy was formulating its position on the real candidate, who for natural reasons was not included in the report.[7] But the choice of Heidenstam is significant to our discussion. Heidenstam, who in the previous year crowned his literary achievement with the publication of the serene collection *New Poems,* was, in a way quite different from Wirsén's sense of the term, a poet with an "idealistic tendency." But his work also fit easily into Hjärne's framework. The choice of Heidenstam corresponded to the "favorable opportunity" the time offered "not to ignore the less populous nations." It is no coincidence that discussion of the 1916 prize focused on Danish and Swedish candidates. The neutrality policy favored the smaller nations outside the belligerent groups and gave the Scandinavian literatures a special chance. The heavier representation of Scandinavia in the list of winners – no fewer than four names if we include the 1920 winner, Knut Hamsun – can be partly explained by the neutrality policy of the World War I years. In fact, even more Scandinavians might have been awarded the prize. In his 1916 correspondence, Tegnér mustered support from two committee members before the decisive meeting; the situation was "so entangled that the result could well be quite unreasonable." One of the alternatives was that one of the available prizes be shared by Heidenstam, Karlfeldt, and Hallström, and the other by "a Norwegian, as yet undecided" – Arne Garborg and Gunnar Heiberg were proposed – "a Dane, most likely Gjellerup," and "a Finn, probably Juhani Aho." With good reason, Tegnér thought that with decisions like that the academy "would definitely compromise itself in the face of the world."[8]

When the Danish proposal was renewed in 1917, Jakob Knudsen had died in the meantime, and the committee was in favor – while continuing to bypass Brandes – of splitting the prize between Karl Gjellerup and Henrik Pontoppidan. Those of Heidenstam's 1890s generation were repaying a debt to their inspirer Gjellerup, who had received scant attention in the literature of his own country. Yet the question remained how the chairman of the Nobel Committee, who did not have any need to express such gratitude, could regard the insignificant Gjellerup as being "in several essential respects" superior to Pontoppidan. The answer is to be found in the type of evaluation that was made in the Wirsén epoch and was still being used.

Under the guidance of a Danish authority (Vilhelm Andersen), Hjärne's renewed reading of Pontoppidan led to a reevaluation. Yet in spite of Hjärne's penitent and more appreciative attitude, his old reservations persisted. With the "key" he acquired–"the poet's concealed sympathy"–Hjärne had a better understanding of the rather disconsolate character descriptions. But what he still believed to be missing, in the face of all this concern with "mediocre and less than mediocre creatures . . . trapped in their narrow outlooks and expectations," is evident in the labored manner in which he tried to express sympathy for the fact that Pontoppidan "never intended to captivate and elevate his readers through the depiction of significant figures and their resolute struggle with life." The view of humanity and the narrative procedures characteristic of the generation who found their inspiration in naturalism remained foreign to Hjärne. The presentation of *Lykke-Per* (Lucky Per) "is conditioned by a sickly determinism" and thus lacked "generally significant content." This is a point of view we recognize. But the storyteller's objectivity also caused concern; "the suppression of individual personality" entailed a kind of objectivity different from the Goethean ideal, here linked with a detailed documentation of features, which offended against the demand for limitation. At the same time that "the keeper of the minutes" took pains to conceal "his own personal involvement," he nonetheless strived "to depict the frailties of his characters most exactly," with a thoroughness that merely tired "the reader who would rather content himself with a few powerfully drawn strokes." Hjärne did make an effort, though, to show that the narrator, while hiding himself behind his characters, "whom he wishes to reveal from within," yet "unveils himself" to the reader who penetrates fully into his works. In such a way Hjärne managed to coax Pontoppidan into an idealistic position. Thus he read into *De dødes rige* (The Realm of the Dead) "an unmistakable, although hardly ever expressed, indignation that compels the recognition of a higher moral world order."

In Gjellerup Hjärne recognized his own values to quite a different extent, for Gjellerup worked toward a coherent worldview characterized by "respect for the ruling spiritual powers of human existence, even if he also shied away from the assertion of the personality's full significance and independence." "The open rift with Brandes" was noted; Gjellerup "could no longer tolerate the frivolous treatment of the fidelities of love and marriage" and felt "repelled by the Parisian prototypes set up for imitation by the new Danish literature." Gjellerup was credited for his break with naturalism; he was drawn instead "to German classicism, whose influence took possession of his youthful predilection for Greek antiquity and Old German heroic poetry." Hjärne's sympathetic commentary ranged from *Brynhild*–"a captivating song of praise in dramatic form, celebrating the sacrificial power of faithful love"–to *Pilgrimen Kamanita* (The Pilgrim Kamanita), in which "the classic poet of Buddhism" appears. So for Hjärne the tendency toward "the ideal" became "the nerve" of Gjellerup's writing. He noted how Gjellerup closed *Vandreaaret* (The Year of Travel) with an idealistic credo by Paul Heyse, to whom he had remained loyal for twenty-five years. It is a significant connection. Gjellerup took his place at the side of Heyse as a late heir of German idealism and German neoclassicism. Hjärne's taste was similarly rooted. In this choice we recognize the Wirsén epoch, which resonated with German idealism, as well as the Swedish 1890s, with their reaction against crude realism; both united in an act of homage to Gjellerup.

The opportunity occasioned by World War I "not to ignore the less populous nations" was thus utilized in 1916 and 1917 to draw attention to Scandinavian authors. In 1919 yet another Scandinavian, Karlfeldt, was chosen; as secretary, however, he refused to accept the honor. In 1920 the same "opportunity" for the small nations was still open, and the prize for that year went to Knut Hamsun for *Markens grøde* (Growth of the Soil), with a degree of competition from Arne Garborg. The seventy-five-year-old Spitteler was given the prize for 1919. The committee stated that "the time ought at last to have come when we can without reservations give a Nobel Prize to the renowned Swiss bard." As we have seen, the reservations were connected with Spitteler's political utterances and the reactions that could be expected from German and Austrian quarters. By 1919 such considerations had been allowed to lapse.

In 1919-20 the war was still exerting its influence, but in another form. For the 1919 "competition" only twelve proposals were submitted – compared with twenty-eight in 1913. This wartime slackening of initiative from the outside world meant that, within the narrower circle of those directly engaged in administering the prizes, a greater use was made of the right to propose; in 1916 the committee members themselves put forward five names. Problems of communication in time of war had also led to a dearth of the "numerous works that could be regarded as necessary for the support of the views submitted with proposals."

The two prizes given in 1920 were not undisputed within the academy. Energetic opposition came from Schück, now a member of the committee. Schück felt that Spitteler's fame could be accounted for only "by confusing, as so often happens in Germany, *intention* and artistic *capacity*, the idea and the execution"; *Der Olympische Frühling* lacked "those qualities that characterize a real epic." Nor did he think that Hamsun's *Markens grøde* could "match up to a Nobel Prize": the novel was undeniably "a significant work of art," but in both this book and in Hamsun's other work Schück did not find "the culture, the well-considered worldview, and the humanity" he demanded from a laureate. Schück's idea of humanity can be seen in his argument in favor of Georg Brandes, whose "worldview was not considered to be of the 'ideal' character that is required of a Nobel Prize winner":

In my opinion the academy has interpreted the word *ideal* much too narrowly, and masses of the great works of world literature, according to this still upheld interpretation, could not have been rewarded if they had been proposed to the academy. To deny a man like Brandes, who throughout his life was engaged in the struggle for ideas – to deny him "idealism" seems to me narrow-minded, and one need only read Brandes's latest books, on the world war, to find how passionate he can be for a world order based upón idealism and justice.

Schück added that the question was not relevant to the evaluation of the writings he had proposed for the award. In Brandes's works on Danish authors, he appeared by virtue of his "superior style," "fine taste," and "psychological penetration ... not just in Scandinavia as indisputably the most outstanding author in his field, but in Europe as one of the most significant, comparable only with the best French critics." Any "lack of idealism" in these works has never, so far as is known, been substantiated.

The other candidate supported by Schück, Grazia Deledda, also fulfilled the Nobel requirement: over everything she had written "there is spread a veil of delicate poetry, of noble, melancholy humanity and sympathy for the human."[9] Schück argued in this way within the framework of Nobel's intentions, which he felt had merely been too narrowly interpreted in earlier practice. What he was in fact arguing against was the Wirsénian interpretation of "idealistic" – an interpretation that excluded the age's most important authors, from Tolstoy to Ibsen. In his own definition of the term, Schück required that a literary work show "a well-considered worldview" and "humanity." These he did not find in *Markens grøde*.

The remarks made by both Hjärne and Schück help to illuminate the literary qualities of the ideal Nobel Prize winner. The kind of evaluation undertaken by Schück and applied to, among others, Grazia Deledda, will be described in our account of the next period, in which we shall also examine the criteria applied by Hallström and Karlfeldt, as reflected in their specialist reports. Here, it need only be added that the neutrality policy was conducted not only internationally but also on a lower level – to settle linguistic and political rivalries first within Finland and then within Spain.

A repeatedly proposed Finnish-language candidate was Juhani Aho, the subject in 1917 of the following balancing act by Hjärne: "His name undeniably deserves recognition. But while I consider that an author who has used Finnish should not without stronger reasons be preferred by the academy to a Finnish writer who uses Swedish, I have chosen to add to the list of proposed candidates the poet Bertel Gripenberg, highly valued on both sides of the Gulf of Bothnia." Prize sharing was here proposed as a way to maintain a neutral position in a tense situation, perhaps also as a means of "toning down" the conflicts. In the following year the matter was postponed, "for both of them are at present, in their literary work as well, strongly affected by the unfortunate circumstances of the time, particularly in their own fatherland." As a result of civil war the Finns had become involved in the need to follow a restrictive and neutral literary policy.

We find a related point of view applied to the Catalan author Ángel Guimerà, who had been on the list since 1907. In 1917 Hjärne wrote: "In this case too I consider that an author who uses the older and time-honored literary language ought to be either placed by his side or rewarded first. It would be harmful if the academy, even against its intention, were to hurt sensitive Castilian national feelings."

In 1919 the idea recurred that "neither [Aho nor Guimerá] should be rewarded before some other author who has written in the earlier literary language of the country in question." The reason was given in words of Hjärne's that summed up well the policy of this period: "The academy's prize-giving policy should not, so far as such things can be foreseen and forestalled, give rise to a further aggravation of such national conflicts, which would clearly be to the detriment of the Nobel Foundation's general aim of promoting peace."

CHAPTER 3

"The Great Style"

In the early 1920s the Swedish Academy lost the final traces of its Wirsénian past. Harald Hjärne died in 1922, and for almost a quarter of a century to come the chairman of the Nobel Committee would be Per Hallström. The academy's secretary from 1912 was Erik Axel Karlfeldt. Other members of the generation who began their literary careers in the 1890s, and whom Wirsén succeeded in excluding, had long since been admitted, Heidenstam in 1912, and Selma Lagerlöf in 1914. Their presence was reinforced by Henrik Schück, admitted in 1913, and Fredrik Böök (1922), the latter having strong roots in the 1890s, particularly those aspects of that decade associated with Heidenstam. On the 1921 committee we find, along with Hjärne, Karlfeldt, Hallström, Schück, and Österling.

What is remarkable is that the kind of evaluation practiced in the 1920s bore little resemblance to the criteria of the 1890s – or perhaps it is more correct to say that the 1890s generation, who occupied the forum, showed aesthetic leanings of a classical variety to a greater extent than may have been expected. The recurring phrase "the great style" can well serve as a motto for the new period. The idea can be glimpsed as early as the prize to Hamsun for "his monumental work *Markens grøde*," but it would not be explicitly expressed until the following years.

The term itself goes back to the anonymous treatise *Peri Hypsos* (On the Sublime) from the first century A.D., but in a later period it was connected especially with Goethe. In Novalis we come across "der grosse Stil der Darstellung, den man mit Recht an Goethe so sehr bewundert" ("the great style of the presentation that we justly admire so much in Goethe").[1] In a 1916 essay Hallström spoke of Goethe's "later monumental style." The Goethean ideal, which had a crucial role in establishing critical norms during the first Nobel period, was being extended in the 1920s to include the "classical realism" (as practiced by the previously rejected Tolstoy) of the nineteenth century. The academy's aesthetic outlook at this time was silently allied with the neoclassical efforts of the 1920s generally, in Europe as well as in Sweden.

Naturally, new interpretations of "idealistic" arose, implying a renewed confrontation between individual members' sensibilities and what was understood to have been Nobel's intention. The result was considerably different from what it was in the first period. The committee no longer promoted a theistic conception of God or a Boströmian view of life and the social order. Philosophically, it was still possible in 1921 to refer, as Hjärne did in his critique of Anatole France, to "the mighty course of generally serious idealism" that began with Plato and could be followed through late antiquity, the Middle Ages, and the Renaissance, through Pascal, Malebranche, and "many philosophical and theological thinkers, romantic, social-utopian, and Parnassian dreamers and poets right into our own days." But Anatole France found sustenance in another aspect of antiquity: "With a sprinkling of Aristophanic humor, of the simpler forms of Socratic irony, and of the scepticism of the younger academic school, he has now and then sought repose in Epicurus' garden of pleasure." Hjärne was describing another tradition, via the Alexandrian world, Petronius, and the medieval wandering scholars to *l'esprit gaulois* – and for a product of that kind of tradition, any question of mastery apart, "the 'idealistic' literary prize of the Nobel will is not intended." A conservative political accent appeared in the same statement: the Clartéist France had "in his pacifistic zeal allowed himself to be drawn quite over the frontier of Bolshevism." A certain moral bigotry could also be detected: Hjärne noted, "not without aesthetic distaste," France's habit "of, like the great master Voltaire, quite unnecessarily involving every sort of banal allusion and piquancy, overmuch reminiscent of the old Priapus."

In the event, the positions taken on Anatole France became decisive for the interpretation of the conditions of the will. Hjärne rejected France and concluded by proposing John Galsworthy; the other members agreed with this proposal – except for Schück. As recently as 1920, after all, Schück had claimed that the academy "interpreted the word *idealistic* much too narrowly," and that using that interpretation would have excluded "masses of the great works of world literature." But he also sought in Hamsun's work "the culture, the well-considered worldview, and the humanity" required of a Nobel Prize winner. Schück continued in the same manner in 1921 when, in an individual memo, he argued in favor of France as "a true humanist" whose education "has permeated his whole being and given him a broad, human, and understanding view of life":

> It is true that he is a sceptic, and those who are fortunate in having found the answer to the riddles of existence could well regard this as a fault, as something incompatible with the Nobel Foundation's obligation to safeguard idealism. But Anatole France has never been an idle doubter

watching with indifference how justice and humanity are trampled underfoot. In the Dreyfus affair he stood in the front rank of those who defended justice against misguided chauvinism and the military caste mentality, and during the Great War he has been one of the few notable men who has not let slip a word of hate.

Schück also claimed that France fulfilled the "idealistic" requirement, provided one did not interpret it too narrowly:

The writings of Anatole France, seen as a whole, must be described as idealistic, so long as one does not confine the term within any confessional restraints. It amounts to a reaction against Zola's naturalism, and against Zola's earthbound analysis of reality France sets the historical tradition, reintroduces romanticism in literature, not the old kind certainly, but a new kind and perhaps more genuine. He tries in each case to *understand* the different periods, to explain and thus, too, to forgive. Perhaps this is not the highest form of idealism, but I may be excused if I do not undervalue it, for it is mine too.[2]

This was an important declaration. It would in future be very difficult to insist on idealism with "confessional restraints" against this more generously formulated humanistic view. His skillful argument at the same time established new but less strict standards with a special appeal to those in the academy with an 1890s background. The criticism of naturalism, the reminder of France's new, "more genuine" romanticism, and the stress on the "historical tradition" could all appeal to Schück's colleagues. Together with an eloquent plea for France as "the greatest stylist in modern France," his defense of an idealist in the widest sense of the term succeeded in turning opinion. The academy's choice for 1921 was Anatole France – "in recognition of his brilliant literary achievements, characterized as they are by a nobility of style, broad-hearted humanity, grace, and a true Gallic temperament." What is significant for the future were the words "broad-hearted humanity." We see here a new and more generous reading of the instructions in Nobel's will.

The new interpretation bore fruit in the following year in the arguments that resulted in the prize going to Jacinto Benavente, whose view of the world "is characterized by humanity," as it was said in an examination of his dramas. But what is remarkable in the 1922 report is the space devoted to the kind of evaluation that was regarded as unavoidable if the terms of the will were to be observed. In the conclusion – after a preference for Benavante had been clearly established – the question is asked whether his receipt of the prize is justifiable "from the point of view of the idealistic tendency in his works." There is first noted "the negative virtue that he does not promote any doubtful ideals, does not attack any values upon which human life is founded. ... He does not preach at all, his art is strictly objective." Benavente had "a view of his brothers and sisters that is, admittedly, often sceptical and critical, but at heart human, and if he ridicules their outward conventionality he does so in the interests of healthiness and the future." Such an investigation based on the criterion of humanity is a far cry from the Wirsénian approach. But the change also affected the very position given to this aspect of the discussion in the report, for the question of whether Benavente can fulfill the requirements of the will was dealt with, almost ostentatiously so, *after* the artistic evaluation, in order to ensure, as the conclusion put it, that as far as the will was concerned, "there are no obstacles in the way of honoring him."

But there is another way in which Hallström's committee displayed a new orientation. Faced with the choice between Yeats and Benavente, it was thought proper "to consider the less familiar, not simply in accordance with our demands but in accordance with its own conditions and in accordance with what we can gather of its significance in the context in which it was created, a context with a tradition and a culture that contribute to the appreciation of the content and form of the works in question." The artistic verdict was undoubtedly dictated by a classical type of aesthetics considered generally applicable. Yet the committee was also willing to be "on guard" against its own limitations, to be aware of the danger of gradually diminishing and specializing the scope of a prize intended to be of world significance "if our greater or lesser ease in assimilating the distinctive characters of the different national complexions is allowed to influence our decisions." The 1922 committee, in spite of its aesthetic limitations, was here expressing ideas important to the future role of the Nobel Prize in a wider international context.

The change of ideas about the "idealistic tendency" was particularly evident in the evaluations of three authors–Thomas Hardy, Johannes V. Jensen, and George Bernard Shaw. Hardy came in for consideration at the beginning of the 1920s, though not, remarkably, in 1921, when the committee recommended Galsworthy (with the rather tame justification that Galsworthy was "capable of developing an even more multifaceted and therefore less hard and sharp characterization of the mentality and behavior of unusual people in their social interplay"). Schück, as already noted, dissented. In his eyes Galsworthy was "a good second-class author, but hardly more." He himself proposed Shaw and H. G. Wells, but "only so that these authors may come into consideration" – for his own candidate was France. It is interesting that Schück had neither Hardy nor Joseph Conrad in mind; indeed, the latter was never discussed in the Nobel context. Hardy, on the other hand, was considered in both 1922 and 1923.

In the Wirsénian verdict of 1910 it was chiefly his bitter determinism and "a strange aversion to God" that had disqualified Hardy. Shortly afterwards, specialist reports on Hardy were written by the two academy members who represented the younger generation of authors, Karlfeldt in 1912 and Hallström in 1913. Karlfeldt saw the picture of fate's cruel play with the characters from a higher perspective, one that included Aeschylus and Schopenhauer. It is clearly from such a viewpoint that he coined the term "pessimistic realism" to apply to Hardy, a term that appeared to open the way to a prize in accordance with Nobel's spirit. *Tess of the d'Urbervilles* was also credited with "international validity": in this book Hardy had "at the instigation of his warm heart, given a contemporarily relevant and full-voiced expression to rebellious thoughts that–all questions of theodicity apart–should constantly occupy oppressed humanity." But there is "too much misery" in *Jude the Obscure,* in which the opposition "to the order of things and their ordainer" shouts itself "hoarse to no purpose." Hardy's spleen "prevents him from seeing the inner connections in what happens, the spiritual threads that lead men, even when they appear to be merely the marionettes of chance." But in the end Hardy was not condemned for any infringement of idealistic doctrine. Karlfeldt's criticism was aimed rather at a limitation in Hardy's view of humanity, a limitation that had its artistic consequences: "With the introduction of chance as a perpetually frustrating power, a large part of the psychological characterization breaks down."[3]

This shift of critical focus in the direction of artistically decisive factors was even more distinct in Hallström's more negative assessment in 1913. Hallström certainly believed that literary history would eventually deal somewhat briefly with "the period of pessimistic realism, whose foremost English representative is Thomas Hardy." But this "is not to say that philosophical pessimism is rejected." What Hallström disliked rather was the impression of coincidence; agreeing with Karlfeldt, he thought the weakness of "Hardy's tragic mechanism" was in "the disastrous power of chance":

> Fate may well be blind and still preserve its propriety, yet if it deteriorates into triviality and pettiness, while the heroes of the tragedies suffer from incurable bungling and carelessness, then there isn't a breath of life left in the literature. What are we to think of people who time and again ruin all their chances by coming too late for trains, by going to the wrong church for their wedding, by putting their letters under doormats, keeping silent when they ought to speak; no matter how it may be on other occasions, etc.? Can any society be responsible for them, and can any world be arranged so that their advocate may be content and happy?

In one aspect, "motivation" was seen to be deficient in Hardy, and that was with regard to the misery that calls forth the accusations against fate and society. In another aspect, the committee found a lack of real dimension in the whims of fate in Hardy's works. These were characterized by a paltriness that "is not rescued through being subsumed into the tragic."

This shift toward artistic evaluation, then, began immediately after Wirsén's epoch, and it had been effected by the early 1920s when Hallström returned to Hardy in his specialist reports of 1922 and 1923. By then, pessimism and the acceptance of the role of chance were not in themselves regarded as disqualifications for a prize whose spirit was "idealistic." Rather, it was a question of the poetical worth of the products emerging from Hardy's "disaster factory. ... One can certainly recognize his stylistic mastery, his unfailing power of describing nature and human life in nature, and his vigor in painting the world as he sees it. But his overall view of the world is distorted, and this fault has the effect of distorting his depiction of character and destiny. It is not true poetry he gives us – what he does give us is in the long run hopelessly wearying and depressing and therefore unpoetic." Schück also found himself "prevented from voting for Hardy." Karlfeldt differed from both his colleagues on the committee in an individual statement: "Since for my own part I must allow Thomas Hardy enormous credit as a portrayer of English landscape and temperament, and since I am convinced that a decision against him would meet with dissatisfaction and sadness in England, which I would not consider unjustified, I wish, without forgetting that the considerably younger Yeats should still be kept in mind, to recommend to the academy that Hardy should be given this year's Nobel Prize."

Österling, too, for all his appreciation of Yeats's worth, found that "justice and suitability" argued in favor of giving the prize to "the elder of the two ... whose contribution to English literature ought to be of even greater significance." He further wished the report to emphasize the poetic value of Hardy's *Late Lyrics and Earlier* "much more warmly" than the specialist had done, "so that Hardy's poetic achievement may be placed as highly as his more widely acclaimed achievement as a novelist." The majority of the academy, however, settled for the younger poet. Five years later Hardy was dead.

When the demand for an "idealistic tendency" was truly put to the test in the case of Johannes V. Jensen in 1925, it was focused principally on the requirement of a humanistic viewpoint of the kind Schück had postulated, in contrast to the earlier "much too narrow" interpretation. The committee's deliberations were based on a specialist report that, as Hallström summed up, gave "eager recognition to the elemental power of the poet's imagination and creativity and to the strength of his personality," yet at the same time maintained "that these qualities are cultivated at the cost of aesthetic taste and, what is worse, of the humanity that, for less one-sidedly materialistic worshipers of 'progress' than Jensen, stands as one of its most precious acquisitions." The keyword is "humanity" – the wording of the 1921 prize is apparent in the argument of the report. The committee accepted the verdict and raised "the question whether that idealism that according to the purpose of the Nobel Prize ought to be demanded of the writer is to be found here at all." It was admitted that Jensen, "with rare consistency," had devoted himself to "an idea" – the perfecting of the human race, that is, "Darwinism's life-sustaining natural selection." Like Schück in his defense of Brandes, this report concentrated on "ideas." Candidates were not being disqualified on account of materialism and Darwinism as such, as in Wirsén's time; rather, notice was being taken of the consequences of that viewpoint on a writer's view of mankind and creation of character. The Darwinian idea was embraced "by a temperament [Jensen's] that with orgiastic joy hails each violent deed in the struggle." But there was quite a difference "between acknowledging this hard law and accepting it as the most exhilarating revelation that has been granted humanity of the mystery of life. . . . Quite simply, it tramples down such values as noble-mindedness, magnanimity, and compassion and consciously or unconsciously accepts cruelty. One ought to have difficulty in defending as ideal, in the normal sense, a viewpoint that bears such fruits."

This basic outlook had consequences for artistic creation that had to be taken into account. Jensen's talents, superior in certain areas, "are reduced through his very diminishment of human feeling, and the works of art are thereby also reduced. . . . The plastically rounded figures of great literature are not born from such confines, or from such a background of stern theory and defiant sermonizing; in their stead appear abstractions that by means of exaggerated activity seek to hide their thinness. The composition will lack repose, moderation, completeness, and clarity." Further, in spite of "considerable aptitude in psychological intuition," the writer worked "with poor raw material. . . . For in advance he had deleted most of what gives wealth to human intellectual and spiritual life; he recognizes as genuine only that which lies on the straight line of development from the gorilla to the student of science. Worst of all is the humor that attempts to exist under such conditions; it becomes quite simply a kind of feeding on the monstrous. All of those features are at their most evident in his central works, his attempts in such a spirit to compose the epic of human development."

It was thus that *Den lange Rejse* (The Long Journey) (1908-22) was stigmatized. A certain recognition, however, was allowed to *Himmerlandshistorier* (Himmerland Stories) (1898-1910), which, even with their typical faults in composition and psychology belonged to "the most powerful products of modern Danish literature, even if in terms of plastic greatness and spiritual maturity they cannot bear comparison with Jakob Knudsen's masterpieces." Jensen was given highest credit for his descriptions of experiences of nature, in a genre that he called *Myter* (Myths) and gathered in eleven volumes, from 1907 to 1944.

By this argument awarding the prize to Jensen was not only found to be "impossible, if we give the least attention to the demand for an idealistic disposition" – the sharpest pronouncement on this question made by the committees of the 1920s. Examination of the artistic consequences was also made, and "doubts" were accordingly expressed about attributing to Jensen's work "a sufficient aesthetic value to justify a Nobel prize."

The interpretation of "idealistic tendency" as having the quality of "humanity" is something we come across again in the evaluation of George Bernard Shaw. In this author, who in Wirsén's eyes was too "brutal," the 1924 report saw "inextinguishably youthful idealism, high seriousness, fresh and genuine humaneness, goodness, and, indeed, even fineness."[4] In 1926 this evaluation was developed further: "Beneath the witticism and the sophistication" there was "a serious and burning intention, eagerly aspiring to liberate the spirits from traditionally dependent attitudes and traditionally ungenuine or half-genuine feelings." In the view of liberation as "aspiring" we can see the distance the committee had come from the Wirsénian doctrine. But these qualities were complemented by Shaw's "human love," a "warmth" that allowed him, "in spite of all his rationalistic raids on intellectual and spiritual life," to retain "a basically idealistic and human outlook." The wording of the award mentioned precisely that—Shaw's work "is marked by both idealism and humanity."

But the verdicts on Jensen and Shaw also contained traces of an aestheticism that had certain parallels with that of the first period—the demand for "the great style." Criticism of Jensen for lacking "plastic greatness," "the firmly molded and rounded figures of great literature," and "repose, moderation, completeness, and clarity" in his composition revealed the committee's affinities with a neoclassical view of literature close to that of the Goethean ideal. The principal requirement of the committees of the 1920s was most apparent in the negative verdict on Shaw finally passed in 1924 under the aegis of Hallström: "He despises every effort at 'the great style,' whose dignity and seriousness call forth his comic imagination, and whose poetic uplift appears to him mere falsehood."

In *St. Joan* the fate of the main character "cannot entirely divest itself of its great style, no matter how anxiously Shaw avoids all pathos. . . . Joan's purity, courage, naive sublimity, and greatness of heart are there in the heroine of the historical drama, without being much disturbed by the forward outspokenness without which she would never have been adopted by Shaw's imagination." The committee saw potential in the "tragic touch" that elevated "the fateful" in her martyrdom—"her lot is that of all greatness." But Shaw's desire also to do justice to the Rouen law court transformed "the naively pious Joan into a dangerous heretic . . . a protestant before the Reformation, who *must* be put down by the obedient sons of the Church"—all of which results in the play "seeming dryly logical and with too little dramatic substance." And disputable views of another kind prevented the heroine's "sublimity" from being realized artistically: "divided as the whole play is between ironic comedy and immediate emotion," it failed to achieve "proper greatness and beauty . . . the mixture is too unharmonious." The composition could be said—as with Jensen—to lack "repose" and "moderation."

When the reasoning of the 1926 report in fact did lead Shaw to the prize, it retained the qualification that his production did not offer "dramatic masterpieces, if we apply the strictest criteria of the art." But there is an awareness in the report of "something quite new, which in more than the usual manner must be judged according to its own special conditions, irrespective of the development of the drama so far. . . . What is new lies not so much in construction and form, which fetches its scenic effects readily and unconsciously from a relatively undiscriminating though uncommonly fresh and brisk theatrical culture; it is to be found rather in the immediacy with which the ideas are turned into action, and above all in the individuality of the temperament and the intellect, which here express themselves with almost unparalleled directness and freedom."

Shaw's temperament, among "the liveliest and quickest that could be found in literature," and, within its limits, his unusually mobile and sharp intellect sought with high-spirited combativeness to reassess, to astonish, to turn conventional notions on their heads: "In this variety of athletics the author displays so little concern for his own dignity that on the face of it his gladiatorial exertions offer not a few resemblances to the trade of the clown."

The author of the report was thus at pains to extend his understanding beyond the "strictest criteria" of the drama and to do justice to a new, agile, and fearless art of the theater that did not worry about its "dignity." What motivated this stretching of the norms was the "serious" and "aspiring" intention behind the means deliberately used to "captivate and win over" a modern public. It was stated that *St. Joan* "stands quite alone as a proclamation of heroism in an age in which heroism can expect scant encouragement" – and that, moreover, much else in Shaw's work "that seemed no more than provocative amusement has at heart something of the same seriousness that reached its highest expression in the heroic *St. Joan.*" Along with arguments in favor of Shaw's basically ideal viewpoint we find attention being drawn to his heroic seriousness, which belongs to "the great style."

It was crucial that the opponent of the narrow limits set upon the idealistic, Henrik Schück, should be in basic agreement with the artistic assumptions of the others involved in this discussion (without necessarily using the term "the great style"). In his advocacy of Grazia Deledda, whom in 1920 he supported against Hamsun, the choice of the majority of the committee, it was precisely the "plastic" ideal that he distinguished. Her depiction of Sardinian nature had a "visuality" of which Schück "has found few equals. . . . Her pictures of popular life are similarly plastic." The unaffected presentation was "almost Homerically simple. . . . The language often has something of the cool and noble beauty of marble." Here we find a combination of two qualities that both Schück and the committee as a whole admire: simpleness and plasticity. But Schück could also go along with the demand for "completeness" in the composition. He admitted that several of Deledda's novels suffered from the lack of a "proper conclusion"; but that fault could not be found in the novels ("perfect" also in this respect) *La Via del Male* (The Road of Evil) and *Elias Portolu,* which he was proposing for the prize. Schück's nomination of Deledda thus took place within the framework of a view of literature shared with the rest of the committee; the disagreements that finally remained when Deleda was given the 1926 prize (in 1927) arose over the application of the criteria. Hallström objected to, among other things, uncertain composition "without inner unity," which made it impossible for him to allow Deledda's fiction "a value high enough to support a Nobel Prize," while Karlfeldt, Schück, and Österling were prepared "to accept a good part" of the criticism yet preferred to emphasize the author's "best qualities," especially in "her later writing, with its refinement and depth ... her ideal conception of life and its moral problems, her sympathy for the suffering, her fine psychology," and – most interesting in the present context – "her gentle and harmonious style" and her skill in "painterly" description. The wording of the award accurately included the current key concept – "plastic visuality."

On the basis of such aesthetic assumptions about "the great style," it was possible in 1924 to identify Władysław Reymont's *Chłopi* (The Peasants) as "lasting art in the great style," a prose epic of more than "national representativeness. ... Through its great and simple presentation" this work was representative of "an entire class of people" and attained "universal interest." Yet such neoclassical aesthetic assumptions were problematic in the face of the new currents in contemporary European literature. We shall see several examples of this happening toward the end of the 1920s. But first we must examine two situations, – in 1922 and 1928 – which each involved a choice and in which those aesthetic assumptions clearly determined the kind of positions adopted in the discussions.

In 1922 there was a difficult choice to be made between W.B. Yeats and Jacinto Benavente, who were comparable "in literary worth alone." Both in their different ways passed muster with regard to the criteria of "the great style." Yeats was presented as "a poet, not only in partly too obscure but partly quite charming poems" (more was not said about his poetry as such) "but also in his plays." The earlier plays also gave delight "through their lyrical beauty, music, and emotion. ... Strict and well-controlled form, dramatic life proper is not his concern. He seeks the great style in his Irish legends and reaches his best in *The King's Threshold,* but even there he achieves his effect more through the depth and refinement of his thoughts and the charm of the feeling, rather than through power and visuality in the depiction of the fates of his characters." Yeats's works therefore disclosed only to a limited extent the tokens of "the great style" – "power and visuality," along with "strict and well-controlled form." But the artistic ideals of the committee left a significant amount of room for lyricism. Here we notice the corresponding demand for simpleness and (in a more elevated sense) popularity, or accessibility; the objection that Yeats's poems were "partly too obscure" is significant. We have already seen a hint of the classical element in this poetic taste: "Homerically simple." Yeats had also written "a solitary little masterpiece" that met the demand – *Cathleen Ni Hoolihan,* "simple and lovely as a flower, popular in the best meaning of the word, and at the same time artistically exquisite." The verdict on Yeats's later work focused on his effort to attain a "great style" but noted that the emotional "power" that belonged to that style was absent: "His later, in its manner very remarkable, attempt to create an austere and archaic drama shows signs of struggle; the simple and high style toward which he feels his way belongs to the origin of tragedy in dance and song, yet hardly gives scope to the free, vigorous heartbeat that is surely essential to full-grown tragedy."

This emphasis on the lyrical aspect of Yeats's drama also served to establish an effective contrast between him and Benavente, who was "through and through a dramatist." Benavente's serious plays were reviewed rapidly, with much value being placed on his objectivity; as noted earlier, "tendentious" writing was a disqualifying factor from this point of view. Benavente was, in "his serious plays," a "dramatic moralist with an objective, clear, and logical disposition, neither a prophet nor a preacher." But it was in comedy that Benavente was at home. In those works the committee called attention to the sense of balance related to objectivity:

> The scepticism and bitterness, for which he is condemned by some critics in his homeland, seem to us, who have had our palates hardened by draughts so much more bitter, not at all violent but distinctive rather through moderation and balance. Benavente's view of the world, clear and firm as it is, is characterized by humanity, just as good a sign of strength in an author as wild gestures and crushing words. By and large it is that strength, expressing itself in simplicity, in a sure sense of limitation, in naturalness, and above all in grace, which gives the most distinguished value to Benavente's art.

Alongside the recently introduced key concept of "humanity" we find here again the tokens of "the great style" – "moderation and balance," "simplicity," "limitation" and "naturalness," all in association with "strength." The place given to "grace" is a little surprising in the context. But in fact this quality was quite amenable to inclusion in "the great style," for "grace, with all that it implies of maturity and harmony and . . . of strength, is an aesthetic quality of high rank and therefore also rare." It was from this viewpoint that Benavente could be assimilated into the Spanish tradition that included, most notably, the comedies of Lopes and Calderon, a tradition characterized not primarily by "the spirituality and lightness of the dialogue

... [but by] the entire movement in the plays, which, following unwritten rules, is characterized by a strange grace."

In the final choice in 1922 between the two great incomparables, Benavente was preferred on pragmatic grounds: partly because of "a geographical distribution of the Nobel Prize," and partly because of the opportunity to honor, after "thorough consideration . . . qualities to which we are not very accustomed, and which do not immediately captivate and delight us." This view was formulated by the committee members against the background of the explicitly accepted necessity of overcoming their own aesthetic limitations.

In 1928 the situation was almost absurd, and it is highly relevant to our discussion. Sigrid Undset had three votes on the committee, and Maxim Gorky had two, Karlfeldt and Österling. As we know, the academy settled on Undset, "principally for her powerful descriptions of Northern life during the Middle Ages." The report lauded not only her "gift of truly bringing to life a distant and forgotten age" but also her rare ability "to depict characters and with sure psychological insight recreate intellectual and emotional life." Objections raised included "detailed and heavy construction . . . confused composition," and "a certain monotony" – in part, sins against the commandments of "the great style." In this case the neoclassical aesthetic view was unexpectedly amplified by the requirement of a kind of cathartic effect: "Although conceived on a grand scale, the tragedy of her characters' fates has not sufficiently achieved the type of liberation demanded of literature in the elevation and cleansing of the imaginatively experienced torments; a religious reconciliation is forthcoming, but not an aesthetic one."

The formulator of this Aristotelian objection was the chairman, Hallström. This criticism was supplemented by Schück, who, in an interesting discussion of the problems of recreating the psychology of a bygone age, found Undset guilty of "unhistorical construction"; her psychology was "neither medieval nor modern." He also thought she lacked the "narrative talents" of a Fielding, a Scott, or a Thackeray – "she does not come up to the standards even of her exemplars, the Icelandic sagas" – and he prophesied that "her novels will in a short time lack readers."

The rival candidate, Gorky, had been reported on negatively several times since 1918, when he was first proposed. With the aid of the specialist report from the eminent Slavonic authority Anton Karlgren, it was possible in 1928 to see how the line of development initiated with *My Childhood* "revealed its remarkable historical and literary significance." The figure of Gorky had acquired "quite a different status from before and inspires quite a different respect and sympathy, even though as a politically active person he is still quite obscure." (The 1918 report had curtly observed that Gorky's "anarchistic and often downright raw writings" were outside the framework of the Nobel Prize, but in 1928 his political leanings were overlooked.)

Gorky's works in the form of memoirs were the books that Karlfeldt and Österling wished to see rewarded. In addition to Gorky's autobiography, the report recommended only two of the earlier stories and *Na dne* (The Lower Depths); the rest of his opus was ruled out. These works contained "a great and genuine depiction of reality," in contrast to "gaudy and false romanticism" courting public attention through elements of "destitution and rawness" in the early stories, and a naturalistic "brutality" in the series of novels: "What was new in them consisted above all in an extensive and wearying account of such aspects of life that the great writers of the previous generation did not consider worthy of detailed treatment."

We shall soon see the 1929 Nobel Committee referring to "the great style" in Tolstoy's "classical realism." In accordance with this norm, certain aspects of life were designated "unworthy" of thorough treatment. But the attempts at "the creation of new figures and types" had not succeeded either "with anything like the certainty and power of which Russian novel-writing has previously shown itself to be capable." It is thus with regard to the balance associated with "the great style" that certain naturalistic features were condemned as "exaggerations."

Hallström feared that the Nobel Prize, even if awarded specifically for the memoirs, "would in the world at large be taken as a mark of approval of Gorky's writings in their entirety and thus provide a dubious advertisement for them, dubious also with regard to the respectability of the members of the academy as judges of literary taste." Schück – who proposed Gorky in order to have his candidacy put to the test, and who found "a truly significant author" in the autobiography and *Na Dne,* a writer who "despite all the dirt in which he moves" still possessed much of the required idealism – finally agreed with Hallström that a prize to Gorky would be misunderstood. He disregarded the fact that Gorky "is or was a Bolshevist"; the academy ought "to have enough spine to stand against a political opinion." But the public would assume the prize had been given for *all* the works. It is interesting that Schück, with support from Karlgren, had a principal objection to the rest of Gorky's work different from Hallström's. He disapproved of the "stereotyped" ideological phraseology – which often got the better of the characterization – the "bad First-of-May rhetoric" in the times of poverty and the "watered-down revolutionary jargon" in the period of agitation.

The 1928 report also had a few lines that are remarkable for their summary justice. Henri Bergson had been recommended by the specialist Hans Larsson and was chosen by the academy in that year as the recipient of the 1927 prize. The disapproval of the committee is important on a point of principle: "The grounds are the same as those so often given before when the question rises of widening the scope of the prize to other than literary works: the difficulty of acquiring a clear view of new areas, from which only by chance and without more general competition, a name here and there and now and then is submitted to the academy." In his history of the Nobel Prize in Literature, Österling clarified the considerations that enabled the academy to overcome these reservations: "It was obvious that Bergson's inspiring influence on modern literature was a principal motive behind the decision." He added that "the great vogue of Bergsonianism at the beginning of the twentieth century was a heartening counterbalance to materialism, and it has been compared to the influence of Schelling's philosophy a hundred years earlier. Unmistakably, it was in harmony with the spirit of Alfred Nobel."[5]

The prizes to France, Yeats, and Shaw were happy results of the efforts made by the Swedish Academy of the 1920s to overcome its earlier limitations. Toward the close of the decade, however, examples of the inadequacy of the aesthetic norms resorted to accumulated. With the criteria of "the great style," it was not in the long run possible to meet the claims of the vital new literature of Europe in the 1920s. The treatment of Thomas Mann's candidacy is a good illustration. That he was given the 1929 prize "principally for his great novel *Buddenbrooks*" is a sensational devaluation of *Der Zauberberg* (The Magic Mountain). When Mann was first discussed in 1924, there was general failure to agree even on the greatness of *Buddenbrooks*. Schück and Karlfeldt were unable to subscribe to Hallström's high estimation, and Österling thought it wisest to await the new work. In the 1929 report Hallström affirmed that *Buddenbrooks* was "a masterpiece in the tradition of bourgeois novel-writing," indeed, "a high point in contemporary fiction generally"; but in considering the aesthetic demands of "the great style," he did have a reservation about the novel: "In human significance, if not in the greatness of its style, it approaches the classical realism of Tolstoy." On the whole the report found Mann's work "uneven," though there were high points in *Tristan* and *Tonio Kröger,* which contained "for a writer of literature a new and bold espousal of life's healthy and prosaic simplicity, as opposed to aesthetic sophistication." The words could imply disapproval of *Der Zauberberg,* which was not even mentioned in the 1929 report. In the previous year the committee, along with the specialist, Hallström himself, had felt it to be sufficient to designate the novel as "remarkable in several ways, of significant content, but from an aesthetic point of view much too extensive and heavy to be counted among Mann's best creations." Two members of the committee–the proposer, Österling, and Hallström–thought, though, that "the most outstanding of Thomas Mann's earlier works are of such confirmed literary value that they could well justify his being given a Nobel Prize." That argument succeeded in 1929–although Karlfeldt gave his vote "with doubt" partly because twenty-eight years had passed since the publication of *Buddenbrooks,* and partly because the latest major work did not seem to strengthen Mann's suitability for the prize. This unanimous repudiation of *Der Zauberberg* was no doubt an expression of the aesthetic values connected with "the great style." Those holding a view of literature that valued "the plastically rounded figures of great literature" and the composition's "repose, moderation, completeness, and clarity" could hardly feel attracted to what caught the attention of European authors: "the bold attempt to extend the scope of the traditional novel to embrace an encyclopedic range of knowledge structured according to the principles of musical form" (Gunilla Bergsten). That following aesthetic principles based on the Goethean ideal should simultaneously have caused the committee to fail to appreciate the foremost adherent of the freer, essayistic, and discursive novel structure in *Wilhelm Meister* is one of the many ironies in the history of the Nobel Prize.[6]

In 1931 the lack of sympathy for the new epic orientation of the time became clearer, as in the case of Martin Andersen Nexø, who rather unexpectedly had to atone for the sins of the avant-garde. He was reproached for the "obscurity" caused by the way in which his "episodes are tossed at the reader abruptly and without preparation," an objection that immediately had wider consequences: "The writer has the modern bad habit of wanting to achieve effects through surprises and illusory vigor, at the expense of motivation and clarity of view." The creation of surprise, or the deviation from the norm, was a leading principle in the aesthetics of the avant-garde in the 1910s and 1920s. The Swedish Academy was loyal to the very norm that the avant-garde declared its intention of violating.

The committee showed another limitation when faced with subtle, extensive psychological analysis. It can be illustrated by the treatment in 1927 of the French novelist Édouard Estaunié, even though he can hardly be said to deserve a place among the pioneers of the age. Recognition was made of his "masterful descriptions of spiritual conflicts, deepened and typified into universal significance." Thus far Estaunié fit the neoclassical ideal. But the form-giving qualities of "the great style" were sought in vain. Estaunié lacked "a sufficiently plastic and multifaceted imagination for characterization, and a sense of reality adequate to enable him to give three dimensions to what he describes." His analysis of inner life was "rich in thought" but gave no "immediate impression of a concrete truth of life," of "a re-creation of human nature, so often irrational, as it is." The writing, rather, resembled experiments "in a sheltered room, in windless air," where the figures were seen either "too long from inside" or simply in passing, and in both cases without "the corporeality that alone creates illusion." It would no doubt have been interesting to see this aesthetic view size up *À la recherche du temps perdu* – if Proust had lived long enough to be nominated.

The committee's most severe limitation, however, was apparent in its handling of poetry. We have so far caught only a glimpse of this in the phrase about Yeats's poems being sometimes "too obscure." Its predilection for a "simple" kind of poetry approaching the nature of folk poetry made the committee quite incapable of appreciating the symbolist and modernist currents in twentieth-century poetry. Its requirements were spelled out most clearly in the recurring discussion of Kostis Palamas, cited here from the 1930 report, which gathered together earlier threads. An important factor in the committee's doubt had been the difficulty of judging the diction of the original while relying for general impressions on translations. But the final unfavorable conclusion was based on other arguments, too. No one doubted that Palamas was "the most outstanding representative of new Greek poetry," but the question was raised whether he had "such poetic worth in the general context of contemporary verse-writing as would justify his recognition with the Nobel Prize." In his rhetorical poetry the committee could see "certainly beautiful offshoots of Victor Hugo's romantic-historical production, which for our age is somewhat distant and alien." A decisive point was that Palamas's poetry was not "simple and genuine"; instead, it exhibited "a naive self-pleasure that allows his ego to take a disproportionate place and a disproportionately high tone in the lyrical discourse." The committee wanted to find, in Schück's words, "Greek folk poetry," in "its plasticity and naive realism" reminiscent of the fragments of Sappho, instead of "the influence of French poetry.... If on such slender grounds as we have here we are going to give a Nobel Prize to an exotic author whose poems one cannot read in the original, we ought at least to have convinced ourselves that it is original and national" (1927).

The search for genuine poetry in the Europe of the 1920s was undertaken in the name of the "simplicity" and accessibility associated with folk poetry. With complete consistency the committee rejected Stefan George, Hugo von Hofmannsthal and Arno Holz, Paul Valéry, Paul Claudel, and Vicente Huidobro. George, for instance, was judged as follows in 1929:

> In the specialist report [by Per Hallström] attention is drawn to this poet's considerable significance in the poetry of his own country and also in that of others, where aspirations are roused to elevate the poetry to austere sublimity of form as well as of content. The great qualities by which he has often, in spite of a somewhat disheartening laboriousness and eccentricity, reached the desired goal, have there been acclaimed, but the altogether too exclusive aspect of his being and emotions has been commented upon, as also the difficulty of the poetic diction.

The committee considered "these limitations in the effect of a poetic oeuvre that is in many respects great" to be so "serious" that it could not agree to support "the otherwise worthy proposal."

The "altogether too exclusive aspect" and the "difficulty" resemble the other negative verdicts. From the specialist report on Claudel in 1926, for instance, the committee cites the "warm appreciation of the poet's strongly religious personality and his strangely intense, poetically rich, and imaginatively powerful, yet also extremely obscure and difficult art" – adding: "No opinion is given on the advisability of awarding this strangely esoteric poetry with the publicity of the Nobel Prize." The committee found that the uninitiated reader could not easily find his way to the undoubted religious and aesthetic values of Claudel's poetry – "the ecstatic inner life of thought and feeling finds its outward expression in a subtle stylization that comes close to distortion" – and that "the French language does not well tolerate deviation from its traditional clarity." The committee was quite incapable of a positive response to such poetry, esoteric both intellectually and aesthetically: "Even just stylistically, Claudel's melodious biblical verses are eventually wearying, and when in addition to the high-toned unnaturalness of the dialogue there is often added the most artificial unreality of the speaking figures, then it is hard to keep interest alive. With all respect for what the poet has to give, it is to be said that one seldom succeeds in drawing immediate pleasure from it." "Unnaturalness," "unreality" versus "immediate" accessibility – the terminology reveals the committee's attempt to get oriented in the new age using aesthetic assumptions from an older period – and naturally enough, not achieving any kind of contact with the new work.

When we turn to Valéry we find that in 1930 there was already, in a specialist report, a clear sign of a stand being taken against his candidacy, although the same report – by Olle Holmberg, subsequently professor of literature at Lund University – nonetheless included "considerable appreciation." The reservations were, reported Hallström, "partly of a practical nature"; it was assumed for good reasons "that such extremely and deliberately difficult poetry as Valéry's, presented to the wide public of the Nobel Prize, would appear to be only confusing, with the exception, of course, of the small circle of the initiated." It had become not simply a question of demanding simplicity and clarity as such. What had surfaced was a consideration for the practical consequences, the thought of the large audience awaiting the academy's decision. It was explained sarcastically that the "initiated" would probably consider themselves above demonstrating the master's greatness "in comprehensive language." The prize giver would "have to stand alone against the shock of the onrush of readers' confusion and questions." This idea, which recurred in the evaluation of Holz, would develop during the next period of the history of the literature prize into a doctrine permeating the discussions. We shall have cause to return in particular to Valéry.

Still less understanding was shown in the 1926 report for the Chilean poet Vicente Huidobro and his *creacionismo*. Indeed his idea of a "transformation of motifs from life" and his title *Horizon Carré* (Square Horizon) were made the butt of a fairly heavy-handed joke. There was also no comprehension of his prose poems in *Las pagodas ocultas* (The Hidden Pagodas), in which the moods were intended "to be more spontaneous and originally natural than any old-fashioned poetry" yet gave the impression of having been worked out by an accountant. The committee's lack of comprehension extended even to the form of the prose poem, which the committee assumed was derived from Tagore's English versions of his own poems – at that time, "an emergency expedient."

As for Hofmannsthal, the committee disapproved not so much of the exclusive elements as the decadent elements in his work, and of "the fluttering between different directions, for the sake of effect" (1919). In his 1919 specialist report, Hallström recognized Hofmannsthal's position as "the most shining representative" of Austrian literature, with few equals at all in contemporary writing when it came to "linguistic virtuosity and formal beauty." His foremost works, however, fulfilled "the requirement of idealism" only if "idealism" was defined as no more than "the purely artistic striving for perfection." Hallström felt that their "lack of idealism from the point of view of content" aroused his doubts, especially when in Hofmannsthal's *Elektra*'s "sickly and brutal sensualism and in the frivolous voluptuousness and wantonness of other works one encounters real signs of decay that contribute to the deterioration of contemporary taste, already disconcerted and foundering." When Hjärne, relying on the specialist report, advised a wait-and-see attitude to Hofmannsthal, he was actually expressing a wider scepticism about the "decadent" currents in literature since the turn of the century. That side of the question was left behind as the 1920s committee developed a more tolerant conception of the idealistic. Instead, they turned their attention to another element that had concerned them since 1919. Although it recognized Hofmannsthal's "exquisite art and stylistic mastery," the committee agreed in 1924 that his "somewhat motley and volatile production, with its much too uneven poetic and human values," did not constitute "sufficiently firm ground" for a Nobel Prize. In the long run Hofmannsthal did not display the calm monumentality and serene maturity that belonged to "the great style."[7]

The Nobel Committee's responses to the symbolist poets as well as to the author of *Der Zauberberg* thus disclosed how its evaluation processes were in no way attuned to the vital trends in early twentieth-century literature. Around 1930 the academy seemed to be a circle of highly gifted and educated people who lacked the tools needed to find what we, wise after the event, are able to see as the fundamental achievements in the literature of that age.

CHAPTER 4

"Universal Interest"

In the 1920s the Swedish Academy was faced more and more frequently with candidates who wrote a boldly associative, strongly condensed poetry characterized by various symbolist and modernist labels. We have already seen several examples of how the Nobel Committee, on the basis of the demand of "the great style" for simple lines, had rejected a number of such oeuvres on account of their "obscurity," "inaccessibility," and "exclusiveness." When in 1924 Reymont's "monumental" *Chlopi* was praised, the committee explained that "through a grand and simple presentation" the novel achieved "universal interest," an expression that, in the context, extended beyond "typicality" to suggest that the work had wide appeal. In judging Arno Holz in 1929, this criterion was applied to his recent "exclusive" poetry. The remarkably strong support for Holz from German universities was proof, the committee found, "of the significance assigned there to the poet's increasingly radical reforms of the principles of German verse." It was then a short step to the reflection that "here we have a purely German affair, at least so long as the poetic result of all these efforts has not achieved a kind of beauty that the ordinary reader finds accessible and convincing. With all respect to Arno Holz's in many ways most remarkable gifts of verbal inventiveness and intensity, the committee has not found his poetry of sufficient universal interest to be awarded the Nobel Prize, whose scope is universal."

From one point of view this important declaration was in line with one interpretation of Nobel's will. The Nobel Prize was intended for those who "shall have conferred the greatest benefit on mankind." It was plausible to equate this "mankind" with the immediate readership of the poetry in question. From another point of view the reference to the "universal" scope of the prize was also a natural defensive maneuver against the new difficult poetry, which broke all the norms of a "grand and simple presentation." In any event, the declaration embodied a program that remained relevant during the following decade. We shall not, of course, forget that the prize winners of the 1930s included innovators like Luigi Pirandello and Eugene O'Neill, but more striking, certainly, were the prizes to Sinclair Lewis, John Galsworthy, and Pearl Buck, who could all speak to "a wider general public."

Behind this policy was an academy with a somewhat altered composition. On the death of Karlfeldt in 1931 Hallström became permanent secretary. Thus, the two leading functions in the academy and the committee, separated since Wirsén's days, were once again united. Since Hallström was, moreover, one of the most trusted specialists, a consolidation of the authority that more than others promoted the aesthetic views associated with "the great style" and general accessibility could be expected. Along with Hallström, Schück, and Österling, the Nobel Committee of the 1930s also included the leading conservative critic Fredrik Böök and Hjalmar Hammarskjöld, who was conservative in both aesthetics and politics. Böök could indeed argue against giving the prize to a candidate who "has been read and admired everywhere" – like Galsworthy – and anticipated the pragmatic outlook of a later period in his idea of "presenting" to the world a great author who had not been boosted by "banal world fame and press popularity."[1] But this viewpoint did not in any way make him a champion of exclusive literature. Hammarskjöld counted himself among the "representatives of the reading public" in the academy, a standpoint from which it was natural to support the universally accessible authors.[2] In 1937 Schück's place on the committee was taken by Torsten Fogelqvist, Karlfeldt's successor in the academy; the popular *Dagens Nyheter* critic, with his air of an adult-education lecturer, also fit the pattern reasonably well.

In promoting the "universal" aim of the Nobel Prize, the academy excluded de facto the whole of modern poetry with its restricted appeal. Only one poet broke through the barrier – and that was Karlfeldt, who in 1931 was awarded the only posthumous Nobel Prize, after several refusals to accept it in his lifetime. But Karlfeldt was a nationally acclaimed poet with no disqualifying "difficulty" in his work; on the contrary, he was safely anchored in an older literary ideal. Just how his universal appeal was envisaged is something we will never know. None of the discussion about members is documented. When Österling in his speech at the Nobel Festival claimed that Karlfeldt, "in a so-called minor language," had created "such jewels" that "even the treasures of the so-called great literatures have only rarely been enriched by," he nevertheless had to admit that elements of Karlfeldt's oeuvre were unfortunately "inaccessible to the foreigner. ... Its most profound qualities and values are indissolubly connected with the character and rhythm of its original language." At the same time he touched rather surprisingly on a possible objection to the traditional character of Karlfeldt's poetry: here was a poet "whose inspiration is drawn predominantly from a past that is disappearing or has disappeared," yet who was "thoroughly unconventional in his means of expression and shows daring innovations, while busy modernists often content themselves with following the latest trends and fads." Here for a moment we catch a glimpse of the Österling who would hail the "pioneers" of literature. But he vanished immediately behind the conservative front that the academy of the 1930s turned toward avant-garde poetry.

The most illuminating example of the inadequacies of the prize policy of the 1930s is the treatment of Paul Valéry. The "practical" argument produced in 1930 was developed in the following year. The decisive point was that "the inaccessibility – a difficulty seemingly intended – has been intensified" through "the poet's exclusively individual handling of form. . . . Although we may well have before us a poetic achievement determined by high endeavor and by strict artistic seriousness, it is still impossible for the committee to grant it such a degree of future importance as a fruitful offering to a wider public that we could meet with equanimity the quite natural bewilderment of that public over the recognition of an author whose work is so inaccessible."

Two years later this kind of argument had become the doctrine we first saw emerging in the 1929 evaluation of Arno Holz. The committee certainly found in the wide body of opinion supporting his candidacy an indication that "in Valéry modern French poetry has its acknowledged leading practitioner"; it noted that the specialist, Olle Holmberg, fully recognized Valéry's "refined intellectuality and the bold independence of his art," but the committee doubted "if the latter can be assumed to retain a lasting quality beyond the experimental." The result was a confirmation of the policy that would be applied throughout the 1930s: "The committee members who previously expressed the same kind of doubts still see themselves unable to recommend for the universally intended Nobel Prize a poetry so exclusive and inaccessible."

These declarations echo summary verdicts such as those on Stefan George in 1931 – "this refined but very difficult poet" – and on Paul Claudel in 1937; the judgment on Claudel made eleven years before throws light on the new negative outcome of his candidacy.[3] Especially representative was the argument in 1932 around Edwin Arlington Robinson, who had been discussed several times in the later 1920s. The earlier verdicts were summed up and specified; the American poet had from the beginning aroused the "lively interest" of the committee members:

> For here it was a question of a poetry individual in form and thought, individual at least in our times because of its ideal tendency, irrespective of the taste and interests of a wider readership. It was with reluctance that we allowed the final decision to be determined by the aspect of Robinson's work that makes it less fitting for a prize, that is, its predominant eccentricity and its difficulty, two faults that have certainly not been fostered for their own sake as distinguishing marks, but that stem from the author's

own constitutional qualities. He usually combines a strong compression of the line of thought with an equally decisive profusion in its verbal dress, often enough resulting in such an unchecked flow of poetical and imaginative images that the reader has difficulty in keeping pace. This obscurity is not in itself unpardonable, since he gives us real thoughts and real poetic values, but it is a great obstacle to fairly general assimilation of what is offered.

The dilemma of the 1930s committee is summed up in these lines. On the one hand, there was appreciation of what was special in form and idea, especially if it contained idealistically inclined integrity. On the other hand, there was a feeling of binding obligation to the demand that a prize-winning writer be capable of achieving "general assimilation." This kind of balancing act had no great future in a period whose significant poetry was to be found in the various branches of symbolism. The phrasing of the committee's doubts reveals how the prohibitive "difficulty" related to an essential component of modern poetry–its associative shortcuts and its profusion of imagery.

Schück rightly noted in 1933 that the academy had rarely found itself able to award the prize to a poet. The "opportunity" both he and the majority of the committee now offered was the Portuguese poet Correia de Oliveira, who, in the eyes of both the specialist and European connoisseurs, was "the most outstanding of today's singers in his language." The assessment is interesting on two points of principle. First, Correia de Oliveira's work was the kind of poetry that both appealed to the taste of the adjudicators and fulfilled the requirement of general accessibility. While admitting that this body of work "lies somewhat apart from the line of development followed by high literature," the committee found that Correia de Oliveira's poetry "instinctively and unaffectedly preserved that idealism that is such an important part of the essence of poetry," and that it was characterized by "emotional immediacy and simplicity. . . . It cannot be called great [but] it is clear and easily comprehended, with a popular touch–the latter a very rare quality nowadays." Both Österling and Böök took an unfavorable view of the proposal, however, and the academy followed their line.

The other point of principle has to do with judging literature from a foreign culture. Linguistic barriers played their part in the assessment of the Portuguese poet, as in the case of Palamas: "The most decisive element of the impression we receive, when it comes to the verse, i.e., the linguistic mastery in the shaping of thoughts and images and the resonance and associative power of the music, eludes direct comprehension." But more important in the long run was an argument put forward by Schück in an individual statement. He was clearly troubled by the fact that several of Correia de Oliveira's poems "strike *us* . . . as rather simple and trivial." (He therefore mentioned in particular the lyrical drama of ideas *Job,* which "even a non-Portuguese must well recognize ... as a significant work of art," at least one full of the desired idealism.) But he suspected that "the Portuguese themselves see the matter differently." It could scarcely be right "to strictly apply only our Swedish taste to the works of authors belonging to peoples whose view of life and general conceptions are remote from ours. ... So far as it is possible for us we ought to try to understand and appreciate their view of literature." We shall return to this important statement in the later discussion of the widening international scope of the Nobel Prize. At the moment another point is of interest, and that is the apparent contrast between the committee's reluctance to extend its understanding to complicated poetry and its readiness to overcome any difficulty that is ethnologically based. Opposition melted in the face of "popularity." What "attracted" Schück in Correia de Oliveira was "the popular and national element in his poetry," which was built "on purely native traditions."

If Correia de Oliveira was poetry's answer to the demand for "universal interest," then his prose counterpart was Sinclair Lewis. The choice in 1930 of this best-selling writer is the telling introduction to a decade in which the committee and the academy sought literary quality in works characterized by "general assimilation."

Lewis was carefully weighed against Theodore Dreiser; both had "the same literary inclination for bold, true-to-life descriptions of people and society," and each had perhaps achieved "lasting monumentality" in only one work: Lewis's *Babbit* and Dreiser's *An American Tragedy*. Thus, they both exhibited the "classical realism" that the 1920s committee related to "the great style." Dreiser was characterized as a "weightily serious" author who in "his unadorned factualness" strictly followed "the tradition in naturalistic fiction introduced by Zola"; underlying his "consistently dark view of life" was "a tenderness for human suffering," which "in the midst of real tragedy reaches greatness through its inspired intuition." Lewis had "quite a different temperament, his cheerfulness and alacrity give a festive air to his crusading social criticism. ... His intelligence is clearer and more supple than Dreiser's, and his culture is firmer; if his psychological intuition is perhaps lacking in depth and range, then he has instead a mobility and quickness, a singular virtuosity in the invention and in the linguistic character of the dialogue that make his scenes more lucid. Dreiser's foremost strength, his all-embracing sympathy, has its counterpart in Lewis's humor, which in its way is equally inclusive."

In this deliberation, which was moving toward a conclusion in Lewis's favor, we can see features of "the great style" – "more lucid" and "clearer" – and the highly valued gift of "humor." These properties also ensured general accessibility; the committee pronounced Babbit to be "a figure of typical significance, of a kind not achieved in contemporary literature – a kind in which the nation with greater or lesser pleasure recognized itself." A decisive point was that in his latest book, *Dodsworth*, Lewis had complemented his criticism of his countrymen with a picture of the European mentality, which "in sometimes brilliant manner gives greater impartiality and balance to his assessment." We recognize the criteria of objectivity and balance. It is not unimportant either that Lewis's other works were found to be "much less uneven than Dreiser's."[4]

The 1932 choice was very similar to that of 1930. John Galsworthy also wrote of "typical" human fates; from his rich gallery of figures there emerged "the history of a whole age ... the disintegration of the classical bourgeois Victorian era into a modern radical anarchy of intellect and emotion"; this "perspective" gave the Forsyte novels "a weight, a range, and a depth that secure for it a distinguished and special place in contemporary literature." Like Lewis, Galsworthy had achieved – continued the committee in 1932 – "greater objectivity." If the committee appreciated the American's humor, it could also value the Englishman's satire. It is interesting that Galsworthy's satirical attitude had to be reconciled with the "idealistic" aim of the prize. From the start Galsworthy had aimed the weapon of his satire "at what seemed to him narrow and hard in the national character, and he appealed instead to justice, sympathy, and imagination as means of liberation from the constraints of the ego. ... One can scarcely say he has attacked real human values; he has been quite free of decadent symptoms." In addition, Galsworthy displayed "the purely artistic idealism ... strictness in the style, contempt for vulgarity and unaesthetic effects."

The committee was aware of the limitations of both Lewis and Galsworthy. Lewis's psychological intuition lacked "depth and range" in comparison with Dreiser's, and Galsworthy's intellect was not of a "large format," even if it was "fine and firm and is put to use in a fearless search for the truth without resort to paradox" (qualities credited to the account of his idealism). In the course of assessing these two realistic oeuvres, whose social relevance was of wide application, the reports implied an awareness in the committee's judgment that it was not dealing with two really great writers but rather with clever painters of characters and society who had a very wide public appeal.

The choice of the Russian emigrant author Ivan Bunin in 1933 has certain parallels to the choice of Lewis and Galsworthy. Anton Karlgren's specialist report affirmed Bunin's significance as "the last Russian prose master with the stamp of the great tradition." A reservation about Bunin, however, had been expressed in 1931: "We do not meet here any great or rich creative power, nor any irresistible or compelling narrative gift, nor any characters who in our imagination take on an intense personal life. ... Thus, the most remarkable qualities of the Russian literary tradition are not to be found here." That reservation reappeared in 1932: it was "only in a somewhat diluted manner" that Bunin's writing "continues the great tradition of

Russian narrative art." It was further noted that the translations did not give "a sufficiently clear picture of the stylistic mastery for which Bunin is credited by his countrymen." The committee was forced to depend upon "cultivated Russian opinion, both among emigrants and at home." Bunin's main proponent on the committee, Österling, cited this writer's "strict artistry." He also stressed that Bunin had "carried on the classical Russian traditions in prose writing," a claim with various implications: it gave belated recognition to a great tradition whose foremost representatives had in their time been passed over by the academy and it implied that Bunin satisfied the general accessibility requirement.

The 1937 winner, Roger Martin du Gard, also seemed to perpetuate a great tradition. In his presentation of Martin du Gard in *Stockholms-Tidningen* on 12 November, Österling called him "possibly the most remarkable practitioner [of the] broad and daring branch of French realism whose roots are in Flaubert and Goncourt"; this "genuinely French narrative art, which for half a century or more has provided world literature with several indisputable masterpieces" was, in Martin du Gard, "for the first time the subject of this particular honor." As with Bunin, this was a belated recognition of a great tradition as embodied in a late representative. The Nobel Committee had earlier – in 1935 – signaled its "interest" in *Les Thibault* (The Thibaults) but had chosen to delay "its definitive treatment" until the series was completed. In 1937 the total work was finished (except for the epilogue), but that did not mean that the discussions that year were free of complications. On the contrary, the committee failed to agree on any name. On behalf of the majority Per Hallström was sceptical of "the modern giant-novel"; *Les Thibault* belonged "from an aesthetic point of view, to a doubtful art form." The depiction of the main character Jacques and of the period atmosphere around him were "a trial of strength," but the narrative as a whole was "wearisome through an excessive desire to include everything." The work was discredited not only by the author's "over-busy and methodical realism" but also by his overly abundant psychologizing. He was not content with giving the reader's imagination "what it needs to be set in motion. . . . He fixes on the page everything he can find to be felt and thought in a given situation" – quite at odds with "the rapid and airy dynamism that characterizes the intellect and the emotions." Here we can see again the reservations about excessively detailed psychological analysis that we earlier saw in the evaluations of the late 1920s committee. Österling was Martin du Gard's man in quite a different manner. In a minority report cowritten with Fogelqvist he was aware that the series as an artistic whole was "uneven and encumbered by certain weaknesses," yet he claimed that the family chronicle in its later volumes "is raised to a new level and encompasses an extended tragic horizon." His emphasis on how the work "with regard to its living strength, universal interest, and psychological richness has scarcely been matched in contemporary literature" would play a decisive role in the academy's final decision. It is of special interest that his skillful argument included the criterion that was so central in this period, that of "universal interest." And as a natural accompaniment we find two other bases of evaluation characteristic of the time spelled out in Österling's newspaper article: Martin du Gard was "in his methods as a depicter of life always ... clear and firm, commendably unaffected in his language, too, where he strives primarily for plastic simplicity and energy." Österling was not yet the spokesman for the "pioneers" of literature, which role would set his mark on the postwar period.

The 1938 prize went to Pearl Buck, the most striking choice of an author of limited caliber yet universal range. Österling touched on her world fame in his presentation in *Stockholms-Tidningen* on 11 November: the prize came "only as a confirmation." These words encapsulate the policy of the 1930s.

The prize was given "for her rich and truly epic descriptions of peasant life in China and for her biographical masterpieces." The first element referred primarily to *The Good Earth,* and the second referred to the recently published works *The Exile* (1936) and *The Fighting Angel* (1937), which, according to Hallström's specialist report, would provide a more secure basis for a prize than was usually the case.[5] The 1938 academy should clearly not be reproached on account of Pearl Buck's later shortcomings; we must remember the perspectives available in that particular year. Yet there is no doubt that the whole affair was conducted with haste. In its report of 8 September the majority of the committee was still in favor of another candidate, the Flemish storyteller Stijn Streuvels; Österling preferred Hermann Hesse, and only one member – Torsten Fogelqvist – was willing to vote for Pearl Buck. Fogelqvist felt that Streuvels's descriptions of the life of common people had been written too long ago to qualify for the prize. Instead, he adhered to the "strongly positive" remarks on behalf of Pearl Buck in Hallström's specialist report and in the Nobel Committee's own statement. Anyone "insisting on a close connection between motivation and proposal" would have expected the committee's statement to "result in a recommendation." Instead, on the basis of a minority report dated as late as 19 September, the academy itself voted to award the prize to Pearl Buck without testing her candidacy over several years, as is the usual practice.

Reactions were strong. In the press there were sour predictions that prizes would soon be going to best-selling authors like Margaret Mitchell and Anita Loos.[6] Things did not go quite as badly as that, but in 1938 the academy did have to deal with a proposal to give the prize to Margaret Mitchell for *Gone with the Wind* – and consequently had to devote a serious discussion to this curious proposal. The episode throws a faint light on a weak aspect of the whole selection system: there is a significant degree of incompetence among those who, in various parts of the world, have the right to nominate candidates because of the positions they hold. But the committee's own judgment was hardly impressive. It reported that Margaret Mitchell's novel recounted the catastrophe of the American South "with exceptional power. . . . Her description of the concrete reality of the world that vanished cannot be highly enough praised." The book also contained "a wealth of powerful and exciting incidents and is infused by an unrestrained energy in the depiction of character." The committee noted, however, that this energy could produce "results doubtful to the sense of reality." It was also remarked that "the harrowing historical drama" had not been imbued with "enough of the tragic conception inherent in it. . . . It could have offered us loftier and more extensive views and above all more profundity." The conclusion was therefore somewhat cool: "The book is without doubt remarkable, and remarkable, too, from a literary point of view, but it nonetheless cannot be regarded as an entirely successful work of art." The proposal, though, was by no means rejected; the committee settled for a wait-and-see attitude. This generous estimation of *Gone with the Wind* – in the year the prize went to Pearl Buck – sharply illustrates the kind of results that the criterion of "universal relevance" could produce.

In its application of the idea of the "universal" intentions behind the Nobel Prize, the Nobel Committee can be said to have *reinforced* aspects we have seen in the reports of the 1920s. In several other respects the discussions of the 1930s were a continuation of those of the preceding decade. We saw the emergence in 1921 of a new and more generous interpretation of the "idealistic tendency": "broad-hearted humanity." That interpretation colored the practice of the 1930s as well. Under its influence there was a continuous reevaluation of Johannes V. Jensen, focusing on his later work. In 1931 his new collection of poems was said to combine "a formal perfection of rare purity and freshness" and "a harmonious and humanly beautiful content. . . . The rest of his later works, as well his view of mankind, have acquired a more humane aspect. The phenomenon is as pleasing as it is surprising and cannot fail to affect the committee's attitude toward an author who is in so many respects richly gifted but who is also so frequently repelling."

The keyword *harmonious*, which appears here alongside the idea of "a more humane aspect," belongs, of course, to "the great style." It is a conception that no longer played such a prominent role in the 1930s. Yet this stylistic ideal reappeared quite clearly in the discussion of Miguel de Unamuno, a discussion that touches interestingly on questions of principle. In spite of the enormous support for his candidacy from all of the Spanish-speaking world and from many countries outside it, and the affirmative support given by the specialist report, the 1935 committee presented a divided attitude. In Unamuno's poetry of ideas could be recognized "simplicity and greatness of style, in its concision it is beautiful and firm." His prose, on the other hand, gave pause with its "mathematical abstraction";

here the committee found "not complete human natures, but isolated ideas that act like physical beings." "The same abstract inclination" was found in the plays. In other words, the author was reproached for lacking the "plastic" depiction of character associated with the aesthetic norms behind "the great style." From a more recent perspective it is easy to understand the limitations implied by the report's reference both to "a not very rewarding experiment" when in one play "the Fedra motif is transposed into a modern and Christian atmosphere" and to "an empty caprice" when in another play Don Juan is allowed to become "a basically asexual figure." This lack of understanding for such departures from the norm reveals the committee's lingering devotion to the classical ideal. Yet the evaluation of Unamuno also gives rather a surprising example of how German idealistic philosophy was still a factor to be reckoned with in the mid-1930s. He was said to base "humanity's longing for immortality exclusively on the individual's demand for a continued existence," a peculiarly Spanish way of stressing "the self-assertion of the individual. . . . It is closer to Germanic idealism to accentuate the demand for eternal and absolute values, beyond and above the life of the individual."

A continuation of the practice of the 1920s can also be seen in the 1930s committee's reluctance to step outside the field of literature. As previously noted, such reluctance had led the committee to set Bergson aside while the academy as a whole had a different view of the French philosopher. In the 1930s the reports constantly reiterated doubts on the question of extending the scope of the literary prize, as for instance in the treatment of Benedetto Croce's candidacy in 1933. The internal specialist, the philosopher Hans Larsson, had given "his unconditional recommendation" and made a point of stressing Croce's unique stature and his influence on contemporary thought. The committee, however, expressed its "hesitation" on the advisability "of abandoning, in favor of other areas, the literary field for which the Nobel Prize is primarily intended, so long as there are worthy proposals in that field." In the same year the same qualification was raised about the Indian philosopher Sarvepalli Radhakrishnan, judged by Larsson to be "a decisively solid and highly admirable thinker" on a level with Croce. This hesitation on a point of principle was also shared by Schück, who proposed, in the event of no literary author being found suitable, that Joseph Bédier, "the foremost Romanist of the day," be considered. This "brilliant stylist," who had demonstrated his mastery in a version of the tale of Tristan and Isolde, Schück placed before Croce, whose "rather heavy style of presentation" he could scarcely describe as having "literary value." Schück let his proposal drop, however, since the other committee members were considering "one, possibly two, literary authors" who, in his opinion, could be seriously considered, that is, Correia de Oliveira and "possibly Bunin." He did have doubts about the "significance" of the latter.

In considering James G. Frazer's candidacy in 1935 the arguments on matters of principle were never raised because the committee adopted the findings of the specialist report – written by Bishop Tor Andræ, a member of the academy who was a leading Swedish scholar in religious history – which recommended rejection. The author of *The Golden Bough* "represents a view of religious history that is now not only largely out of date but also, in a fundamental sense, infertile." Nor in assessing Sigmund Freud, proposed in 1936, was it found relevant to rediscuss the question of policy. The Swedish Academy was quite simply not the appropriate forum for an evaluation of "Freud's significance for humanity" – such an evaluation lay in the domain of medical science. The committee had no hesitation, however, in attributing to him "an admirable and natural literary style." Attention was also drawn to "the keenness, flexibility, and clarity of his dialectics." But it was suggested that "the flexibility of his intellect is no longer to be seen" when, in his basic approach to the interpretation of dreams, he arranged his material to fit "the Procrustean bed" of his system:

> He proceeds mechanically and quite uncritically to untangle the confusion of dreams into a grossly simplified symbolic language whose main components relate to male and female sexual organs. Whatever forms are conjured up by the vision of the dreamer are reduced by Freud through a purely geometrical process of simplification to one or the other of the two organs, which in turn become a Scylla and Charybdis that allow nothing past. Almost anything can be deciphered thus, but the method becomes too convenient and the results are undeniably monotonous and unrewarding.

Freud himself was judged to be "at the mercy of a sick and distorted imagination" to a greater extent than his patients. His inability to break free for a moment from "his fixed idea" of the Oedipus complex hardly recommended the practical value of his therapy. And at this point the generally negative report widened the scope of its criticism:

> In a historical perspective the fact that our age has imbibed his wisdom so extensively and with such fascination will come to be regarded as one of its most characteristic and most questionable features. As an argument in favor of a Nobel Prize in Literature, such a fact carries little weight. Still less so in this case, where literary authors in particular have been trapped by his teachings and under their influence have created gross effects and indulged in simple-minded psychologizing. He who has so corrupted even the least of these should hardly be honored with laurels due to an author – no matter how much he may have produced as an author in the course of his scientific pursuits.

Among other candidates outside the literary field in that same year was Ludwig Klages, whom the committee also praised for the high quality of his style: his language "unites the strictest objectivity with a fire and vigor and power that one would expect to be indeed rare in the field." In that respect

Klages could "fully measure up" to the indispensable requirements that "weighed very heavily" in the 1927 choice of Bergson. But on the matter of his vitalistic philosophy – a subject on which Hallström, author of the report, expressly disclaimed expert knowledge – the report arrived after some pages of exposition, at a somewhat reserved and sceptical conclusion: "It is to be feared that his message does not arouse any strong idealistic current in our day, and that its negative aspects are more likely to be influential. This would hardly imply the resurrection of some kind of golden age for humanity, scarcely even the appearance of the happy human animal on the arena, but rather the proliferation of the type of unhappy and confused human animal that is already sufficiently represented in our age. Approval of such a tendency would not be compatible with the spirit of the Nobel Prize."

Quite different feelings were expressed about the Spanish linguistic and literary scholar Ramón Menéndez Pidal, who had been a candidate since 1931 and was regarded by the committee as a "brilliant representative" of contemporary Spanish literature. But the limitation of the prize, on principle, to "literature as such" determined the position adopted toward him from the start, a position that remained unaltered.

It would, however, be surprising if the practice of the 1930s was no more than an extension and accentuation of the tendencies apparent in the 1920s. In fact, there are two events in which we can see omens of the radically different judgments that would be made after World War II – the prizes to Luigi Pirandello and Eugene O'Neill, and the discussion of Hermann Hesse's candidacy. Pirandello was awarded in 1934 "for his bold and ingenious revival of dramatic and scenic art" – words that anticipate the Österling era of the late 1940s onward. These words, however, originated in Hallström's specialist report, in which – as it was repeated in the committee report – the most outstanding and most typical dramas were discussed "not without criticism" but with a definite conviction that Pirandello had made "a remarkable and independent attempt to renew the world of the stage." One objection was that Pirandello's ideas "rather tenaciously circle round the problem of the ego's identity and composition, but it cannot be denied that the problem is profound and significant, and that it is treated with a true wealth and acuity of thought and with a great capacity for variation." Pirandello's dramatic opus, which included "quite often works of genius," was illuminated, as a whole, "by those rare qualities, lightness, immediacy, and, not seldom, grace. . . . One has the agreeable impression that what was given has been given in joy, without brooding and toil." Hallström, a veteran of the theater, had an eye for Pirandello's distinctive character; Schück, on the other hand, dismissed him as "a clever fabricator" whose dramas "will quite soon be forgotten." Pirandello was truly a "renewer" and *Sei Personaggi in Cerca d'Autore* (Six Characters in Search of an Author) has, ever since its appearance, exerted a considerable influence on European theater through its play with illusions and its break with realism. The 1934 prize was, indeed, the only really splendid accomplishment of the 1930s committee. Happily, Pirandello possessed an "immediacy" that kept him from being rejected on the all-powerful criterion of "general accessibility."

The prize to Eugene O'Neill in 1936, however, was not the committee's work; Schück won over the academy to his minority opinion when the committee for the second time in succession concluded its discussions without arriving at a proposal. The basic argument already existed in the 1934 report. The reason for the committee's wait-and-see attitude could be found in the specialist report by Per Hallström, which the committee summed up as follows: "This versatile and much acclaimed production offers us a variety of artistically remarkable things, but scarcely anything that from start to finish is properly matured." O'Neill's theatrical experimenting was certainly not met with the same sympathy as Pirandello's; instead, the committee saw in O'Neill's work "effects that do not rest upon means that are essential and legitimate to the drama," causing the art form of the drama to deteriorate, a situation for which O'Neill, however, was "only partly to blame. . . . On the whole this process is apparent in the playwriting, which, restless and aiming at instant public success, hardly gives scope in our days to a stricter, firmer, and more refined culture." In these last words can be glimpsed the ideal – "the great style" – that was not found in O'Neill. He was allowed a place of honor among his contemporaries on account of his "effort to reach higher, as far as the currents of the age would allow." His "poetic seriousness" and "energy" were apparent in *Mourning Becomes Electra,* although only the first two parts of that play had "the impress of perfection." Several other plays gave a "sometimes totally dispiriting impression."

Schück accepted the objections up to a point: O'Neill "undeniably lacks culture, and even his best plays suffer from doubtful aesthetic deficiencies. . . . Yet he is a great poetic force. Over the first two parts of *Electra* there is a strong tragic atmosphere of a kind that few modern authors have managed to attain." The complaint that the last part of the trilogy weakened the effect can also be directed against the Aeschylean model. Further, the first act of *Anna Christie* was "quite splendid. . . . It could hardly have been better written by Strindberg, and the little fantasy-play *Emperor Jones* is sheer poetry." Such examples could be produced only "by a real poet, and it is indeed this pure poetic strength that ought to take precedence, not the greater talent, which certainly avoids faults yet does not possess merits." With such arguments Schück persuaded the academy to accept his point of view, not in 1934 but in 1936. He did not, as was the case with Pirandello, press for O'Neill as the dramatic renewer but as "the greatest poetic force."

In the reports of the 1930s several of the more adventurous authors of the time were reviewed. Aldous Huxley appeared in 1938; since he had come to "recognize irrational moral forces as indispensable to worthwhile human existence," he could certainly be counted "as a suitable spokesman for idealism"; yet doubts remained that in view of his earlier "destructive onslaught on all the sources of spiritual life ... he can offer anything truly fertile." Karel Čapek was a recurring candidate. As the 1935 report shows, the committee had been "more favorably inclined" than the specialist Anton Karlgren, but further study had caused it to agree with the criticism of "the author's laxity and emptiness in his philosophical ruminations" and of the lack of "soundness in his descriptions." Expectations "of Čapek's advance to greater status as an author" had not been fulfilled, but "his fertile imagination and wealth of ideas" persuaded the committee nonetheless to keep his candidacy alive. In 1938 notice was taken of his novel *Prvni parta* (The First Rescue Party), which appeared to be the "most mature work in Čapek's entire oeuvre ... free from his customary striving after effects and his rather indiscriminate hunting for ideas" and a work that, "in its profoundly serious treatment of universal social-ethical problems," was fully up to the measure of "its hard-won ideas. ... The novel's idealism appears to be incontestable." In order to judge whether his performance had achieved "clarity of thought and power" suitable to a worthy presentation of its ideas, however, it was decided to wait for a translation into "some generally accessible language"; the evaluation rested, in the meantime, on the specialist report. But the occasion never arose for such a renewed consideration – Čapek died in 1938.

The most interesting name among the innovative authors was, however, that of Hermann Hesse, proposed by Thomas Mann. The initial discussion took place in 1931. In spite of the unusual stature of his personality and "his exceptionally perfect stylistic and linguistic mastery," Hesse fell short in two respects. His "idealistic tendency, in its way unusually clear and strong, leads to a complete ethical anarchy, which is hard to reconcile with the views of the founder of the prize." Nor had he achieved "a sufficiently rich and, with regard to his descriptions of life, a sufficiently comprehensive novelistic standard." The implications of the latter shortcoming were spelled out in Hallström's specialist report:

> His narrative gifts ... are seldom adequate to the creation of characters, they lack dramatic imagination and concentration, and furthermore, they lack the ability to individualize his personages through their dialogue. His leanings are chiefly musical and romantic, and when it comes to outward reality it is only the landscape that is rendered with plastic visuality and firmness, while the humans interest him merely as souls, with regard to which even his fundamental conception of their chaotic composition fails to stimulate a sharp distinctiveness.[7]

Again we can see the desire for a "plastic" and "well-rounded" type of characterization. Hesse's new divided image of man, with its element of expressionistic stylization, was measured with a yardstick that belonged to

Goethe's classicism and Tolstoy's realism. A great deal of eloquent and sensitive analysis would be needed to overcome this resistance to the author of *Der Steppenwolf.* Hesse was again one of the candidates in 1938 (when Pearl Buck won the prize) and in 1939 (when Frans Eemil Sillanpää won). Thanks to his new books he had achieved "a high rank among contemporary poets," but without it being possible to call him "a poet of truly great stature" (1939). In that year Österling obtained Fogelqvist's support in a minority report that not only took account of the later poetry – "some of the most remarkable to be found in the German language today" – but also called attention to the period around *Der Steppenwolf,* when Hesse appeared "as a boldly exploratory artist with a new spiritual orientation, an intensely sensitive interpreter of contemporary anxiety and of the play of demonic forces." Österling cleverly made a point of how Hesse, in the midst of "his modern problems," yet preserved "the connection with noble German traditions." In his latest prose work, *Gedenkblätter* (In Memoriam), his narrative gifts had reached "a calm perfection and a noble clarity of classical effect" – a form of words that appealed to the academy's residual classical ideals. It was added – as an implied polemic against the objections that had been raised against Hesse – that the story "Tragisch" (Tragic) was "a beautiful demonstration of the nature of his loyal idealism." Österling and Fogelqvist also utilized the current political situation. Just after the outbreak of war, Hesse, the Swiss citizen and refined humanist, occupied a special position: "Doubts as to principle need not arise, if the prize is now given to a master of the German language who is resident in a country that belongs to the neutral cultural reserve. Such an honor would have a special further justification in that Hermann Hesse in his capacity as a nonpolitical author is moreover a worthy and sympathetically original representative of beleaguered but persistent humanism."

There is a hint of Österling's postwar policy in his evaluation of the "boldly exploratory" artist with a "new spiritual orientation." But the time was not yet ripe for giving priority to renewers. The essential moral and aesthetic doubts about Hesse remained. One of the committee members, Hjalmar Hammarskjöld, even stated that he was "quite unable to participate in the award of a Nobel Prize to an author whose principal and best-known work is of such a subversive and . . . morbid character as Hesse's."

Dealing with the candidacies of Hesse and Sillanpää was in fact the final test of the criteria applied by the academy of the 1930s. It has been assumed that the 1939 prize was politically conditioned, a question to which we shall return. In the meantime, we can note that the Finnish prize was the result of a complicated situation in which, on 26 October, the academy had to take its stance on three candidates – Hesse and Sillanpää, of course, and also the Dutch humanist Johan Huizinga. According to a report by the secretary – about which more will be said in Chapter 7 – Hesse received two unqualified votes, from Österling and Sigfrid Siwertz, while three other members made Hesse their first choice and Sillanpää their second. Up until that time, that figure was the highest achieved by any candidate, but we shall see later that thanks to the workings of the election Hesse's position was illusory. At all events, this was probably the maximum support Hesse could count upon. The doubts were much too strong. It was actually the academy's hesitation over Hesse that opened the way for the 1939 prize to go to Sillanpää. This was the epilogue concluding a decade whose aim had been to award authors whose work was of "universal interest."

CHAPTER 5

"Pioneers"

The postwar series of prize winners shows a radical break with the prewar record. The choice of Gabriela Mistral in 1945 did not really belong to the new period because from 1940 onward a large number of nominations came from every corner of Latin America; she could well have been given the prize in that year if it had not been for the freeze imposed by the Swedish government from 1940 to 1943.[1] Her significance to our discussion – apart from the fact that a poet had at last been chosen – is that she broke the European and North American domination for the first time since 1913, when Tagore was the recipient.

But more than that had changed. The 1948 prize was given to T. S. Eliot "for his outstanding, pioneer contribution to present-day poetry" – these words indicate a new atmosphere in the academy. The postwar period was the age of the great innovators. The academy's adopting the criterion of innovation was not altogether new: Pirandello was awarded the 1934 prize "for his bold and ingenious revival of dramatic and scenic art," but given the tendency of the 1930s to favor work of a "universal" nature, this award was the exception to the general rule. A similar line of thought can be glimpsed in 1944 when the prize went to Johannes V. Jensen, who had earlier been strongly opposed by the academy. He was finally awarded the prize "for the rare strength and fertility of his poetic imagination with which is combined an intellectual curiosity of wide scope and a bold, freshly creative style." Jensen's bold, innovative style was still only one element in the total evaluation, but the notice taken of it suggests that a new basis for evaluation was in the process of being established.

The key term "pioneer" was associated above all with Österling, secretary to the academy since 1941 and from 1947 chairman of the Nobel Committee, of which he had already been an active member for a quarter of a century. His stamp was clearly visible in the new policy, which broke with earlier practice in its aim of singling out bold and renewing kinds of authorship. The series began with Hesse (1946), Gide (1947), Eliot (1948), and Faulkner (1949). Naturally, as we shall see, several members argued in favor of such a direction; but it is not unfair to refer to the postwar decades as the age of Österling.

The watershed can be discerned in 1945. That year's prize was to be Paul Valéry's – but he died in July. After this "stroke of bad luck for the Nobel Committee," there was some support for the idea of giving the prize posthumously; Österling successfully argued, however, that such a gesture, instead of being applauded, would be criticized for being too late.[2] The academy was no longer the one that in the 1930s had rejected "such exclusive and difficult poetry." Among the new members were Hjalmar Gullberg, Pär Lagerkvist, and Gustaf Hellström. On the committee were Hallström, Österling, Hjalmar Hammarskjöld, Böök, and Siwertz. Österling, Siwertz, and Böök fought for Valéry, Böök with a personal recommendation already made public: Valéry's poetic contribution was "so original and significant," and his prose "so brilliant and rich in ideas," that the prize would be justified.[3] With words like these the resistance to "exclusiveness" was beginning to fade. This concentration on artistic renewal was especially significant considering the large and vital contingent of poets and novelists in the academy. As early as 1939 Siwertz joined Österling in favor of Hermann Hesse, and as we shall soon see, Hellström was a driving force behind William Faulkner's prize. On several occasions Gullberg prepared the ground for awarding the prize to poetry, which had previously been regarded rather grudgingly. Österling in his old age emphasized how much this powerful contingent of authors in the academy meant for the new postwar policy.[4]

Valéry's role as touchstone was inherited by another "difficult" poet in the symbolist-modernist tradition, T. S. Eliot, who was first proposed in 1945 by Österling. Hallström wrote a negative report, the main lines of which are already known. He admitted that there were both beautiful passages and deep thought to be found among the associative complexities, but his final conclusion was negative, citing the preciosity and the hermetic character of Eliot's work.[5] His criticism echoed the judgment passed on Valéry in the 1930s.

Eliot had to wait in the wings for a time. In the meantime, two other controversial nominees were carried forward to the prize, Hermann Hesse and André Gide. During the 1930s Hesse had been reproached for "ethical anarchy" and defective characterization. For those acquainted with Österling's efforts to introduce Hesse to a wider public – from his preface to *Der Steppenwolf* (1932), via a series of interpretations in *Tonen från havet*, to his review of *Das Glasperlenspiel* (The Glass Bead Game) (1944) – it can be no secret who acted as pilot for Hesse around all the obstacles and forward to eventual recognition, who was the admirer of his boldly regenerative art and his careful advocate. Österling's skillful pleading of the case for Hesse can be read in his Nobel speech; as so often happens, the speech brought into the light of day words and arguments that had hitherto been confidential. Hesse was "a good fighting man" who "in a tragic age has managed to defend the hallmark of true humanism." At the same time he was an author "with a right of domicile in a country that chose to belong to Europe's neutral preserve" – a strong argument so soon after the end of the war. But in the long run another emphasis was more significant. Österling talked of Hesse's "increasingly bolder productions" from the time of a personal crisis, with "its most magnificent documentation in the fantasy-novel *Der Steppenwolf.*" It was this devotion to boldness and renewal in literature that was to be Österling's special mark. We may add that he held this view retrospectively, for in his history of the prize a couple of years later he regretted that Ibsen never received it and that "Nobel's roll of honor will forever lack the name of one of the very greatest figures in the world's dramatic literature." Österling's ambition, then, was to see this roll of honor include the great pioneers of literature.

Such an attitude is perhaps not so clear in the 1947 choice – André Gide. Although "undoubtedly regarded as the foremost name in France," Gide had nevertheless been "a highly controversial man, who from the beginning was to be found in the frontline of intellectual agitation," according to the Nobel speech, in which the turns of phrase echo the arguments used in the academy by Österling. What matters here, however, is not the efforts to guide around potentially obstructive prejudices an author who was found provocative. More important is the idea of *renewal* associated with the author of *Les Faux-Monnayeurs* (The Counterfeiters) – the inner examination and reexamination that made him seem to be a Proteus "assiduously experimenting with pole and anti-pole in order to strike living sparks," as a phoenix "constantly swinging up from the burning nest," but above all as an innovator whose "influence ... has extended over several generations and ... still gives no sign of exhaustion." Without it being explicitly stated, this tireless and much imitated experimenter appears nonetheless as one of the pioneers whom Österling was anxious to reward.

Such implications, discreetly signaled in 1946 and 1947, were spelled out clearly in the case of T. S. Eliot in 1948. Österling's acclaim of this "pioneer within modern poetry," moreover, gave an elegant solution to the conflict between exclusiveness and universality, which had caused such insuperable difficulties for the academy in the 1930s. Eliot had "from a highly exclusive and deliberately isolated position gradually come to exercise a very widespread influence"; his poetry had succeeded "in cutting, with the sharpness of a diamond, into the awareness of our generation." Österling recapitulated Eliot's own argument that poets in a complex culture must be complex, too. Of special interest in this context is the fact that the speech placed Eliot's "magnificent experiment in poetry," *The Waste Land,* alongside "another pioneer work, which had a still more sensational effect on modern literature, the much discussed *Ulysses,* from the hand of an Irishman, James Joyce." With this reference to the greatest omission of the 1930s Nobel Committee, Österling extended the 1948 acclaim of Eliot to cover the other pioneering work that was "closely allied" with *The Waste Land,* "in both spirit and mode of composition."

In fact, he extended this acclaim even further. Österling recalled the moment exactly twenty-five years before when Yeats had stood in the same place: "The honor now passes to you as being a leader and a champion of a new period in the long history of the world's poetry." The new poetic phase being honored in the person of its leading exponent was modernism, now for the first time brought into the purview of the Nobel Prize. The change was apparent at the very opening of the speech. The majority of those who had won the Nobel Prize in Literature were "representatives of a literature that seeks its natural contacts in popular consciousness, and in order to achieve its aims uses means that are more or less close to hand." But Eliot was "an exception," a poet who had chosen the narrow and exclusive path "into the awareness of our generation." It was no coincidence that Eliot was stepping into the place so inopportunely left empty by Valéry's death. The apostrophe to the author of *The Waste Land* was also an apostrophe, by implication, to all of the great adherents of the symbolist-modernist tradition, which stretched from Mallarmé into recent times.

The following year's prize – not presented until 1950 – went to a prose writer of equally radical significance. William Faulkner's immense influence on narrative fiction, not least on the French *nouveau roman* and on Latin American "magical realism," still cannot be fully estimated. The 1950 academy could know nothing of that, of course. But such an outcome was anticipated by the academy's focus on a writer who, it was felt, had distinguished himself as a great experimenter. Hellström, who wrote the specialist report, summed up his views in his speech to the prize winner. He maintained that Faulkner, as a depth psychologist, was "the unrivaled master" among living Anglo-Saxon novelists, with "fantastic imaginative powers and ability to create characters" unequaled by his fellow writers. He also focused on Faulkner's "continuous renewal. ... Scarcely two of his novels are similar technically." Faulkner was thus "side by side with Joyce, and perhaps even more so ... the great experimentalist among twentieth-century novelists." This renewal included his "perfect command of the resources of the language. ... The same desire to experiment is shown in his unrivaled mastery, among modern British and American novelists, over the richness of the English language, a richness derived from its different linguistic elements and the periodic changes in style – from the spirit of the Elizabethans down to the scanty but expressive vocabulary of the Negroes of the American South." This appreciation of the "experimentalist," shared by other members of the academy, was not necessarily correlated with the "pioneer" quality. In the case of Faulkner, the academy lacked the longer perspective offered by Eliot's achievement, but, as with the previous year's prize, this one recognized a literary force that could reasonably be expected to exercise a refreshing influence.

Obviously, such high regard for pioneers could conflict with other criteria. The committee's postwar practice was characterized on the whole by choices between the great "pathfinders" and the solitary "masters," between those whose work appeared as a point of intersection in the wider context of literary history and those who had perfected a tradition and created significant work of a kind that was sufficient unto itself. The tension between these two types of choice is obvious in the list of prize winners. After a series of awards to experimenters, which culminated with the awards to Eliot and Faulkner, came four prize recipients who by contrast were solitary masters. The wording of the award to Winston Churchill referred expressly to "his mastery of historical and biographical description," but the prizes to Bertrand Russell, Pär Lagerkvist, and François Mauriac could be regarded from a similar viewpoint: significantly, Lagerkvist was rewarded "for the artistic vigor and true independence of mind with which he endeavors in his poetry to find answers to the eternal questions confronting mankind." This idea of artistic "vigor" – the similar phrase applied to Mauriac the following year was "artistic intensity" – was an overall criterion for the kind of writing that appeared to be in steady competition with that of the pathfinders. But, of course, a pioneer could also be hailed as a master, as happened in 1954 when Hemingway was honored for "his mastery of the art of narrative, most recently demonstrated in *The Old Man and the Sea,* and for the influence that he has exerted on contemporary style."

Even such a brief review of the wording used in the prize presentations can show how particular usages of the term "pioneer" could limit its significance. The term was applied not just to writers who, like Eliot, had gained a wide international importance. The pioneer criterion could also be used in the recommendation of authors who within their national or linguistic borders had been of great significance to their followers. In quick succession, in 1955 and 1956, prizes went to two authors of such a kind: to Halldór Kiljan Laxness for "his vivid epic power, which has renewed the great narrative art of Iceland," and to Juan Ramón Jiménez for "his lyrical poetry, which in the Spanish language constitutes an example of high spirit and artistic purity." Gullberg clarified the word *example* in his speech to the laureate. The Jiménez who first appeared on the scene was "no bold regenerator," but the later Jiménez, who turned his back on his earlier work and could now be characterized by "his formal experimentation," had become an enormously significant influence on the poetry of the Spanish-speaking peoples: "Rafael Alberti, Jorge Guillén, Pedro Salinas, and others whose names are now part of the recent history of Spanish poetry have been his disciples; and to their number we can also add Federico García Lorca, as well as the Latin American poets, with Gabriela Mistral at their head." This line of reasoning shows how Gullberg must also be counted among those who gave decisive weight to the role of renewer. But at this time others, including Dag Hammarskjöld and Eyvind Johnson, also used terms like "innovative significance" and "pioneer."[6] Österling was rather cool, however, toward Jiménez; he had a higher regard for the literary critic Menéndez Pidal.[7]

This oscillation between pioneers and solitary masters continued throughout the postwar period. The brilliance of the solitary figure was often referred to in terms of "vigor" or "intensity." In contrast to Jean-Paul Sartre, whose work "has exerted a far-reaching influence on our age," Samuel Beckett, with his "new forms for the novel and drama" in the depiction of "the destitution of modern man," and Vicente Aleixandre, who represented "the great renewal of the traditions of Spanish poetry between the wars," we find Ivo Andrić rewarded for "the epic force with which he has traced themes and depicted human destinies drawn from the history of his country"; Mikhail Sholokhov hailed for "the artistic power and integrity with which, in his epic of the Don, he has given expression to a historic phase in the life of the Russian people"; Aleksandr Solzhenitsyn given the prize for "the ethical force with which he has pursued the indispensable traditions of Russian literature"; and Isaac Bashevis Singer distinguished for "his impassioned [literally, "intense"] narrative art which, with roots in a Polish-Jewish cultural tradition, brings universal human conditions to life." Pioneers dominated from 1946 to 1960, starting with Hesse, Gide, Eliot, and Faulkner and concluding with Boris Pasternak, Salvatore Quasimodo, and Saint-John Perse. That Pasternak belongs in this category is clear from remarks made by Österling in a 23 October 1958 radio broadcast: he described Pasternak as "a pioneer with modern inspiration" and a renewer of the Russian language. In general it can be said that as the great renewers of modern poetry, fiction, and drama gained recognition, this criterion became less important. The modernist tradition gradually became so well established that it was no longer felt to be necessary to emphasize the avant-garde aspects of a Pablo Neruda, a Harry Martinson, or a Czesław Miłosz. These authors belong not to the heroic period of modernism but to its rich harvest.

In 1964 two contending pathfinders were set against each other; both of them had, from such a viewpoint, merits and deficiencies. "The final contest," wrote Karl Ragnar Gierow to Erik Lindegren on 9 October, "will be between Sartre and Auden." The wording of the prize to Sartre would mention his wide influence; Gierow also made the point that *Les Mots* (Words) "seems to presage a new and vital stage in his authorship." Against Sartre it could be said that "he is more of a debater than a properly creative artist." As Österling said in his 22 October radio presentation, "the message remains the essential thing" in a "realistic" dramatic form. In other words, Sartre was a philosophical pathfinder, not a pioneer like Pirandello or Faulkner. W. H. Auden, on the other hand, was counted among the *literary* innovators. To his advantage, continued Gierow, was the fact "that – unlike the other two [Sartre and Sholokhov] – he belongs to the century's innovators" (and in addition, "his critical writings display an unusual degree of sharpness and awareness"). On the negative side, "his best period is now rather far back in time." The whole situation was complicated by the question of to what extent the committee should consider different nationalities (of which more in Chapter 9): "Only the most compelling and obvious reasons could justify giving the prize for the fifth time [since the war] to the same country." Apparently, compelling reasons were found. In Gierow's words, "the more likely of the two principal candidates" proved victorious on 21 October – only to turn down the prize a few days later.[8]

Gradually, however, the signs increased that a new generation was taking over from the old. Just a decade after the beginning of Österling's new policy, Dag Hammarskjöld exclaimed, in reaction to the choice of Churchill, Hemingway, and Laxness, "Oh – if only we could show a touch of daring!"[9] For him the attitude toward Perse epitomized the division between the generations: Österling "seems to prefer the youthful work"; Sten Selander (to whom he was writing) could go "as far as *Anabase* anyway"; he himself was "enthusiastic only from *Exile* onward."[10] This distinction was not entirely just: Hammarskjöld could not, of course, see Österling's role in the matter as clearly as we can with our historical perspective on the evidence. But he did touch on one important factor: the demand that the prize go to innovators was more frequently made by the younger generation, while the previous guardians of the same criterion looked on sceptically.

In reality the Nobel Committee of the early postwar period never abandoned the theoretical reservations about "exclusive" poetry that had characterized the committees of the 1920s and 1930s. The sequence of "difficult" poets – Jiménez, Pasternak, Perse, and so on – raised certain problems. In Österling we can discern something like an ambivalence between the claim that pioneers should be rewarded and the reservation on principle about esoteric poetry. It was Salvatore Quasimodo who came close to the ideal, a poet who, as Österling said in his speech, was "one of the renewers of modern poetry," with a natural sense of belonging to the classical tradition, but at the same time a poet whose "human pathos irresistibly breaks through the hermetic form in which he was at the beginning restrained." The latter remark was in fact the view of the committee, which Österling made public with his speech.

Österling's mixed feelings can be detected in his attitude toward Saint-John Perse, the 1960 prize winner. It is well known that Dag Hammarskjöld was Perse's main advocate. The energy and persistence – probably unique in the annals of the literature prize – with which year after year Hammarskjöld tried to win supporters for his cause – founded on a very thoroughly considered view of Perse's significance – is evident in the correspondence now available for study in the Royal Library at Stockholm; the picture is supplemented by the set of letters preserved in the Lund University Library. (Here is also evidence of the astonishing amount of work he devoted to the examination and refinement of Lindegren's translations.) As is known, Hammarskjöld translated his idol himself and composed the brilliant specialist report in 1955 that provided the basis for the final verdict on Perse (and whose main features are known).[11] From our point of view what is particularly interesting is how Perse, struggling ceaselessly with the existential problems, was presented as at the same time a renewer and a "preserver" of a great lyrical tradition – a kind of surrealist free of all doctrinaire fortuitousness who was also in line with the classical French verse tradition as developed by Baudelaire, Rimbaud, Mallarmé, and others up to Claudel. It was a very skillful argument that both seized upon Perse's role as a "renewer of form" and offered the chance to hail the great French tradition of which he was "the foremost living proponent" (thus making good on earlier omissions as Hammarskjöld mentioned in letters to Österling in 1956, in which he recalled that "both Claudel and Valéry departed without reward").[12]

Österling gave due measure to these points in his speech. Perse was "one of modern poetry's foremost pioneers," as well as a poet who continued "a glorious line in French poetry and above all the rhetorical tradition of its classics." In his homage to – significantly – the "pioneer," Österling seemed nevertheless on this occasion to be of two minds, because for him the difficulty of Perse's work had prevented his unqualified appreciation. As Hammarskjöld had put it bluntly several years before, Perse was "out of the question, being 'much too exclusive.' "[13] Österling also found "the inexhaustible imagery" of Perse's rhapsodies to "be tiring because of the concentrated effort that the poet demands of his readers." Yet the speech demonstrated how Österling tried to overcome his fundamental misgivings. Perse was the author, "certainly ... of highly individual creations, linguistically and intellectually complex, but their master is by no means exclusive in the sense of resting within self-sufficient limitations"; on the contrary, his voice wished "to be an expression of the human, in all its variety and continuity, and of the eternally creative human spirit that through the ages has contended with the equally eternal resistance of the elements." In this way Österling found a compensation for the sublime poet's heedlessness of "response and common human contact": this "isolation and distance" amounted to "a vital condition for ambitious poetry in our age." In spite of "all his apparent reserve and his frequently difficult symbolism," Perse was thus in the final analysis "a poet with a universal message to his contemporaries."

This was another echo of the 1930s criticism of difficult poetry with its lack of universal response, now heard from the man who more than any other had made himself spokesman for the great literary pioneers. Yet Österling overcame his doubts, precisely in the spirit of this innovative zeal. As a criterion, however, innovativeness gradually became more problematic. In 1967 it was time for a new pioneer, the author of *Hombres de maíz* (Men of Maize), the first great work of "magical realism." The awarding of the prize to Miguel Angel Asturias was, as *Frankfurter Allgemeine Zeitung* (20 October 1967) emphasized, a recognition of the international significance of the Latin American novel.[14] But this novel was characterized not only by what the wording of the prize called its roots "in the national traits and traditions of Indian peoples of Latin America." Asturias had also, as Österling noted in his speech, "completely freed himself from the routine of old-fashioned techniques of storytelling"; influenced at an early stage "by Europe's modernist breakthrough," the author showed, in his explosive style, "a clear affinity with French surrealism." Nevertheless, Österling showed a lack of warmth that makes us suspect that he was not among those who worked most energetically to see the prize go to Asturias. As we shall soon see, a younger generation was now making its presence felt.

In 1969, nine years after Perse's prize, came a still more difficult test of the criterion of "pioneer." That Samuel Beckett really was a controversial figure can be gathered from the fact that on this occasion Österling did not give the speech to the prize winner – an omission of striking significance. The substance of his criticism was evident in Karl Ragnar Gierow's speech, which to a great extent was a rebuttal of the idea that Beckett's pessimism should have disqualified him from receiving a prize intended for work of an "idealistic tendency" – probably one of the last occasions when this condition was central to the discussion.[15] It was only at "the depths" that "pessimistic thought and poetry can work their miracles," said Gierow. He emphasized Beckett's deep sense of human worth and found a "source of inner cleansing, the life-giving force, *nevertheless,* in Beckett's pessimism. . . . It houses a love of mankind that grows in understanding as it plumbs further into the depths of abhorrence, a despair that has to reach the utmost bounds of suffering to discover that compassion has no bounds. From that position, in the realms of annihilation, rises the writing of Samuel Beckett like a miserere from all mankind, its muffled minor key sounding liberation to the oppressed and comfort to those in need."

The earlier public account of Beckett's selection, however, is not quite correct in giving Gierow a unique role in the matter: it was suggested that he swayed the academy to his point of view by his persuasive eloquence.[16] That account ignored the fact that other members of the committee had already openly expressed attitudes very like those of Gierow: Artur Lundkvist, for instance, had argued in an essay that Beckett's annihilation myth gained, "by sheer force of contrast ... the character of a creation myth," and that nothingness became "in a way liberating, stimulating." In *Diarium Spirituale*, Lars Gyllensten claimed that "Beckett is, of course, an optimist – he lays bare the vitality, the creative power that remains when all has been scraped away that can be scraped away without life itself disappearing." It may be added that such a positive view of Beckett was by no means lacking among other members of the academy.

If Gierow's speech suggested conflicting attitudes toward Beckett's pessimism, it nonetheless allows us to see a degree of continuity with Österling's line of thought, which in a wider perspective is more important: Beckett "has pioneered new modes of expression in fiction and on the stage." This argument continued the main principle associated with Österling.

But the 1969 choice also offered a glimpse of a process of rejuvenation taking place in the academy, marked by the fact that Gierow, permanent secretary since 1964, took over as chairman of the committee in the spring of 1970. Österling was still playing an important role, but the initiative now quite naturally passed to a younger circle, represented by Gierow (elected 1961), Gyllensten (1966), Lundkvist (1968), and Johannes Edfelt (1969). The continuity apparent in the basic modes of evaluation was, however, striking. It was not only Gierow who spoke of pioneers. Among the others, Lundkvist especially was a spokesman for this point of view. In 1962, six years before he occupied chair number eighteen, Lundkvist attacked the academy for its choice of John Steinbeck, "one of its greatest mistakes," and his reasoning was that, "if attention had been focused on the *renewal* of narrative fiction, then Steinbeck would at once have been out of the picture in favor of authors like Durrell, Beckett, or Claude Simon, who from an artistic and psychological standpoint are much more central." When the prize went to Solzhenitsyn in 1970, Lundkvist was among the sceptics, and for similar reasons. In 1983 he supported Claude Simon, who, he alleged, had had "a greater influence and much greater significance" than William Golding; Simon had "carried forward the tradition from William Faulkner to the new French novel and [had] further influenced the whole range of recent Latin American literature."[17]

But obviously Gierow and Lundkvist were not alone at this time as supporters of Österling's "pioneering" motto. Several members had in a variety of contexts expressed similar views.[18] It was Gyllensten who stood for a somewhat different emphasis, which will be examined in the next chapter.

Lundkvist's indiscretion in 1983 illustrates the tension naturally associated with an emphasis on the value of innovation. In his eyes someone with the key role of a Claude Simon was unquestionably in a higher class than someone who may have been in his or her own way a "good writer." We do not need to quibble here about the tendentious adjective "good" – what concerns us is the perpetual tension, throughout the postwar period, of the choice between innovators (pathfinders) and solitary masters. The dilemma of the choice between those who stood for vital renewal and those who explored their existence, their experience, and their subject matter with personal intensity is explicit in the documentary evidence of the 1970s.

We can also see this dilemma in the personal ambivalence of someone like Gierow. In pleading for Beckett he fastened on the innovative aspects of the Irishman's achievement. The extent to which he could argue for the other choice is apparent in his 1972 speech to Heinrich Böll. In the wording of the prize, this winner had "contributed to a renewal of German literature." In our context, however, that description could readily be misinterpreted. Gierow was sketching the outlines of the historical background to Böll's oeuvre–the hungry years in Germany, an existence in ruins, in the stranglehold of dictatorship–and indicated the kind of German miracle that a new generation of poets, thinkers, and scholars stood for: "The renewal of German literature, to which Heinrich Böll's achievements witness and of which they are a significant part, is not an experiment with form–a drowning man scorns the butterfly stroke. Instead, it is a rebirth out of annihilation, a resurrection, a culture which, ravaged by icy nights and condemned to extinction, sends up new shoots, blossoms, and matures to the joy and benefit of us all. Such was the kind of work Alfred Nobel wished his prize to reward." The renewal referred to here is different from that of the pioneers, represented in German literature rather by the experimentalist Günter Grass. Here–with a direct appeal to Nobel's intentions–preference was given to the foremost representative of a moral renaissance from the ruins of the Third Reich.

Claude Simon's role as a pathfinder received a rather discreet emphasis when he finally won a majority in 1985, after having been a strong candidate since the 1960s. (In the French press it has often been claimed that the long delay in giving the prize to a French candidate was a reply to Sartre's "insult" in 1964. In the evidence there is nothing whatsoever to support this suggestion–the academy simply does not think along such lines. We should not overlook the fact that the 1969 prize was awarded in two languages, for Beckett was also a French author.) In his speech, Gyllensten depicted Simon as a representative practitioner of the *nouveau roman* in France: "The new writers were against the more conventional fiction and broke its rules that a novel should have a realistic story and move along in a lucid and coherent way in time." The wording of the prize implied such renewal when Simon combined "the poet's and the painter's creativeness with a deepened awareness of time in the depiction of the human condition." The painterly element suggested the overriding simultaneity that placed the past and the present alongside each other on the single plane of the canvas. Or as Gyllensten put it: "In a picture everything is contemporaneous. The flow of things that follow each other is brought about by the beholder's co-creative feeling moving over what actually exists as a single coherent now."

These words allude to a method for which Simon had been of immense significance in recent narrative fiction. The stress on the "poet's" creativity drew attention to the daring linguistic innovation in Simon's work, to what Gyllensten called "a close and evocative web of words, events, and environments," with separate elements gliding together and coalescing "according to a logic different from what the realistic continuity in time and space prescribes," an art in which "the language begins to live its own life." His stress upon the role of the poet is a reminder that Simon's novels belonged among those densely associative and luminously visionary texts that occupy a prominent place in the innovative fiction of our time, akin more to poetry than to epic discourse.

One passage in the speech implied reservation: in its depiction of war and its description of erotic relationships, Simon's work showed "a fixation on violence and violation." Against this picture of humans "exposed to destructive passions and selfish impulses," however, there were "contrasting elements of another kind: ... of tenderness and loyalty, of devotion to work and duty, to heritage and traditions and solidarity with dead and living kinsmen. In particular there appears as a contrast of a consoling or edifying kind the devotion to such as grows and sprouts independent of man's lust for power and overweening enterprise." And here the artistic dimension returned: "First and foremost we meet this growth, this vitality and this creativeness and this viability in language and memory, in the shaping, the renewal, and the development of what is and was and what rises again inspired and alive through the pictures in words and story for which we seem to be more instruments than masters."

"Language" and "memory"—we are back in those areas where the innovative creativity of the poet and the painter work together in "a deepened awareness of time."

In the continuous homage paid to the pioneers, there was apparently a troublesome lacuna, which critics have not failed to remark upon: the pioneers of expressionism and of surrealism were missing.[19] (The omission of Dadaism has also been mentioned; but that episode was, of course, short-lived, and the French variety at least was soon assimilated by surrealism.) As for expressionism, it is easy to be misled. Its great masters—poets like Georg Heym and Georg Trakl—were, after all, dead by the time the First World War was fully under way (Heym died in 1912, Trakl in 1914). This did not prevent one critic from bemoaning the absence of a prize for the latter.[20] There were the not altogether obvious candidates like Gottfried Benn and Theodor Däubler; the former was in fact considered in 1956, but he died in the summer of that year, and the latter was turned down as early as 1928.[21] Neither were ever referred to as examples of great neglect by the academy.

The committee's objection to Däubler's poetry–"mystical, obscure, and difficult"–reminds us that modernist poetry could not count on any understanding from the academy of the day. The expressionist inheritance, however, was taken over by a new generation that included poets like Paul Celan and Nelly Sachs; they appealed to an academy with a different sensibility. Österling probably had Nelly Sachs's roots in the expressionist tradition in mind when in his speech to her in 1966 he declared that her "symbolic language combines modernistic daring of inspiration with echoes of ancient biblical poetry." Such a characterization could have fitted the only significant woman poet of expressionism proper, Else Lasker-Schüler. It can be added, however, that Österling was personally not convinced of Nelly Sachs's stature.[22]

As for surrealism, we see more clearly that it was a later generation that received recognition–and was explicitly given preference over the orthodox old guard. Pablo Neruda's poetry, given the 1971 prize, has been regarded as surrealistic. A few years before, Lundkvist saw Neruda as almost a parallel to the French representatives of the tradition; in Neruda's *Tentativa del Hombre Infinito* (Attempt of Infinite Man) and Tristan Tzara's *L'Homme approximatif* (Approximate Man) the titles "are as like each other as the styles." But a distinction does emerge: in an essay Lundkvist said that "it is a question of judgment whether we wish to regard Neruda as the greatest contemporary poet." Similarly, Gierow argued, in his speech to the 1977 winner, that on the one hand Vicente Aleixandre was the member of his circle "who came closest to the new doctrines from Paris," and that on the other hand "Spanish surrealism" had in him "given to French surrealism what the latter had always lacked–a great poet."[23] The observable shift in the matter of poetic method is important to our discussion. Against automatic writings this poet set *la conciencia creadora*–the creative consciousness. Gierow returned to the idea in his speech to Odysseus Elytis in 1979. The significance of the new great period of Greek poetry was to be seen most clearly in this poet: the exciting meeting between surrealism and inherited myth. Gierow balanced the poet's definition of surrealism as "the last available oxygen in a dying world" against his statement that he was definitely "never a disciple of the surrealist school." Surrealism "released" Elytis's writing, but the poet dissociated himself from "automatic writing, with its unchecked torrent of chance associations." In fact, Neruda, Aleixandre, and Elytis all belonged to that second generation of surrealistically inspired writers who–like André Breton himself–abandoned the doctrinaire attitude toward automatic writing and made use of the new associative freedom and the possibilities of highly charged metaphor in order to achieve more expressive ends. The position arrived at by the academy means the results of this modified surrealism were given a higher value than those of the orthodox phase.

The poetic avant-garde thus received its recognition from the Nobel Committee in the postwar period. The modes of selection we find in the 1930s had allowed no place to symbolist or modernist poetry, scarcely even to poetry at all. The list of winners in the new period was to have opened with Valéry. Instead, poetry in general came to be represented by Gabriela Mistral, and the more exclusive type of poetry, a few years later, by Eliot. One of the most important features of the history of the Nobel Prize in Literature since the war has been the recognition of a series of difficult but brilliant poets who have consistently belonged to the great modernist tradition, which the earlier epoch had stamped as "hermetic." If a certain ambivalence remains, we can still see attempts to overcome it. The reorientation, however, was even more far-reaching. The Nobel Committee – and with it the academy – appeared ready in a manner quite different from before to listen to divergent voices, to give innovators a justified recognition, and to promote exclusive but distinguished writing. The whole idea of "promoting" unknown but important work to a wider public has recently played a large role, and it is to this idea that we turn in the next chapter.

CHAPTER 6

"A Pragmatic Attitude"

In the 1970s the Nobel Committee's promotion of the great innovators had to be reconciled with another aim: making judgments based on a "functional" or "pragmatic" viewpoint. This viewpoint is derived from the idea that when we talk about authors and scientists of a quality high enough for them to be discussed as potential Nobel Prize winners, we are talking about quality that cannot be measured. "The prize, whether in literature or in another subject, is not a prize for the best person in the world in a particular field – for such a person simply does not exist." The words are Lars Gyllensten's and come from his well-judged reply in *Göteborgs-Posten* (24 June 1984) to the critical views that had recently been put forward by the Chinese writer Tsu-Yü Hwang. After making some striking examples – "How is an astronomer in the field of radio physics to be compared objectively with a specialist in electron transmission in semiconductors?" or, "Who is best, Dante or Cervantes?" – Gyllensten outlined a reasonable way of handling the problem:

> It is a matter of finding people who are good and who deserve the prize – and of doing so in a historical perspective, with the knowledge that posterity may well decide one should have done otherwise. Some of those who are worth a Nobel Prize will receive it – for the most part, we hope, those who are well worth it and for whom the prize can be of benefit to themselves and their work – while others who are worth it will not receive it. A pragmatic attitude toward what one can do and what one can expect is no bad thing in the context.

This pragmatic attitude was not limited, however, to what the academy *could* do; it became the basic program for what the academy *should* do in dealing with noncomparable achievements at a high level of quality. The instigator of this new reading of Nobel's will – for that is what is involved – was primarily Gyllensten himself. We can see the process, above all, in two statements of principle, from 1969 and 1971, respectively, in which he put forward what to begin with was a minority viewpoint.

The forum for the expression of such an opinion had already emerged in 1969. As we have seen, the process of choosing that year's winner, Beckett, was not without complications, and composing a single report reflecting the opinions of the majority on the committee proved to be difficult. The outcome was that the individual memos were passed on to the members of the academy. This procedure, at that point something of a temporary expedient, was found to be a great help in clarifying the issue, and indeed it became a permanent feature of the selection process. The delivery of individual reports gave the other academy members a better chance of coming to an opinion based on the separate views competing with each other within the narrower group. The reform, carried through under the aegis of Gierow after 1970, can be said to have moved a larger part of the discussion to the academy.

This new framework created a forum for written statements such as Gyllensten's in 1969 and 1971 and also for a continuous and multifaceted discussion of prize policy in a form that proved more lasting and exact than purely oral debate. Gyllensten's position on current candidates cannot, of course, be reported, but the principles governing the more specific views can be quoted because he himself has made them public on several occasions.

Gyllensten's starting point was Nobel's "so-called functional attitude to the purpose of the prize" – "the donator's wish that the prize should be given to someone who is still in a creative period of his life, so that the further development of his work may be expected to follow from the encouragement of the award." Gyllensten recalled the criticism that had been made of honors bestowed for achievement already complete and concluded:

> The prize must not be a medal for services rendered – if it were then it would be a conservative gesture out of touch with present and future tendencies – but rather a kind of investment in – and as such, of course, entailing a degree of risk – the advancement of an oeuvre that still *can* be advanced. And this must be relevant both for the recipient of the prize and/or the line of development or research that the recipient's work represents in contemporary literary life, and for readers and other authors at the frontiers of literature.

This functional viewpoint was extended in the 1971 statement, which cited "two objectives" discernible in Nobel's will: "a demand for *quality* in the recipient and a demand for *usefulness* in the prize." As for the former, any "pretension to picking out the first among noncompatibles" had to be rejected, since "independent and creative efforts, with their own visions, objectives, and claims to new ground, amount to achievements that by their very nature defy comparison." This "sober, less sensational" view of the role to be played by the demand for quality led to the second criterion – the usefulness of the prize. Aligned with this we find the condition "that the prize should recognize work with contemporary relevance" – this being the interpretation given to the original requirement that the work awarded should have been carried out in the course of the preceding year. More important from our point of view, however, is Gyllensten's interpretation of information from the witnesses to the will that, according to Nobel's insistent and repeated explanation, his purpose was "not simply to reward already completed achievements but equally to create propitious circumstances for *continued efforts* and *further development* of 'the promising aptitudes' evident in the works to hand":

> Interpreted narrowly, this would mean supporting promising aptitudes in the prize-winning scientists or authors. Interpreted more widely, it ought to be possible to argue in favor of "works" rather than of people, and thus also to regard those aspects of the works that in themselves are productive, innovatory, promising, and capable of future development, irrespective of who may later come to build further upon them or in some other way benefit from them. Such a view is self-evident in the assessment of scientific achievements and their significance, as, for instance, in Nobel's own field of technical innovation – a comparable form of assessment can, of course, often be effective in the field of literature.

After discussing how these and other considerations could be applied in terms of "a few general rules of thumb of a pragmatic kind," Gyllensten asked some questions about the constructive aspects of the prize:

> Which of the nominees have produced substantial works of such quality that reading and writing "mankind" would benefit from our promotion of these works through rewarding them with money and prestige and the consequent publicity? Not the best work – for none is best where there is no common measure – but at least very good work. Not something past its best – but something still alive and promising and capable of benefiting from the prize. And such benefit arising from a prize to literary work can take many forms – for example, an original and innovatory *author* can be given the means to continue; a neglected but fertile *literary genre* can be given attention and support; an insufficiently recognized linguistic or cultural sphere (or other human endeavors and enterprises) can be encouraged by the fact of its *literary manifestations* being supported by the prize.

This pragmatic perspective on the role of the Nobel Prize is thus from one point of view an interpretation of the last wishes of a man who was himself an innovator with a keen sense of practical purpose. From another point of view it can be seen as a crystallization of Gyllensten's own thoughts as an author and a medical researcher; in other words, it can be seen in the same intellectual context as his own work, in which C. S. Peirce's pragmatism and his own scientific training were vital elements. This hardly means that such a view was unprecedented in the history of the academy, still less that colleagues of like mind were not to be found among its current members.

An early expression of a pragmatic attitude can be seen in Hjärne's arguments in favor of Selma Lagerlöf in a letter to Tegnér of 26 December 1903. After stressing the "idealistic tendency" of her work, he added:

> Further, the Nobel Prize would now be of great value to her writing. She needs proper security, freedom from the necessity of tiring herself out composing serials, stories for Christmas supplements, and so on. Nobel clearly intended his prizes to support continued work. And that is most likely to succeed if they are given to authors at the height of their powers, though in principle I would not be opposed to the idea of deserving older writers, who can still manage something, receiving their due encouragement as well.

This resembles what Gyllensten called "a narrow interpretation": supporting the promising author personally. But Hjärne combined this with a wish to draw attention to work that was not yet internationally renowned: "It is more worthy of the academy to take the initiative, on its own responsibility, in raising an author out of the mass, rather than, once some fellow has already become 'world famous,' to come running behind with its bags of money for the consolidation of his estate." In addition to this aim, which has become important in recent times, Hjärne had a more provincial and practical idea: the academy would, through its recognition of Selma Lagerlöf, "enhance its position here at home in a most decisive manner." This initiative initiative from 1903 was not altogether isolated; in a letter to Wirsén of 13 October 1908, Hjärne used the same argument in support of Eucken: "We would thus demonstrate that we were not afraid to select a worthy recipient on our own account, without feeling we ought to wait until we can come with our diploma and our pennies simply to crown a world reputation already safely established."

Hjärne in fact succeeded in getting Selma Lagerlöf the prize, over Swinburne, but it was no happy start for the pragmatic line of thought. He was not very consistent on the subject either. When one day it fell to him to write the committee report, he based his reasoning, as in 1914, on "those authors who have won renown in a wider world."

A happier manifestation of the desire to "raise" a less-than-famous oeuvre is found in Heidenstam's support of Tagore in 1913: "For the first time, and perhaps also for the last time in the foreseeable future, we would have the chance to discover a great name before it has already spent years haunting the newspaper columns." The idea had a touch of journalistic zeal to be first with the news: "If we are to succeed in this, then we cannot afford to delay and waste time by waiting for another year."[1] In a letter to Hallström of 28 August 1927, Heidenstam also expressed a wish for a discovery of a less obvious kind, but he does so without keeping a beady eye on the calendar; again, he was supporting a poet, this time the Greek nominee Kostis Palamas: "It would be pleasant if once more we could leave the beaten track and in some less familiar language come upon a great poet whom it would be unjust to neglect. It seems to me that in this case we have the chance of such a discovery."

A few years later the idea was revived by a man close to Heidenstam, Fredrik Böök, who declared it would be "defensible, indeed praiseworthy" of the Swedish Academy to "draw attention, in the view of the world, to a great author" (in this instance, Paul Ernst). Böök argued against the current choice and outlined a new policy for clearly pragmatic reasons; the prize "ought to fulfil a mission":

> Galsworthy is a popular and world-famous figure whose undemanding novel sequence has been read and appreciated everywhere. A Nobel Prize to him will not have the slightest significance, either for himself or for literature. The Swedish Academy has often and quite naturally honored successful international writers, and to a striking extent authors of widely read novels have been specially favored. It seems to me much more satisfying if the prize can justifiably be given to a significant and highly individual author who stands somewhat apart from banal world fame and press-inspired popularity. With this in mind, I find that no prizes have redounded to the honor of the Swedish Academy more than those to Tagore, Spitteler, and Yeats.

The idea of "drawing attention" to a significant author who stood "outside the noise of the marketplace" was, however, alien to the customary practice of the 1930s. In the immediate postwar years, on the other hand, pragmatic ways of thinking returned. In *Nobel: The Man and his Prizes,* Österling touched on "the purely practical benefit" of the prizes in an age when an internationally known novelist had an income much higher than the amount in question:

> It would be a justified reaction to this commercialization if in the future the Nobel Prize awards were to favor writers who do not enjoy the benefit of such a market and who, for the sake of it, do not compromise their literary standards. Only in that way would it be possible to come a little closer to Nobel's own wishes and to aid dreamers who are handicapped in their careers as writers by their struggle for daily bread. In the long run it would be better if the prizes were thereby to lose some of their present character of decorations, even though public opinion, both at home and abroad, seems to demand to a surprising degree that in the prize awards the honor should be principally stressed – for the general public naturally does not like to be surprised by names it has never heard of before.

Here already we can see the scepticism, which later declarations of the prize's pragmatic intent would share, toward the decorative "function" of a Nobel Prize, and we can also see the wish to act in the practical Nobel spirit and give the awards a promotive function. This more utilitarian approach could be interpreted, however, on two levels. Österling confined himself to the narrower assumption that support should be given to the uncompromising but economically handicapped author himself. The later extension of the concept to also include "a neglected but fertile *literary genre*" or "an insufficiently recognized linguistic or cultural sphere" was not yet part of the picture.

Österling had a few years before already offered a sample of such a pragmatic viewpoint when, during the discussion that followed Valéry's untimely demise in the summer of 1945, he aired other possibilities. In a letter to Hallström of 10 August 1945 he wrote, after dismissing Jules Romains's novel sequence as "an intellectual performance and a gigantic collection of documents" of "doubtful" artistic value, "I would place Werfel higher as a delineator of character, but in his case a prize would mean nothing at present – it corresponds approximately to the royalties from one film. I did not propose Hesse this year, but perhaps in spite of everything he would have been a worthy subject, as one of the last surviving writers of the genuine romantic, noncommercial type."

When the next year Österling resumed his support for Hesse and guided him forward to the 1946 prize, he still had his idea of the noncommercial author. His letter leads us to a quite natural conclusion – that the emphasis on bold innovators and the pragmatic attitude can be very well combined. In fact, several of the prizes to the more exclusive authors can be viewed from this standpoint, long before the "functional" concept became a declaration of principle.

Österling was not alone in holding such opinions. On several occasions between 1952 and 1962 the committee members submitted individual reports supporting a pragmatic view, including Sigfrid Siwertz in 1954. Removed from its Nobel Prize context (which must remain confidential), the principle as outlined by Siwertz may be presented thus: Over the years Siwertz had acquired the feeling that "all too often we keep to the world-famous and neglect hidden merit." He stressed the benefits of encouraging "a narrower cultural circle" and spoke in favor of the kind of candidate whose choice would let the academy really "do something." Six years later, in a variation on the same approach, Siwertz thought that the academy "ought to step outside the usual dominant cultures and give the prize to someone off the literary beaten track." This time he had a particular name in mind (his proposal refers to "this time round"). His overall feeling that great but lesser-known writers had been neglected and his desire to "do something" with the prize were more an attempt to achieve a better balance than an attempt at radical reform. Dag Hammarskjöld concurred; glancing over the list of candidates in 1955, he found it "liberating" to come across Malraux and Perse "after these broad-footed composers of epics on the verge of best-seller fame." He argued against the risk of letting Perse "follow Claudel and Valéry unrewarded to the grave while we trudge along in the footsteps of the ambitious reading circles."[2]

These expressions of the pragmatic view throw some light on a number of postwar choices. As well as world-famous pioneers like Eliot and Hemingway and well-established "followers" like Mauriac, we find several poets of very limited range, such as Jiménez, Quasimodo, and Perse, and regional figures who could have achieved a worldwide public only through the prize, such as Laxness and Andrić. Such choices could, in Österling's words, surprise an international public with "names it has never heard of before" yet could "favor writers who do not enjoy the benefits of the market and who, for the sake of it, do not compromise their literary standards."

That the honoring of pathfinders could be combined with pragmatic help is evident not least in the example of Jiménez. The give-and-take between the different criteria is also evident in the 1971 declaration that the prize should be of use to "reading and writing mankind." The reference to works being "productive, innovative, promising, and capable of future development" applied fully to the "writing" members of mankind. Those pathfinders (with their beneficent influence on younger colleagues) who were the focus of so much attention in postwar discussion of the prize were incorporated quite naturally into the pragmatic model.

A discreet hint that the intention of drawing attention to less familiar poetry was entertained by a majority of the academy in the later 1970s was given by Knut Ahnlund (himself involved in the matter) in an article on Isaac Bashevis Singer in *Svenska Dagbladet* (25 October 1978): "It sometimes happens that a Nobel Prize attracts public attention to the work of a relatively obscure author. Judging by the surprise caused in Sweden by this year's choice, there should be a good chance of the prize achieving this effect – one that is by no means unfamiliar to the selectors."

That Artur Lundkvist was of like mind is clear from a few words in his article "The Nobel Prize to Whom?" in *Svenska Dagbladet* (12 October 1977): the true purpose of the prize "is to direct attention to achievements that have not been sufficiently regarded." He returned to the idea in his presentation of Elytis two years later. To the expected outcry following this choice of a poet who was unknown to most he replied: "Isn't there some point then in discovering something new and drawing attention to something that could possibly be worth getting to know? Making such discoveries can perhaps quite simply be seen as part of the selectors' duty, without their being labeled on that account as high-faluting elitists moving in the rarified atmosphere far above the heads of 'the people'" (*Svenska Dagbladet*, 19 October 1979).

Lundkvist was thus in sympathy with the idea of "drawing attention" to an author unknown to the majority. But the words "discover something new" make it clear that innovation remained a decisive criterion for Lundkvist. The pragmatic approach was for him something that could defend innovators against pressure from the best-selling authors. Once more we see how the two principles are mutually compatible, this time balanced in Lundkvist's typical manner.

Since Lundkvist's formulations of the pragmatic approach to selection recurred in a number of striking newspaper articles in the years 1977-79, this approach has tended to be associated with his name. The picture was more complex, however. Following earlier hints of this view in statements by Heidenstam, Böök, Österling, and Siwertz – and several choices of prize winners reflecting a pragmatic spirit – it was Gyllensten's declarations that laid the groundwork for the new practice. What appeared at first as the opinion of an individual member soon turned out to be an articulation of what several thought. A breakthrough for the pragmatic view can be seen in the surprising choice in 1978 of Isaac Bashevis Singer, a writer not widely known. This choice and the three following – Elytis, Miłosz, and Canetti – constitute a pattern that in its way was as surprising as the launching of the "pioneers" between 1946 and 1950.

But of course pragmatic evaluation may well have played a part in the preceding years without thereby having a dominating influence. The 1969 choice was to that extent in line with the developing practice. Beckett's work was still growing and its productive role in the literature of the period evident. The younger group who, in the exchange of views on Beckett's pessimism eventually carried Österling's conception of the "pathfinder" on to a further stage, were aware, as we have seen, of the life-giving force that in spite of everything rises from total reduction, and of the stimulus generated by this author who "has pioneered new modes of expression in fiction and on the stage."[3]

This intention of *promoting* the work of an author or a literary area is more relevant to two other prize recipients in those years: Pablo Neruda (1971) and Patrick White (1973). Both prizes were well in keeping with the wish to direct attention to "an insufficiently recognized linguistic or cultural sphere." Australia had, of course, been overlooked, and the two prizes that had previously gone to South America were hardly in proportion to the rich and dynamically expanding literature of that continent. Both Neruda and White were also authors in their prime, with new works in the offing. A more specific motive seems to have influenced the 1976 choice. As we shall see in Chapter 8, Vicente Aleixandre was given preference, to the surprise of many, over Rafael Alberti. Among the arguments in favor of Aleixandre was that the younger writers gathered around him during the difficult years and that he thereby had a unique importance for the rebirth of poetry in Spain. This prize could draw attention to an important contribution that had been largely ignored in the literary surveys.

The breakthrough year – 1978 – also provided the well-chosen occasion for a public clarification. When that year's choice was announced, Gyllensten told journalists that the academy's function was "to promote significant authors and encourage the spread of their works." This effort on behalf of important but insufficiently recognized literature was linked with the commercialization of cultural life: if the Nobel Prize could act as a counterweight to that commercialization, then it would be fulfilling its purpose.

The positions taken by individual members are, of course, difficult to illustrate. Traces of expressions of principle of this kind have not been left in the reports and minutes. Nor does our usually unfailing source, the Nobel speeches, disclose any direct information on the matter – after all, an address to a recipient is hardly the occasion for suggesting how the prize will help to raise a neglected achievement from obscurity. Yet indirectly the principle could be formulated quite clearly, as in Gyllensten's speech to García Márquez. It opened with the sentence, "With this year's Nobel prize in literature to Gabriel García Márquez the Swedish Academy cannot be said to bring forward an unknown writer." After a brief account of the enormous international success achieved by the "almost overwhelming narrative talent" of this master of language, Gyllensten returned to his opening point: "Nor can it be said that any literary unknown continent or province is brought to light with the prize to Gabriel García Márquez." Latin American literature, long renowned for its vigor, "has won acclaim in the cultural life of today." In this way García Márquez was presented against the contrasting background of the immediately preceding series of prizes, which had called attention to unknown authors or neglected literary provinces.

International press comment has to a certain extent accepted the importance of such a policy – and has also been aware of the fact that the policy has been practiced. In *Le Monde* of 12 October 1979, just before the announcement of that year's prize, Françoise Wagener commented in a general article on the prize, "What's more, the Nobel Prize ought, as in the case of Singer last year, to reveal to the public at large an important but little-known author. What is the use of breaking down doors that are already open by giving the prize to international best-sellers?"[4]

Many newspapers recognized that this principle was followed in the 1978 choice. How the new signals were understood is shown most clearly, however, in the responses to the choice of Miłosz in 1980. In *Expressen,* Nils-Åke Nilsson, a specialist in Slavonic literature, distinguished a pattern: "The academy has followed the line that has been discernible for several years now: the selectors have looked for authors who are less well-known, who are not already the objects of heavy promotion and advertising ... Without a doubt they have come upon a treasure" (10 October 1980).

One of Sweden's leading critics, *Dagens Nyheter's* Bengt Holmqvist, found it "hard to imagine many better choices" and welcomed the principle that had thus been given expression: "Miłosz is certainly not a well-known writer. But there is – as Artur Lundkvist in particular has been in the habit of pointing out – very little purpose in rewarding those who have already been richly favored by success. A more reasonable use of this spectacular scholarship is undoubtedly to let it help spread knowledge of a significant but insufficiently noticed body of writing. . . . Such is the work of the new prize-winner" (10 October 1980).

The new type of prize winner was well described by Salman Rushdie in his article on Elias Canetti in the London *Sunday Times,* "The Invisible Master," on the occasion of the 1981 choice. The function of the prize was neatly defined in his closing words: "Thanks to the Swedish Academy, he is unlikely to remain, for much longer, the 'Dr. Who?' of our literary world" (18 October 1981). Laying greater emphasis on the promotional aspect, Lorenzo Mondo in *La Stampa* wrote (after regretting that Borges had been passed over) that that year's happy choice "has the merit of being a sophisticated choice, not one conceded to general opinion, and therefore it honors literature and justifies the Nobel Prize, which like all other prizes is primarily intended to spread the work of significant authors. Canetti is, we may say, an author whose works circulate almost clandestinely, in spite of the fact that his name has acquired a quasi-mythical status" (16 October 1981).

When, after awarding the prize to two celebrities, García Márquez and Golding, the academy chose Jaroslav Seifert in 1984, *Le Monde* (19 October 1984) noted that the selectors had carried out their duty to the full: to direct the attention of world opinion to an author who perfectly embodied the soul of his country but who so far had remained unnoticed outside his native frontiers.

Ultimately, however, the pragmatic principle is one of many in an intricate play of forces. It does not, therefore, exclude the choice of a well-established master. Gyllensten's comments to the international press in 1978 have been taken as an explanation of why Graham Greene had once again been passed over that year. A similar idea was expressed in an editorial by Ingmar Björkstén in *Svenska Dagbladet* (20 August 1978). Even before the choice of Singer, he interpreted the academy's aim to be to call attention to "what for various reasons has tended to remain in the shade rather than to what already speaks for itself." He concluded: "The principle excludes an author so firmly established as Graham Greene [and] threatens the equally deserving Doris Lessing." Max Frisch "likewise is in the danger zone . . . and what about Günter Grass?" Such a conclusion derived by contraries may lie near at hand but it is not the less incorrect. The pragmatic program by its nature discountenanced the international celebrity, just as it did the author whose prime work was far in the past. But this argument is only one of many;

in fact, there has been a pattern of alternating between "discoveries," homage to internationally significant pathfinders, and rewarding already recognized solitary masters. The selection of García Márquez and Golding between Canetti and Seifert illustrates this dynamic process. The idea of not rewarding "something passé" had been balanced by recognition of the fact that many of the authors likely to be considered would have reached a relatively high age before the greatness of their contribution and its importance in a wider perspective began to be clear. An analysis of the pragmatic principle can thus throw light on several of the choices made in recent years, but the academy's decisions still maintain their classic stamp of unpredictability.

CHAPTER 7

"Political Integrity"

During the postwar period a number of Nobel Prizes in Literature have given rise to discussion of their political implications in the climate of the cold war. The literature prize has also, like the peace prize but unlike the scientific prizes, spotlighted questions of values and viewpoints that are often sensitive issues in the wider world. At the same time the Swedish Academy for its part has on many occasions expressed a desire to stand apart from political antagonisms. The guiding principle, in Lars Gyllensten's words, has been "political integrity."

Part of the explanation of the sometimes heated debate generated by the choice of prize winners is to be found in the fact that in many quarters there has been a misunderstanding of the Swedish Academy's autonomous position vis-à-vis state and government. Making a distinction in relation to the practice of East European states has on several occasions been necessary – for instance, in a contribution to *Dagens Nyheter* (22 February 1984) on the subject of Nikita Khrushchev's claim in his memoirs that it was he who – via a Swedish minister – had advised the academy to give the prize to Sholokhov. A journalist who reported this claim found it confirmed the prize to Sholokhov as "one of the saddest episodes in the history of the Nobel Prize." Gyllensten replied (27 February 1984) that there was not the slightest evidence of pressure from Khrushchev in the academy correspondence, or in the minutes, or anywhere else. Another part of the article, however, had wider implications:

> In communist countries the academies are government-controlled organs. Their actions express the political will of the state power. Our Swedish academies, among them the Swedish Academy, are private associations, and freedom from political control is for them an affair of the heart. Nor is there any wish on the part of the government to interfere in the Nobel Prize deliberations; that would simply create political and diplomatic complications.

Such a situation is difficult to understand for those in communist and totalitarian states. But for the Swedish Academy, as for the other institutes that distribute Nobel Prizes, avoiding the influence of political powers is axiomatic. The prize to Sholokhov may have been wise or unwise – Nikita Khrushchev has neither honor nor blame with regard to the fact that it was given.

It is thus quite unthinkable that the academy would have acted on a diplomatic level and tried to find support for the choice of a prize winner in the government of his or her country. Pasternak himself helped to spread the rumor that in 1954 the academy sounded out the Soviet authorities on the idea of giving him the prize and actually sought their permission. In 1981, on behalf of the academy, Gyllensten was able to dismiss the rumor as quite groundless: "Enquiries of the kind referred to were not made and are never made." In the same spirit in which he replied to the Sholokhov rumors, he was referring to the academy's political integrity and independence from political power.[1]

A position of autonomy in relation to the state is one thing; the possible political overtones of a choice of prize winner is something else. To what extent have the decisions of the committee and the academy had a *de facto* political content? That is a complex question that must be divided into its several components. We can begin with three statements on the matter from three of those closely involved, statements made over the course of seven decades. Bishop Gottfrid Billing made a point of principle in a letter to Wirsén on 16 July 1902 on the subject of a proposal to divide that year's prize between Ibsen and Bjørnson; he first referred to Wirsén's view, with which he agreed: "It is true that the awarding of the prize must not become a question of national politics. But it is equally incontrovertible and unavoidable that it has and will have a political aspect. This lies in or follows from its international nature. The academy may disregard political views as much as it wishes – its prize giving becomes an international affair that will be judged in the international press, etc. from various national viewpoints."[2]

From this evaluation of the problem in the time of the union crisis, let us move ahead to the somewhat resigned view expressed by Dag Hammarskjöld in the age of the cold war. In a letter to Erik Lindegren on 26 October 1959, he wrote of the impossibility of "achieving either rationality or full justice" in an institution like the Nobel Prize: "It's a matter of chance how proposals emerge, and it's a matter of chance how half-political judgments come to intersect with private evaluations."

The third voice comes from the agitated days of October 1970 when Solzhenitsyn was awarded the prize. In an interview in *Aftonbladet* on 10 December 1970, Artur Lundkvist referred to the academy's claim that the prize was untouched by political shadows and described that attitude as "somewhat naive. ... All prizes are political in their effect, if not in their intention." (Not unexpectedly, an editor gave the interview the tendentious headline, "It Was Politics That Gave Solzhenitsyn the Prize.") Statements such as Lundkvist's must be reconciled with equally strong views on the academy's integrity. How right is either side?

To begin with, we can affirm what is obviously correct in Billing's view–that an international award like the Nobel Prize has, unavoidably, "a political aspect." But that is not really what the recurring press debate has been about. That honors given to representatives of the literature of different countries in a world full of tensions acquire a political dimension is, of course, a truism. Equally obvious is Lundkvist's claim that the prize is "political in its effect." The interesting question is whether Nobel choices have also had political intention, and whether the actual political effect was foreseen and included in the selection process.

Billing immediately brought matters to a head. He spoke not only of the decision's unavoidable *effect*–that a prize "becomes an international affair," judged in the international press from sundry biased viewpoints, irrespective of how much the academy "may disregard political views"–but of the political *intention:* "As a by-product, which must not be determinative but is yet not to be despised, of the proposed [sharing of the award between Ibsen and Bjørnson], I regard the friendly gesture to Norway that could be seen to lie in the award, and the good effect that should have, especially in the present, when, so to speak, we have begun to cross between the Friendly Islands."

Wirsén's reply is part of the argument against Ibsen, but it touched on principles: "I believe . . . that we are doing not only the wisest thing but also the most just in never using this prize as a political tool or bargaining piece; the result in any case would always be uncertain, at the same time as the procedure offends against the impartiality of a literary tribunal." That is a statement of great relevance. This desire for "impartiality," which haunts the early judgments, became a doctrine in the 1914 declaration that outlined the policy of literary neutralism during World War I. That policy was connected to Nobel's wish to encourage those who had "conferred the greatest benefit on mankind"; a prize with such an end in view could not be allowed to appear to "favor any particular nation." Fourteen years later Schück made a clear declaration of such integrity in his deliberations on Gorky. He had proposed Gorky, he said, with no regard for the fact that Gorky "is or has been a Bolshevist"; the academy "ought to have enough spine to stand against a political opinion." When the secretaries were Österling, Gierow, Gyllensten, and Allén, the academy's expressed desire for political integrity was quite distinct. Characteristic was the 1984 statement by Gyllensten that the academy wished to keep itself immune to all political, diplomatic, or in any other way nonliterary considerations.[3]

The problem was in what limitations this principle of political integrity could impose on particular cases. The question we must ask about a number of crucial choices is whether there was a subsidiary political intention in the decision. Can we, in Billing's words, distinguish a calculated political by-product, or can we at least detect a political effect that the academy chose to ignore?

Two questions must immediately be put aside for separate study. As we have already seen with Ibsen and Bjørnson, a proposal for a shared prize can well have political overtones; that issue will be the subject of a separate chapter. But the very desire to spread the prizes to the different literatures of the world has a political aspect; that question will be the subject of another chapter.

Our examination of the problem will be limited to the postwar period. Chapters 1 through 4 cast an indirect light on the consideration of political factors made during the earlier periods. Here it is enough to remind ourselves that, from the treatment of Tolstoy onward, Wirsén's "impartiality" was balanced by the idealistic considerations that, in his view, the will prescribed. A system of selection in which state, throne, and altar are values to defend against criticism has, of course, political implications. It is not necessarily concerned, however, with foreign policy. That the prize was given to Bjørnson "to lessen tensions with Norway," as Robert J. Clements maintained in "Is the Nobel Prize for Literature Political?" in the *Saturday Review* (4 December 1965), is thus a meagerly supported claim.[4] The 1903 report, on the contrary, stressed that the academy "in the question of Bjørnson's suitability neither wishes nor ought to concern itself with political views of any kind, but determines its procedure in this case exclusively on the basis of its opinions of the worth of the literary production of the candidate." Quite absurd was the notorious reasoning of Girolamo Ramunni (*La Recherche,* October 1983); he related the decisions to, among other things, the commercial aspect; he alleged that the first three Nobel Prizes awarded to French authors were made because the French market "is indispensable to the realization of the industrialization program."[5] Considerations of that kind are totally alien to the academy's deliberations.

The conservative view was preserved during the chairmanship of Hjärne, but without that element of bigotry that readily appeared in the first decade. The praise of nationalist outlooks characteristic of that decade was also more restrained under a chairman who saw the total Western cultural inheritance as a force much stronger than the achievement of any individual nation. On the other hand, a new political element had surfaced: the academy sought to avoid "outbursts of bitterness" in the world being directed, through the choice of prize winners, "at our country." Adopting a restrictive policy in the award of prizes to candidates from the belligerent countries was, naturally, a political act in its own way. Both of these political factors were nonetheless subsumed under the desire for "impartiality."

The period covered by Schück's declaration by and large maintained conservative criteria. Not everyone in the circle had the same dispassionate attitude toward a Bolshevik – on the contrary, Hjärne, as we have seen, held it against the Clartéist Anatole France that "in his pacifist zeal" he had "allowed himself to be drawn quite over the frontier of Bolshevism."[6] The verdict of "not guilty" on Benavente in 1922 revealed, however, how the red pencil proceeded among the politically engaged candidates of the time: "He does not preach at all, his art is strictly objective." A passionate political involvement was disqualifying above all as an infringement of the demand that candidates be free of "tendencies." Perhaps this criterion was the strongest element of political judgment in the earlier period. In any event, we can dismiss as pure imagination claims that obedience to the League of Nations was rewarded with a Nobel Prize. The award to Yeats in 1923 was thus supposed to be motivated by the fact that Ireland had accepted a boundary agreement with London and applied for membership in the league, and the prize to Reymont in 1924 was supposed to have been determined by the fact that Poland had accepted the Geneva decision on the division of Silesia (Ramunni).[7] Extravagant hypotheses of this kind are irreconcilable with not only the Swedish Academy's autonomy from the state but with its policy and practice. In several instances reasoning of this type has been based on an embarrassing ignorance of elementary history – like Clements's assertion that political suspicions were brushed aside when the committee in 1936 accepted the proposal of the fascist-dominated Italian Academy, so that Pirandello collected his prize while "the black-shirted legions he never condemned were already bombing the civilian population of Ethiopia." The slight hitch in this line of thought is the fact that Pirandello got his prize in 1934, well before Mussolini's attack on Ethiopia. (Nor is there any sign in the documentation that political doubts were brushed aside.)[8]

From a political point of view the most questioned prize of the first four decades was the one given in the autumn of 1939 to Frans Eemil Sillanpää. As already mentioned, this has often been regarded as a politically motivated decision. Many have found it difficult to understand an award to an author whose literary value was so "completely insignificant" – without, that is, considering the Soviet threat to Finland.[9] In his history Österling gave support to such an assumption: "It should not be surprising if in its decision the academy was somewhat influenced, whether consciously or unconsciously, by the contemporary situation, i.e., Finland's heroic fight against an overwhelmingly superior power."[10] This observation is slightly anachronistic. Sillanpää was chosen on 10 November, and the Soviet attack did not occur until 30 November, although the threat was, of course, building up throughout the preceding weeks. On 8 October there had been press references to imminent negotiations in Moscow on what were as yet unpublished Soviet claims; on 1 November the newspapers reported these claims to be a demand for a naval base at the entrance to the Gulf of Finland and an extensive border readjustment on the Karelian Isthmus. The gravity of the situation was intensified with the news of Finnish evacuation (11 October) and a "further enhanced" state of readiness (12 October). The idea of a political influence on the prize was therefore highly plausible. Yet the heart of the matter is to be found in quite another direction.

Sillanpää was no newcomer to the Nobel discussions. He had been a nominee since 1930 and the subject of seven consecutive specialist reports by Hallström, whose attitude was on the whole rather qualified: "an exquisite mastery in the description of what the eye can observe, but no really strong narrative art or characterization" (1935). Yet there were those within the academy who wanted to see a prize go to Finnish literature – preferably a shared prize of the kind that had crossed the minds of the 1917 committee. The moving force was Heidenstam who, in a letter to Hallström on 10 November 1935, argued in favor of that year's prize being shared between Sillanpää and the Finnish-Swedish author Jarl Hemmer. The idea generated serious discussion but failed to win a majority. In 1939 opinions on the likely winners were, as we have seen, divided. In the committee's report of 26 September it was admitted that agreement had not been reached. Two members recommended Huizinga, two Hesse, and one the Flemish novelist Stijn Streuvels. The report cited the previous objections to Sillanpää but also gave the substance of the more positive evaluation made by "some" of the committee members as well as a certain degree of support among other members of the academy. A majority opinion, however, had "so far not materialized," and the committee "for the present" decided not to recommend the proposal. The supporters of Sillanpää within the rest of the academy were not willing to rest content with this somewhat resigned attitude; it is clearly this persistent group that was responsible for the fact that Streuvels – who after all had found only one advocate – was exchanged for Sillanpää when preliminary voting got under way on 26 October. In this first round – just at the time when news was coming in of the threat to Finland – a majority of seven out of the twelve present wanted to withhold the prize. As a second choice, in the event of a decision to award the prize, three of those favored Sillanpää. At the same time there were five, led by Österling and Siwertz, in favor of Hesse. An analysis of the result still shows that Sillanpää had already won, provided it was agreed to give the prize at all. The situation may be briefly summarized as follows. All support for the problematic Hesse was mobilized in the five votes. As he could not muster a majority, three of those voting for Hesse, with Sillanpää in second place, transferred their allegiance, while a couple of odd votes for Huizinga, from the opponents of Hesse, were rerouted in the same direction. Together with the three votes already given to Sillanpää – plus that of the faithful Sillanpää advocate Heidenstam – there were now a total of nine votes, and the way was open.[11] The outcome was primarily a result of election arithmetic that was dictated by hesitation about Hesse. No reference to the Soviet threat is visible as a motive, either in the minutes or in letters. That does not, of course, exclude the possibility of sympathy for Finland having some influence on various academy members, in the fall of 1939 as well as throughout the decade-long discussion of Sillanpää's candidacy. The most tangible political elements, however, were the facts that the choice was between three citizens of neutral states (an echo of the neutrality policy of 1914) and that in the end it was decided to make an award in spite of the international situation.

It was not, however, until the postwar period – during the cold war – that the political aspect of the Nobel Prize in Literature became a recurring subject of debate. The question is of less relevance in the case of the prizes to the pioneers in the late 1940s. On the other hand, there was a critical period, 1953-58, when prizes went to Churchill and Pasternak, and there was a preliminary internal discussion of Sholokhov and a response to the candidacy of Ezra Pound. The prize to Sholokhov in 1965 again raised the temperature. The period from Solzhenitsyn and Neruda in 1970-71 to Miłosz in 1980 and Seifert in 1984 gave rise to many commentaries on the alleged political character of the prize.

Dag Hammarskjöld's remark in the late 1950s about "half-political judgments" was prompted by the unease and disapproval he felt about a couple of decisions in 1955, the year when he first participated in the process and when his concern about the present case was greater than his familiarity with the procedure. "Churchill-Hemingway-Sholokhov: is the Swedish Academy a literary committee in the Foreign Office?"[12] Let us begin with the prize to Churchill. To what extent *was* it a diplomatic gesture? It is known that he had been a candidate since 1946, the year after he had handed over power to the victors in the 1945 election.[13] As can be gathered from letters from Österling to the historian and academy member Nils Ahnlund in 1948, it was Ahnlund who was entrusted with the specialist report on the two proposed "historians," Churchill and Trevelyan.[14] The degree of Ahnlund's "lively interest" in Churchill's candidacy is apparent in a later Österling letter (2 October 1953) to him just before the actual decision; Österling asked Ahnlund if, in his capacity as a historian, he would take on the task of making the speech to Churchill in the event of the committee's recommendation being accepted – no doubt also an indication of Österling's own limited enthusiasm. (The task in the end went to Siwertz). Österling further alluded to "various objections" made when the matter was first discussed in the academy. These are not specified, but their nature is hardly secret. Since 1951 Churchill had again been prime minister of Great Britain – and he was still regarded as the winner of World War II. There was, however, a political element in the very postponement. The fact that Churchill was not finally chosen until 1953, after many years of discussion, means that it was felt that a sufficient distance from his wartime exploits had been gained, making it possible for a prize to him to be generally understood as a *literary* award. The reaction from many quarters showed that this was quite a vain hope.

There can be no doubt that the committee and the academy attributed exceptional literary merits to Churchill. In Ahnlund's eyes it was mainly as an orator that Churchill deserved a prize; the historical works on their own account perhaps do not measure up to the requirements, but they do serve as a suitable frame for the public oratory.[15] The same virtue carried particular weight for Siwertz, as is clear from his speech on the achievements of the prize winner: "Churchill's mature oratory is swift, unerring in its aim, and moving in its grandeur. There is the power that forges the links of history. Napoleon's proclamations were often effective in their lapidary style. But Churchill's eloquence in the fateful hours of freedom and human dignity was heart-stirring in quite another way. With his great speeches he has, perhaps, himself erected his most enduring monument."

These lines exemplify Siwertz's picture of "a Caesar who also has the gift of wielding Cicero's stylus." The problem was how this Caesar, a mere eight years after the war, could be mentally separated from the Ciceronian prose, how that power that had forged "the links of history" and sent out its appeal "in the fateful hours of freedom and human dignity" could for one moment be forgotten in the midst of the great oratory. Furthermore, in 1953 Churchill was in spite of everything prime minister and leader of one of the key powers in the cold war world; from that point of view as well, his suitability was questionable. It can be asked if any of the academy's choices has put its political integrity at such risk. At any rate, *one* well-known conclusion was drawn: ever since, candidates with governmental positions, such as Malraux and Senghor, have been consistently ruled out.

Hammarskjöld's irritation over the political aspect of the prize to Hemingway in 1954 was, on the other hand, unjustified – and was indeed to a certain extent disavowed by his remark to Selander in a letter of 11 March 1955 that Hemingway's countryman Robert Frost "should have got the prize instead." Hemingway had been a likely candidate for some time, and it was his masterpiece from 1952, *The Old Man and the Sea,* that clinched the prize. I have not found the slightest hint of a political intention behind the 1954 decision, neither in the reports nor in correspondence, nor in any other material. In his capacity as "one of the major influences on contemporary style," Hemingway naturally takes his place in the series of pioneers honored by Österling's academy.[16]

It is more interesting to turn to Hammarskjöld's contribution to the pattern of choices in 1955. On 12 May 1955 he wrote to Selander: "I would vote against Sholokhov with a conviction based not only on artistic grounds and not only as an automatic response to attempts to pressure us but also on the ground that a prize to a Soviet author today, involving as it would the kind of political motivations that would readily be alleged, is to me an idea with very little to recommend it." The ominous reference to "attempts to pressure us" need not be interpreted as an allusion to any Soviet approach over and above a normal nomination submitted by a person or institution entitled to do so. (It is certainly not a confirmation of Khrushchev's allegation; his apocryphal advice calls for comment rather in connection with the 1965 prize.) In May 1955 what we have may well be a recommendation within the circle, based on a higher artistic evaluation than Hammarskjöld's, a recommendation that in the period of the "thaw" he imagined to be politically charged. The matter went no further in 1955. When the final candidates were aired in September, Sholokhov was not one of the serious contenders.[17] *One* point that can safely be made about that statement by the newly elected but still rather uninitiated Hammarskjöld is that we can see him thus defending his integrity in the same way in which the academy defends its integrity. A second point is that for his own part, by saying no to "a prize to a Soviet author today," he revealed a willingness to let political considerations play a part alongside his literary judgment.

The choice of the prize winner in 1955 was politically sensitive in a different manner – though still with a communist author in the leading role. When Halldór Kiljan Laxness was named, certain French and American commentators saw a connection between this choice and the beginnings of the détente of which the Soviet leaders had given proof in Geneva. Kjell Strömberg has already shown how such an accusation is quite unfounded. *L'Express* was content to see the future of the literature prize compromised by a purely political gesture in favor of a local mediocrity, but *L'Humanité* rejoiced in this celebration of literature, the communist cause, and peace.[18] In truth, the decision entailed no celebration whatsoever of the author's political views. On the contrary – as Österling let us understand in his radio program on 27 October – there had been reservations on the ground that the author's ever-present social and political involvement was at times so strong that it threatened the artistic qualities of his work. We can well recognize here the reaction of an older academy to an author's "tendencies." But in 1955 the objection was not to the possible danger to "impartiality" but to the way in which the author's "Marxist convictions, however honest they may be, lead in many instances to anachronistic views that disturb and damage his perspective on reality."

During those sensitive years of the 1950s there was also discussion of a candidate whose politics were of quite another color – Ezra Pound, who had been interned as insane in order to be saved from a death penalty for treason. In the correspondence from 1955, now accessible, his name recurs; he appealed to the academy because of his "pioneering significance."[19] On that point, however, Österling expressed a qualification in his article "The Case of Ezra Pound" (*Stockholms-Tidningen,* 21 September 1959): "In his time Pound has signified more as an inspirer and as a renewer of style than as an original poet." In 1955 doubts were also felt about Pound's later *Cantos,* which included much that was "quite incomprehensible simply because of the abundant use of Chinese," according to Hammarskjöld in a report to Österling on the various soundings taken in the matter.[20] His conclusion was that a Nobel Prize could readily "be taken as an attempt at overt pressure" and would thereby help to create a bad "aura of publicity" around Pound. He recalled that Pound was "a man who is in certain respects mentally ill" and warned that giving him the prize would risk "the most bizarre and compromising remarks." In Hammarskjöld's opinion, the academy "should bide its time, first working for his release, and then considering his development as a free man." The academy followed his advice – in fact, in his 1959 article Österling mentioned that "Dag Hammarskjöld, commissioned to do so by the academy, has made considerable efforts to negotiate with the legal authorities on behalf of Pound." The letter cited above shows just how Hammarskjöld planned to bring about Pound's release through contacts in the U.S. State Department and through the influence of W. H. Auden and his circle; the idea was for Pound to make a formal admission of guilt and in exchange to accept release and exile.[21]

The crux of the problem, however, was neither the question of literary reservations nor that of his internment in a mental hospital, but rather the fascist involvement that initially brought Pound to this pass. In his 1959 article Österling referred to *A Case Book on Ezra Pound* and recalled that on the Italian radio network Pound attacked the Allied leadership, praised Hitler and Mussolini (who ought to have led the Allies), applauded the mass extermination of the East European Jews, and threatened the Americans that their turn would come. All of this discredited the later *Cantos;* "the evil spirit raises its head everywhere." The conclusion was clearly spelled out by Hammarskjöld in a letter to Pär Lagerkvist in 1959:

> I have no objection to a Nobel Prize being given to an author who is mentally unbalanced, provided the conditions for being given a prize are fulfilled. But what is frightening about Pound is the special form his mental illness has in one respect taken, when he has fallen victim to an anti-Semitism whose prerequisites and quality bear the same character as the anti-Semitism in Germany or the racial hatred in the American South. I regard that as such a "subhuman" reaction that it ought to exclude the possibility of a prize that is after all intended to lay weight on the "idealistic tendency" of the recipient's efforts. I do not know exactly what the words "idealistic tendency" mean, but at least I do know what is diametrically opposed to what they can reasonably be assumed to signify.[22]

One would imagine that the reservations felt in the 1950s would in the course of time lose their force, but that did not happen. The poet and critic Karl Vennberg raised the question again during an exchange with Lundkvist in 1979. He saw it as "a weakness on the part of the academy that it did not dare to challenge the world by disregarding Ezra Pound's fascist aberrations and giving him a Nobel Prize." Later he asked if it would "have been shameful to have given Céline a Nobel Prize. ... The private politics of an author amount after all to an aberration that dies with his historical epoch. ... Not even the worst Marxists, for instance, any longer condemn Balzac for being a reactionary ruffian." Lundkvist was unable to follow Vennberg "in his pseudo-radical broad-mindedness." He "can't see how the limited merits" of Pound's and Céline's writing "could make up for their shameful outpourings of psychopathic hatred and evil."[23]

The extent to which the criterion implied by the words "idealistic tendency" has affected other politically sensitive deliberations is hard to illustrate, given the current lack of open access to the source material. We can best gather something of the manner in which the spirit behind these words has made itself felt – as now interpreted, after the event – if we focus on an aspect that is apparent in several discussions of authors who have worked in totalitarian societies. The demand for "integrity" that the academy imposed upon itself has been, in a certain sense, extended to the nominees. Not that an "impartial attitude" has been required of the potential prize winner; the prizes to Laxness, Quasimodo, Sartre, Asturias, Solzhenitsyn, Neruda, and García Márquez all show the extent to which postwar criteria have moved away from the earlier demand for "objectivity." On the other hand, there has often been praise for the artist's independence in the face of totalitarian power. The arguments used in several of the situations involving a candidate – for or against – in the communist sphere of influence reveal a significant pattern. From that point of view we can examine the controversial prizes to Boris Pasternak in 1958, to Mikhail Sholokhov in 1965, and to Aleksandr Solzhenitsyn in 1970.

It was natural that the attention given to Pasternak's prize should have centered on *Dr. Zhivago,* published first by Feltrinelli in Italy in 1957 and made available soon thereafter in translation in the entire Western world; in the Soviet Union, as is known, the author's attempts from 1954 onward to get the book published had failed. Yet Pasternak had been annually nominated for a Nobel Prize as early as the years 1946-50, at that time in his capacity as one of the leading Russian poets.[24] Already in 1947 he was the subject of a specialist report by the eminent Slavonic scholar Anton Karlgren, who drew attention to his position as the foremost representative of Russian poetry. At the same time a certain emphasis was placed on the way in which Pasternak, the least Russian and most Western of Soviet authors, was in his poetry the most "exclusive."[25] It is thus the *poet* Pasternak who first appeared as a serious candidate, and the first phrase in the wording of the award – "for his important achievement ... in contemporary lyric poetry" – indicated this essential part of the justification for his prize. In his 23 October radio presentation of Pasternak, which was closely linked with the committee report upon which agreement had been reached, Österling also spoke of Pasternak as "a modern-minded pioneer" and a renewer of poetic language. More interesting from a political point of view is Österling's observation, in the same talk, that the earlier Pasternak was "an individualist who went his own way and never played any official role in the Soviet Union," an author whose "artistic integrity" seemed to have been respected to a certain extent during the years of his somewhat withdrawn life, when outside the Soviet Union he became increasingly recognized as "one of the significant poets of the age."

The idea of the artist's "integrity" recurred when Österling characterized *Dr. Zhivago* as a work "raised above all party-political boundaries and, rather, antipolitical in its overall humane outlook. ... Through its pure and powerful spirit it can also and to an unusual degree be said to fulfill the requirements that from the beginning have been laid down for the Nobel Prize in Literature." One can see in these words the care he took to depoliticize the implications of the choice. Yet there is no question of his argument being a diplomatic gesture aimed at the international audience. By referring thus to Pasternak's strong artistic integrity, Österling was publicizing the judgment upon which the academy had come to agreement in its decision. How this moral independence was placed in the literary context indicated in the wording of the award – "the great Russian epic tradition" – was clarified by Österling in his radio talk: "As a document of its age the novel stands comparison with Tolstoy's *War and Peace,* and as a poetic work it also often invites such comparison with that monumental predecessor."

There are traces in Österling's presentation of an awareness of the political complications and of a wish to tone down the image of Pasternak as a critical author: "Here it ought to be noticed that the writer is telling his story not to accuse and not to protest. He does not criticize the Revolution itself but rather its opportunists and camp followers." On the other hand, there is nothing to suggest that the members of the academy foresaw the strong Soviet reaction or suspected how precarious the outcome could be for Pasternak. That *Dr. Zhivago* could not be published in the Soviet Union seems to have been regarded as a temporary phenomenon. When one of Pasternak's biographers, Guy de Mallac, speculated that the academy made political and diplomatic approaches in advance to the Soviet Union via Andrei Gromyko and to the U. S. government via John Foster Dulles, we can only say that such ideas not only conflict with the spirit and practice of the Nobel Prize,[26] but they also presuppose that the academy had anticipated the complications to which its decision would lead. At the time when it was voted on, the prize to Pasternak had no such character: it was honoring a pioneering poet and epic novelist of great humanity and Tolstoyan stature. Far from regarding him as a critic of the Soviet system, the academy saw in him a high degree of artistic integrity deserving of discreet protection against political misunderstanding.

When Sholokhov's turn came in 1965, it may have been natural to see his choice as politically conditioned – as an attempt along the lines of Sartre's suggestion of the previous year to create balance. At that time Sartre saw the prize as something reserved for authors in the Western bloc and for rebels in the Eastern bloc.[27] In reality Sholokhov had been a serious competitor to Pasternak ever since 1947. The specialist Anton Karlgren had chosen, however, to give preference to Pasternak, partly on account of his poetic merits and partly on account of the psychological qualities in his prose, which was reminiscent of Western renewers such as Proust. The idea of placing Pasternak before Sholokhov won support in the academy as well. Sholokhov remained a candidate and only had to wait until the time was ripe for a new Russian prize. It is somewhat ironic that in 1964 his candidacy was weighed alongside that of Sartre himself; that year, Gierow believed he was the only one willing to favor Sholokhov. In the following year Sholokhov's moment came; even in the preliminary voting round, eight out of thirteen votes went to him.[28] In his speech Österling remarked on the delay: the award to *Tikhii Don* (And Quiet Flows the Don) was "rather late in the day," but, he added, "not too late to add to the roll of Nobel prize winners the name of one of the most outstanding writers of our time."

Even if the source material could be quoted, it would be too insubstantial to provide any conclusions about the possible role of political considerations when the decision was finally reached. But Österling's speech illuminates our line of inquiry. With only a few words he glided over Sholokhov's later work – that is, that period in which Sholokhov played the part of a literary figurehead in Stalin's Soviet Union. Instead, naturally enough, he emphasized the masterpiece *Tikhii Don* and pointed out that at the time when this enterprise was undertaken, it was "a daring step, a step that at that point in his career also meant the settling of a conflict with his own conscience." The "controversial aspects" of the subject matter have to do with the fact that the chronicle, whose four parts appeared at protracted intervals between 1928 and 1940, was "long viewed with some concern by the Soviet critics, whose political affiliation made it difficult for them to accept wholeheartedly Sholokhov's quite natural commitment to his theme, that of the Cossacks' revolt against the new central authorities; nor could they easily accept his endeavor to explain and defend objectively the defiant spirit of independence that drove these people to resist every attempt at subjection." When Österling stressed how Sholokhov set about his controversial effort to understand this revolt against the system, he was discreetly replying to criticism of the academy for its choice of a party boss. But Österling's remarks have a greater significance in the bigger picture – the one that also included Pasternak – and one of greater importance than the simple question of whether the academy performed a balancing act by compensating for the choice of Pasternak by awarding a prize to the Communist party's literary favorite. When Österling directed attention to Sholokhov's bold choice of a subject that, from the party's point of view, was inflammatory, he was in fact ascribing to Sholokhov the political integrity that was a vital qualification in a politically charged context. Österling's summary treatment of the later work can be seen in that light: that work was not only of less interest than the epic of the Don Cossacks, but it revealed an author who had lost much of that precious independence. Limiting the award to Sholokhov's "epic of the Don" was thus eloquent.

The choice of Solzhenitsyn has in various quarters been interpreted as a response to the pressure of newspaper opinion, sometimes domestic, sometimes international. Strömberg described the well-orchestrated Swedish press campaign, for which Swedish P.E.N. acted as the mouthpiece in its proposal in 1970, but neglected the fact that a choice of prize winner is not the work of a single year but rather the result of deliberations extending over a long period. The Soviet reaction seems to be even more confused. On 14 October 1970, *Literaturnaya Gazeta* not only accused the Nobel Committee of having yielded in general to the pressure of international journalists, but it even believed it could identify a particular Russian exile periodical as being especially influential. In his reply of the following day – reported in the press in many other countries but never in *Literaturnaya Gazeta* – Gierow reminded readers that periodicals were not called upon to initiate proposals, and that "no heed is paid to the press debates and expressions of opinion in various parts of the world, which more or less regularly precede the choice of a prize winner." Nevertheless, the first Soviet reaction, a 9 October report carried by Tass from the Writer's Union (which had in the previous year expelled Solzhenitsyn), had already claimed there was a political aspect to the choice: "It is regrettable that the Swedish Academy has allowed itself to be drawn into an unworthy spectacle that was staged not at all to advance the spiritual values and traditions of literature but was dictated by speculative political considerations."

Lundkvist, well-acquainted with the work of the academy, also claimed, as we have seen, that the prize to Solzhenitsyn had political overtones – but with the idea that such a prize "may have a political effect." Nothing in the records, however, suggests that either the committee or the academy in 1970 foresaw the violent Soviet reaction or anticipated that their choice would be regarded as so politically charged. In the Nobel Prize deliberations, consideration is, of course, given to the consequences a prize may entail for a recipient, and with particular care in a case like Solzhenitsyn's. According to the memoirs of Gunnar Jarring, then Swedish ambassador to Moscow, Gierow took the unusual step of writing to the ambassador to gain some idea of Solzhenitsyn's position: "The question relates of course only to what may happen to him personally." On that point Jarring felt able to give a reassuring answer. There were good reasons, too, for viewing the situation positively. Solzhenitsyn had been personally left in peace. The open letter to the Kremlin from Russian scientists and scholars, among whom was Andrei Sakharov, had been published abroad without repercussions to its signatories. And rumor had it that Yury Daniel was to be freed. At the same time there was cause to believe that the Soviet authorities, after the prize to Sholokhov, would hardly look upon a prize to Solzhenitsyn with such disapproval. When the matter was being discussed in the academy, a likely assumption would have been that while a prize to Solzhenitsyn would not be greatly appreciated by the Soviet authorities it would not incite any intervention. Such an assessment of the political effect of the decision turned out, as we know, to be incorrect.

Jarring also had another message for the academy. Already in the spring of 1970 he put it to Gierow that it would perhaps be "wiser to wait another year and see what has happened in the Soviet Union." In October he developed the idea further by suggesting to Österling that a prize to Solzhenitsyn "would lead to difficulties for our relations with the Soviet Union." He received the reply: "Yes, that could well be so, but we are agreed that Solzhenitsyn is the most deserving candidate." Jarring reiterated his hope that the academy would postpone the decision for one or more years, but Österling did not agree. This exchange illuminates a fundamental fact: the academy has no regard for what may or may not be desirable in the eyes of the Swedish Foreign Office. Its unconventional inquiry, in Gierow's letter, was concerned solely with the likely effects of the decision for the candidate personally.[29]

The exchange also offers a good example of the way in which a political "by-product" may be taken into account – not, of course, that the academy intended the possible disturbance in Soviet relations, but it was aware of the risk and chose to take it.

A more subtle determination of the political undertones of the decision is to be found in Gierow's speech to the prize winner. He spoke of "the ethical force" with which Solzhenitsyn "has pursued the indispensable traditions of Russian literature." The academy had chosen to honor a moralist of great integrity, and moreover, a successor to Tolstoy and Dostoyevski. In his speech Gierow relied heavily on *Pravda*'s reaction to *One Day in the Life of Ivan Denisovich*. In addition to citing his narrative art, which "is reminiscent at times of Tolstoy's artistic force," the periodical had noted what we may call the author's profound humanity: "Why is it that our heart contracts with pain as we read this remarkable story at the same time as we feel our spirits soar? The explanation lies in its profound humanity, in the quality of mankind even in the hour of degradation."

Gierow focused particularly on the way Solzhenitsyn speaks to us "of the individual's indestructible dignity." With a fine artistic percipience he also managed to link Solzhenitsyn's allegedly conventional methods with this leading viewpoint. He referred to Solzhenitsyn's "polyphonism":

> Solzhenitsyn has explained what he means by polyphonism: each person becomes the chief character whenever the action concerns him. This is not just a technique, it is a creed. The narrative focuses on the only human element in existence, the human individual, with equal status among equals, one destiny among millions and a million destinies in one. This is the whole of humanism in a nutshell, for the kernel is love of mankind. This year's Nobel Prize for Literature has been awarded to the proclaimer of such a humanism.

We can be certain that Gierow's words touched on what had been central to the academy in arriving at its decision. He is also aware of the political implications of such an ethical stance on the part of a writer in Solzhenitsyn's situation; of Solzhenitsyn's address to us on "the individual's indestructible dignity" Gierow said, "Where that dignity is violated, whatever the reason or the means, his message is an accusation but also an assurance: those who commit such a violation are the only ones to be degraded by it. The truth of this is plain to see wherever one travels." Solzhenitsyn's humanism becomes an "accusation" in places where the individual's dignity is violated – that is its political corollary. With a diplomatic touch Gierow extended the perspective: this author's words "are valid round the world." I believe that Gierow's meticulously judged formulations balanced primary and subsidiary motives in a way that reflects the intentions behind the decision. A great humane author was awarded, one whose moral stance had political implications in a society where human dignity was violated. But it was this humanism, and not the criticism of a particular political system, that the prize focused upon.

The following year's winner, Pablo Neruda, provided a political problem of the opposite kind through his contributions to the Stalin cult. It is symptomatic that Lundkvist, in his presentation in *Dagens Nyheter* on 7 March 1971, introduced Neruda as one who "reproaches himself, not without reason, for having been politically credulous"; he was "blinded by his vision . . . led astray by an excess of hope." The two samples of Neruda's poetry that accompany the article illustrate Neruda's distance from Stalin. Lundkvist appeared to feel obliged in general to tone down the entire political aspect of the poet's work. Neruda, "for long . . . a forerunner of political poetry," did not show one of his "happiest features" in this kind of involvement: "It appears rather as a sacrifice he has offered, at the expense of his most essential gifts, which are attuned most to nature, to elementary and concrete things. It is in that direction his poetic imagination is so incredibly penetrating. And it is with regard to that aspect of his sensibility, above all, that he can be described as a genius."

In his speech to Neruda, Gierow also discreetly made the point that the poet had distanced himself from Stalin: "The territory of terror was found to lie in more than one part of the globe, and Neruda saw this with the indignation of one who feels himself duped. The erstwhile idol who was set up everywhere in 'the stucco statues of a mustachioed god in boots' now appeared in an ever more merciless light, as did the similarity in methods and trappings between the two leader figures whom he called just Mustache and Little Mustache."

The intention behind these attempts to give a moderate view of Neruda's earlier political leanings was clearly to protect Neruda from indiscriminate criticism from the right and to help create a more balanced view of his actual position. But what was finally of the greatest importance was the poet's integrity. An author who had declared his loyalty to an absolute dictator – whether of the left or of the right – lacked the spiritual independence that had come to be a vital component of the prize winner's identity.

This issue is also relevant in the case of Jorge Luis Borges. During his discussion with Vennberg (*Svenska Dagbladet,* 20 December 1979), Lundkvist responded to the rumor that he would have prevented a prize to Borges on the ground that Borges "had expressed his gratitude to the dictators Pinochet and Videla, because more than others they had defended Western culture. . . . I don't want any unnecessary mixing of politics and literature – whether it concerns Borges or Ritsos. I have translated and introduced Borges, I have a great admiration for him, especially as a poet, but I am also aware of his limitations and I think his worth is greatly overestimated in certain quarters. When it comes to his political blunders, this time in a fascist direction, these make him in my opinion unsuitable on ethical and human grounds for a Nobel Prize."

The extent to which Borges deserved criticism on the political grounds referred to by Lundkvist has been, as we know, a matter of dispute; we know at least that on a number of later occasions he dissociated himself from the South American dictators. And Lundkvist's opinion cannot be taken automatically as representative of the academy. Yet it is important that one who was more than others in a position to promote a South American candidate chose to demur in this way.

A recurrent feature of the armchair politicizing that surrounds the literature prize is a type of nearsightedness, both geographical and chronological. Criticism of interference in the internal affairs of a country is not seldom characterized by national egocentricity, which we can see in the cases of both Heinrich Böll and Patrick White. The 1972 prize to Böll caused irritation in certain West German circles, where it was seen as support for Willy Brandt and the Social Democratic party in the domestic political power struggle. The extensive documentation of the discussion in the academy of Böll's candidacy contains not a trace of such a perspective. In the broadest sense, the academy took a cultural and political view, which Gierow encompassed skillfully in his speech to Böll: his position in the spiritual renewal of post-Nazi Germany and as the originator of "the aesthetics of the humane" made him a figure embued with the spirit of Nobel.

The prize to White was also construed as a contribution to a domestic debate. In Australia the prize was seen as an international recognition of the newly installed Labour government's progressive attitude toward cultural politics.[30] This is as fanciful as the idea of an interference in the party conflicts of West Germany. The only political aspect that can be detected in the 1973 prize is a wish to attain greater international coverage, and more particularly, a desire to draw attention to a new literary continent.

The type of recognition presumed in this case is simply not to be found in the reports, in the correspondence, or in the general discussion of the candidates. That the prize to Aleixandre in 1976 should have been thought of as a declaration of the respectability of the regime in Spain is just as groundless as the suggestion that the choice of Elytis in 1979 was a tribute to the new Greek democracy. A more meaningful political question about both prizes is why shared prizes (Aleixandre and Alberti, Elytis and Ritsos) were not awarded in order to avoid any impression of political partiality. That question will be taken up in the next chapter.

Another type of nearsightedness has been chronological: some suspicions of the academy having a political purpose have not accounted for the time involved in each nominee's candidacy. The discussion arising from the prize to Czesław Miłosz is a good illustration. "Has Miłosz been given the 1980 prize because Poland is politically in fashion?" asked *Der Tagesspiegel* (10 October) and many others. However, François Bondy felt able to reveal in *Die Weltwoche* on 15 October that for the initiated Miłosz had been the most certain candidate before there was a Polish pope or any "Danzig events."[31] Artur Lundkvist confirmed this chronological sequence in an interview in the London *Sunday Times* on 23 November; asked if he was really insisting that the Polish strike had had no influence, he replied that Miłosz had been on the list for three or four years and had been shortlisted in May 1980 – in other words, long before the strike.[32] The strike caused several members to hesitate, said Lundkvist, but he added that it would have been equally impossible to drop Miłosz because of the events in Poland.

In the Soviet Union the prize to Miłosz was regarded as a decidedly political gesture. In the eyes of *Literaturnaya Gazeta,* Miłosz was "a rather middling poet and a bitter anticommunist" who had been rewarded "precisely for his anticommunist stance."[33] To one who has had the opportunity to study the documents, this accusation is quite absurd. The wording of the award referred to Miłosz as an author "who with uncompromising clear-sightedness voices man's exposed condition in a world of severe conflicts." These words focused primarily on the existential dimensions of the human predicament – with the contemporary international tensions nonetheless in the field of vision. Gyllensten's speech, closely echoing his comments as a committee member, also stressed aspects of exile that are more important than the narrowly political. For the stranger Milosz, "physical exile" was "really a reflection of a metaphysical or even religious exile applying to humanity in general." With "the fervor of the Preacher or of Pascal" he strives "to make us intensely aware that we are living scattered abroad. ... The tensions, the passion, the contrasts – the diaspora at once freely acknowledged and enforced – are the true meaning of our human condition." The human condition – it is one of Kierkegaard's foremost disciples who was now pointing out the existential dimensions in a great contemporary author. But this perspective corresponded to the humanistic tradition of the Nobel Prize in Literature. From that point of view it was essential that Milosz's political defection be thus formulated (after a reminder of how during the cold war the political climate had altered in a Stalinist direction): "With his uncompromising demand for artistic integrity and human freedom, Milosz could no longer support the regime." Uncompromising integrity and a call to rally round human values – these are qualities that the Swedish Academy, following the spirit of Nobel's will, has repeatedly sought in combination with great artistic achievement. And just as repeatedly, this mode of evaluation has collided with the Soviet view of literature. Justifying a prize by focusing on not only an author's interpretation of the human predicament but his integrity is quite simply beyond the grasp of Marxist-Leninist aesthetics, which interprets such a focus as mere camouflage for political intentions.

When the prize to Jaroslav Seifert was announced in 1984 it immediately gave rise to speculations among the gathered journalists that it was a political rebuke of the government of Czechoslovakia. Gyllensten denied that there was any ground for such speculation; he added that every human activity may be viewed politically, but that the academy's overriding concern was literary. This observation did not, of course, prevent conclusions being drawn in a variety of quarters about the politics of the choice. A recurring idea was expressed by the author (and translator of Seifert) Harry Järv in *Sydsvenska Dagbladet* on 12 October: the prize to Seifert "has implications beyond Seifert himself without that entailing any devaluation of him as a poet: it is the first occasion on which the prize has gone to a Czech, and it happens at a time when the Czech authors and the Czech people could well do with a token of encouragement." The newspaper *Arbetet* (12 October 1984) likewise conceived of the prize as "a mark of support to the sorely constrained and persecuted Czech literature. . . . Therefore, the Swedish Academy's choice is a political act."

The press statement issued to coincide with the announcement of the prize provided some commentators with the support they wanted to find. Quoting Gyllensten's words that it is possible to take a political view of every literary work and every human action, the Belgian *Le Soir* (12 October 1984) claimed that the members of the academy had done exactly that when they wrote:

> It is human beings who create society. The state exists for the people, not vice versa. In Seifert's view of life there is an anachronistic element – a protest against everything that reduces men's and women's opportunities in life and reduces them to cogs in some ideological machine or restrains them with the prudery of this or that propaganda. This may perhaps seem inoffensive to those who have never themselves had to experience oppression and want under a coercive political regime (to us here in Sweden, for example). But Seifert has never been inoffensive. His poetry, this visibly abundant cornucopia, has also been and is a political act.[34]

Arbetet also considered these lines a "political verdict" on Seifert's work. That is a misunderstanding. The press statement emphasized what Seifert's "Song to Prague and Woman" "has also been and is," that is, "a political act," and amplified in what manner, more closely examined, it was so. We are given a presentation of Seifert's life and work, including the obvious political aspects, but not a political verdict on his achievement. Likewise, in making the choice the academy was clearly aware of the political implications of Seifert's work, but that is different from saying such an awareness determined the result. As Gyllensten insisted, the academy's decision was primarily a literary matter. It was inescapable that such a choice would have a political "effect." The academy foresaw such a result yet nonetheless, and for literary reasons, chose Seifert; it is only in this limited sense that the decision may be termed "political." It can, however, be denied, with good reason, that the choice had a political "intention."

As with Miłosz, a closer examination reveals elements of greater import than any political maneuvering. Seifert protested "against everything which reduces men's and women's opportunities in life," uncompromisingly defended "literary and cultural freedom," and evoked a world different from that of "coercion and deprivation." It is just this kind of endeavor that fits in with the humanistic tradition of the Nobel Prize. On a political level, expressions of this tradition can often be interpreted as distinct political stances. But it is more reasonable to view the choice of prize winner in the light of the overall criteria, according to which it is the writer's *integrity*, not the role of dissident that from time to time may follow from that, and the writer's defense of human values, not its practical consequences, that stand at the center of the academy's attention.

The process of judgment, while "primarily a literary matter," does not, of course, prevent subsidiary evaluations from gradually forming a pattern. Such a pattern is apparent in the sequence Singer-Miłosz-Canetti-Seifert. At first sight one could see here what a newspaper headline proclaimed about the choice of Seifert: "The Swedish Academy Greets Central Europe." Or the choice can "be seen as a token of respect for the Central Europe that – to borrow Milan Kundera's words from a well-known essay of his – must be redeemed from oblivion through our refusal to accept the definitive division of Europe into a West and an East."[35] Closer examination, however, reveals a more complex pattern, a pattern relevant long before Kundera wrote his essay. It is not a question of some politically definable region or some third way in the tug-of-war between East and West. It is rather a question of authors who with great personal integrity have given voice to an old culture that had either been swept aside by oppressors or whose continued existence was severely threatened. These authors have thus spoken, out of their sorely tested experience, on behalf of the basic human values. In the difficult area of Central Europe, in other words, a number of authors have emerged who express an attitude toward life in keeping with the humanistic tradition of the Nobel Prize. Such a pattern, though, reveals only part of the truth. The prize is in the end not given to an attitude toward life, to a set of cultural roots, or to the substance of a commitment; the prize has been awarded so as to honor the unique artistic power by which this human experience has been shaped into literature.

This discussion can be extended to include the 1987 winner. In his speech to Joseph Brodsky, the academy's permanent secretary, Sture Allén, downplayed the significance that "political disputes" have had in Brodsky's work: "The problem is raised to a more general level: man's duty to live his own life, not a life determined by the categories and norms of others." The speech aimed – as have so many previous speeches – at an existential objective above that of political differences of opinion. What was essential for Brodsky in the meeting between Russian and Anglo-American was thus seen not in political but in human and artistic terms. Allén quoted Brodsky's remark that his access to two languages was "like sitting on the top of an existential hill with a view over two slopes, over humanity's two tendencies of development"; Allén added: "The East-West background has given him an unusual thematic richness and a multitude of perspectives. Together with the writer's thorough insight into the culture of former epochs it has also conjured up a grand historical vision."

The choice of a Soviet dissident, who could be recognized as one of our age's great poets only after he had begun his life of exile in the United States, had political implications of which the academy was naturally not unaware.

Anxious to avoid misunderstanding on that point, the secretary drew special attention to the human and literary aspects of the choice. Once again emphasis was placed on the author's "integrity" when faced with the political hardships of "trial, internal banishment, exile." But paramount in the academy's estimation was "the magnificent joy of discovery" in "this richly orchestrated poetry." Once again the decisive factor was the poet's supreme artistic power in developing his humane view of life.

CHAPTER 8

Shared Prizes: "A Mutual Fellowship"

The issue of dividing the Nobel Prize in Literature between two recipients is liable to have political implications. When in 1902 Gottfrid Billing highlighted the inescapable political dimensions of the award, he was speaking in connection with the idea of Ibsen and Bjørnson sharing the prize. The political aspect was most immediately apparent in the prize being a gesture of "friendliness to Norway" at the time of the union crisis, but the very idea of sharing the prize had political implications. The compromise of a shared prize was thought to indicate certain reservations the academy had about the gesture of recognition: "That the academy should approve of Ibsen's later writings, no one should suppose, any more than that the same academy should sanction Bjørnson's political activity" (i.e., his anti-Swedish agitation). Political deliberations of a like subtlety were apparent in the critic Bengt Holmqvist's argument (*Dagens Nyheter,* 23 November 1977) that the 1977 prize should have been shared between Vicente Aleixandre and Rafael Alberti. The sole prize to the former had "naturally come to be understood in its special political aspect: as a particular recognition of the so-called inner emigration in Spain at the expense of the resistance movement." With a similar argument two years later, Holmqvist claimed that the 1979 prize should have been divided between Odysseus Elytis and Jannis Ritsos.

An extreme – hypothetical – case of a shared prize discussed as an expression of political justice appeared in a statement (*Dagens Nyheter,* 9 June 1984) by the Egyptian author Yousuf Idris; after an apparently confused conversation with a Swedish ex-party leader, he aired the absurd notion that he "would gladly accept a prize shared with an Israeli author! A new variation of the Begin-Sadat Peace Prize! The literature prize as a political demonstration! Do they think like that, those who give the Nobel Prize?"[1] No indeed, they don't. But the discussion of prize-sharing that – often with political overtones – gathered momentum in the 1970s involved many misunderstandings as to the likely conditions, the methods of evaluation, and the actual practice. Some comment is necessary.

The problems of a shared prize have followed the Nobel deliberations from the very beginning. As early as 1901 the committee expressed a commitment in principle to undivided prizes "when possible." The Norwegian compromise that crossed the minds of Billing and several others was rejected in the Wirsénian reports of both 1902 and 1903; the latter referred to "eager deliberations" in the previous year and "an occasional suggestion" in the present year: "But the committee has finally agreed to the idea that – quite apart from the question of Ibsen's chances of an eventual majority in the academy – a division of the prize could readily be misunderstood, since each of the named authors is too significant to receive only half a prize."

Common to the differing viewpoints of Billing and the committee was the idea that a divided prize signaled reservations about the value of the writings in question. No such idea, though, was behind the first shared prize, that given to Frédéric Mistral and José Echegaray in 1904. The committee had already unanimously proposed Mistral when committee member Carl Rupert Nyblom's unsuccessful translation of Mistral's *Mirèio* was presented. In letters Wirsén expressed fears that the public might see the translation as something produced by order of the academy and that the readers – not least the King of Sweden – would be surprised at the decision; because of such purely domestic doubts, he wanted to withdraw the proposal and go for Echegaray. Before the decisive meeting, though, he could count on only six votes out of twelve for the idea. Sharing was a compromise in a stalemate situation: "Even though in principle I have no great liking for the sharing of prizes, I still think that in the present crisis the solution is a good one. Partly because it neutralizes, as Hjärne has maintained, potential unpleasantness in consequence of Nyblom's translation, and partly because an attempt has been made to please the admirers of both Mistral and Echegaray."

In these depressing proceedings it is hard to see where the principles were. On consideration, the 1904 solution gave cause for scepticism about prize-sharing, as we read in a letter of 28 October 1917 from the diplomat Carl Bildt to Karlfeldt. Bildt had often heard Spaniards complain that the prize had never been given to one of their countrymen, and when he had "retorted that it has been given to Echegaray, the reply has always been: 'No, only a half.' " His attitude – on the basis of his perspective as Swedish envoy in Rome – was that prize sharing created "two categories among winners . . . If we solemnly declare that half a prize is as much of an honor as a whole prize, our protestations unfortunately have no effect on the public's emotionally determined belief in the opposite." Sharing was "really a compromise" that "belongs to political life. . . . It registers unwillingness either to undertake a sufficiently thorough examination of the performance of the different candidates, or to bring two approximately equal voting groups to agreement." Bildt drew the conclusion that, "chiefly for our own sake, we ought to avoid this expedient, which is more convenient than it is satisfying for our reputation."

The letter voiced the "serious doubts" that, as we shall see in the 1919 report, several members raised on the matter of prize sharing. Another who "greatly dislikes a division of the prize" was Selma Lagerlöf.[2] A frequently cited reason was that "repeated divisions must gradually lower the ideal worth of the Nobel Prize," as it was put in the 1905 report. When, like Tegnér in that year, one called for a sharing of the prize–in that case between the two Polish candidates, Eliza Orzeszkowa and Henryk Sienkiewicz–the idea was put forward as an "exception." What is interesting is that here for the first time we encounter an argument that would later be vital. "In a much closer manner" than was the case with the previous year's divided prize between Mistral and Echegaray, both the Polish writers "belong together: not just through bonds of nationality but also through the close relations of their respective oeuvres." At the same time Tegnér shared the general reservations, which is obvious from the fact that he considered it to be "rather a suitable kind of recognition of the prize winners that these exceptional cases should follow each other, one pair immediately after the other, . . . The diminishment in honor of having received only half a prize will not be felt so much if it soon after affects, or has just affected, other authors whose renown is worldwide."

The idea that a divided prize devalued the honor was expressed in a couple of debates in the 1910s. In 1912, when the choice was between Gerhart Hauptmann, Karl Schönherr, and Carl Spitteler, the majority of the committee thought that Hauptmann alone should receive the prize. But if the academy decided to divide the prize, the combination Schönherr and Spitteler was recommended, since it was believed that "a shared prize would not be a sufficient honor for Hauptmann, who in his literary production is much stronger than the two others" and who "has spoken and speaks to a much wider public." A similar line of thought can be glimpsed in correspondence between Heidenstam and Karlfeldt in October 1917; Karlfeldt favored the Danish proposal: "If Brandes cannot get the prize"–and at the most he could count on two to three votes in the academy–"it ought to be shared between Gjellerup and Pontoppidan." Heidenstam admitted that a shared prize "would weaken the impression of a stab in the back to Brandes." As has been pointed out, the gesture was obviously meant to indicate tactfully that two authors were needed to balance the hapless critic.[3].

A reasonably eloquent passage in the 1914 report lets us see how academy members of the time struggled between their fear of devaluing the prize through sharing and the stipulation in paragraph 4 of the statutes that they should evaluate "works, each of which may be considered to merit a prize."

It may further be objected that the reduction in the amount of the prize for each of the recipients weakens its significance as what we are in the habit of calling a "world prize," irrespective of the founder's declaration that both of the rewarded works ought "to merit a prize." It may nonetheless with reason be maintained that the significance of the prize in itself, whether or not it is regarded by a greater or lesser public as a "world prize," must be measured not specifically according to its monetary size but according to its intention and usefulness as emanating from the Nobel Foundation, which even by means of shared though still substantial awards – together with the honors attached to them – can enable two outstanding individual talents to labor successfully in the service of mankind, when it proves to be impossible to distinguish a single great achievement that would fully outweigh both of them.

In spite of the reference to the clear requirements of the will about the individual quality of works sharing the prize, and in spite of the argument that the significance of the prize did not reside in the amount of money given, the reasoning was that prize sharing was acceptable when it was not possible to find one equivalent "great work." It was just this division into "two categories," however, that had been feared and that was at work when Hauptmann was balanced against Schönherr and Spitteler, and when Gjellerup and Pontoppian were balanced against Brandes.

As we have seen in our discussion of literary neutralism in World War I, quite a different attitude toward prize sharing prevailed during that period. Both candidates, the Finn Juhani Aho and the Catalan Ángel Guimerà, were the subjects, in 1917 and 1919, respectively, of debate on the implications of maintaining that "neither of them should be rewarded before some other author who has written in the earlier literary language of the country in question," as it was said of Guimerà. Their sharing the prize with an author who used "the older and time-honored literary language" was suggested in both instances as a means of not offending sensitive national feelings. The idea recurred in the 1930s when a shared prize was considered between the Finnish-writing Sillanpää and a Finnish-Swedish author, first Bertel Gripenberg, then Jarl Hemmer.

After the Danish prize in 1917, half a century passed without a shared prize, although the idea was aired from time to time, as when Österling argued for awarding the prize to both Dreiser and Lewis in 1930. The reasons for this restrictive policy right into the 1950s were summed up well by Österling himself in his comment on William F. Lamont's article "The Nobel Prize in Literature" in *Books Abroad*. Looking over the first half-century of the history of the prize, and with the help of an international jury of 350 members, Lamont had arrived at a list of 150 deserving prize winners and drew the conclusion that each prize should have been divided into three, on lines similar to the practice of the scientific awards – to which Österling responded: "But here a principle distinction must be pointed out: the scientific prizes sometimes must be shared for the simple reason that several researchers have worked together on the same project and the award therefore cannot reasonably be given to only one of them. The literary achievements, however, are never the result of any kind of teamwork."

Repeated sharing could well have had weighty consequences for the status of the literary prize: "Such mass-production of literary prize winners – three or four per year – would be a sure way of lessening the renown of the prize and turning it all into such an indifferent affair that it could scarcely give rise to debate either in Oklahoma or elsewhere." (*Stockholms-Tidningen*, 2 May 1951).

Emphasizing even more the principles involved, Österling had affirmed the academy's practice in *The Literary Prize*, published in the previous year; he speculated, for example, that Pontoppidan would seem to posterity a weightier figure than Gjellerup: "The fact that such a comparison becomes inevitable is one of the drawbacks of a divided prize; in subsequent years the academy has, in fact, avoided this procedure that in the public mind may often have the effect of reducing to one-half, not only the monetary value of the prize, but also the honor of receiving it." The correspondence shows that this view was shared by many of those involved. For instance, in considering "the Icelanders," "the Laxness couple" – a combination that would be out of the question a month later – Dag Hammarskjöld argued against sharing, in a 22 September 1955 letter, "for the impression is often that the sum of two is less than one."

After fifty years of restraint in the matter, the academy decided on a shared prize twice – indeed, within a relatively short interval. In 1966 Shmuel Yosef Agnon and Nelly Sachs shared a prize, about which the now available correspondence shows a certain degree of doubt. Nelly Sachs's translator Erik Lindegren was so sure of her worth that in 1965 he argued for putting her in an undivided second place after Asturias. (At the same time Agnon was, in Lindegren's eyes, "the only modern Hebrew author with a place in world literature.") Österling was more cautious; Nelly Sachs's theme "is certainly powerful enough," but he "can't help comparing her historically with the great poets who have received the prize (or who did not!)," he wrote to Lindegren. This doubt seemed to lead discussion in the direction of a shared prize. Such a solution is, in fact, the starting point for literary historian Henry Olsson when, in a letter to Lindegren, he discussed whom she "can share with"; instead of Agnon – "much too odd to be considered" – he wondered about Ingeborg Bachmann, Anna Akhmatova, and Erich Kästner.

There seems to be a lack of clarity here about the principles governing the sharing of prizes, an uncertainty that demands clarification, especially since so many proposals for shared prizes are now being made. One such possibility was raised by Lindegren in the 1965 letter to the committee chairman already cited: "For a long time now the academy has been extraordinarily restrictive about rewarding Swedish authors. For my part I would like to see a Nobel Prize shared between Eyvind Johnson and Harry Martinson. They are truly the opposite of everything that could be labeled 'provincial.' "

In 1967 the eventual winner – Asturias – was also featured in a proposal for a shared prize. Gierow, who mentioned this in a letter, said that those on the committee who were willing to consider it regarded it as an expedient, a way out of a difficulty; it seemed that a shared prize would "on all counts . . . meet with scant approval." (That does not prevent the proposal – according to which Asturias would share the prize with a prominent fellow writer – from seeming now to be considerably forward-looking.) Then in 1974 the idea was realized of giving the prize to Johnson and Martinson. As soon as two years later – according to Francisco J. Uriz in *El País,* a man said to have reliable sources – the academy considered dividing a prize between Aleixandre and Borges.[4]

The Swedish Academy, of course, has been fully aware that increased resort to prize sharing would entail a new policy, justified by the wider area the prize now has to cover, but in any event demanding an extended theoretical basis. In the years 1974-76 the principles for prize sharing took shape – first, in two of Gierow's reports as committee chairman (1974 and 1975), then in contributions from Johannes Edfelt and Artur Lundkvist, and finally in a formal decision after a discussion in the academy at the meetings of 22 and 29 January 1976. The actual nominees and their grouping cannot be disclosed, but the views aired are hardly so sensitive. Since these views were in part merely interpretations of the statutes, and since they have in part already appeared in print, it is no infringement of confidentiality to repeat them here. The whole discussion is well caught in Gierow's summation of the January deliberations in his 1976 report:

> It was not any real conflict of opinion, either within the committee itself or in the academy as a whole, that brought about the discussion, but the need for some clarification, unclouded by the thought of specific would-be prize winners. The differences of opinion that did surface did not dictate the outcome and amounted mainly to the fact that while some found the idea of prize sharing quite suitable, perhaps even desirable, others considered that, with regard to both the ideal and the material value of the prize, the academy ought to observe the greatest restraint. It was further confirmed on the one hand that in certain conditions neither the statutes of the Nobel Foundation nor the practice of the academy place obstacles in the way of dividing a prize in two – though not three, as far as the literature prize is concerned – and on the other hand that in the present, and no doubt continuing circumstances, i.e., the steadily expanding literary area requiring attention, the expedient of a divided prize, desirable or not, would come to be more and more often unavoidable.

On the matter of conditions for prize sharing, the academy was unanimous: (a) each of those sharing a prize must individually be worthy of the prize; and (b) between their work there must be a mutual fellowship that makes it clear why the joint prize has been given to them.

The first condition comes directly from paragraph 4 of the statutes: "A prize may be equally divided between two works each of which may be considered to merit a prize" (where practice has accentuated not the single work but rather the total production). But the statutory requirement is one thing – the public response may be quite another. Practical wisdom on that score was apparent in Gierow's recommendation of 5 June 1972: "The impression of a divided prize can easily be, as we all know, that neither winner has deserved the whole prize. The expedient can be resorted to only when it is clear, preferably outside the academy as well as in it, that both recipients are worthy of the prize, but that if the one should receive it then the other would be excluded."

The second condition – only briefly discernible in the earlier period – is not supported by the statutes but by the practice that had begun to take shape. Representing this view of prize sharing are remarks in Österling's speech to Agnon and Sachs in 1966. The prize was being "awarded to two outstanding Jewish authors . . . each of whom represents Israel's message to our time. . . . The purpose of combining these two writers is to do justice to the individual achievements of each, and the sharing of the prize has its special justification: to honor two writers who, although they write in different languages, are united in a spiritual kinship and complement each other in a superb effort to present the cultural heritage of the Jewish people through the written word. Their common source of inspiration has been for both of them a vital power."

Not only did this careful argument reveal a reasonable diplomacy about taking this unusual step, but it was embued with Österling's basic caution in the matter of shared prizes, a caution that in this special case could give way to particularly compelling reasons. The emphasis given to spiritual kinship and common roots can be said to put into words that demand for a mutual fellowship that was to characterize the intensified discussion of the issue in the 1970s. The 1914 Nobel Committee, as we have seen, viewed prize sharing as part of its neutrality policy, as one of the expedients available to help the academy "as far as it is able, to exercise a restraining and counterbalancing influence on the excesses" that nationalism in contemporary literature and "the competition for power" could so easily generate. Prize sharing with the aim of pouring oil on troubled waters – the gesture that Idris had in mind – is no longer conceivable, given the spirit and practice of the Nobel Prize in recent years. That spirit and practice require some kind of mutual fellowship between any two candidates in question.

To this must be added Gierow's argument from 1972 – "that if the one should receive the prize then the other would be excluded." That is exactly the situation that emerged two years later when the choice was between the candidates Eyvind Johnson and Harry Martinson. A prize to the one would have definitely excluded the other.

Two episodes in recent decades are of particular interest with regard to the principles involved; they occurred in 1977 and 1979. Both the committee and the academy had, of course, carefully considered the options of shared prizes mentioned by Holmqvist. In the earlier case two writers from the Spanish generation of 1927 undoubtedly fulfilled the requirement of mutual fellowship. But in the end, Aleixandre alone was found to represent – in the words of the award – "the great renewal of the traditions of Spanish poetry between the wars." In what respect was he found to be superior to the other surviving poets of the group? We gather part of an answer from a newspaper article (*Svenska Dagbladet*, 8 October 1977) by Knut Ahnlund, the committee's specialist in Spanish-language literature:

> That this token of recognition, which is a tribute to Spanish poetry, should be given to Aleixandre in preference to Rafael Alberti, is perhaps surprising to many. But there are several good arguments in favor of Aleixandre. He was not quite so dazzling and precocious as his younger friend, but the center of gravity in his life's work lies much closer to our own time than that of Alberti, who reached his peak with *Sobre los Angeles* (About the Angels) long ago. Alberti is more popular, his songs can be heard when people congregate, but Aleixandre has probably had a deeper influence on readers' minds and development. Few poets still alive belong in such a high degree and with such full right both to the present and to literary history. Few have had such an importance for the regeneration, and the continuance of literary life, in a country that has experienced its golden age being drowned in blood and that now after forty years of quarantine can see its poetry set free.

Ahnlund's article naturally had parallels with his report and thus voiced arguments that found a place in the discussion. That these were, on one point, significant for the result is clear in Gierow's speech to Aleixandre; that point was Aleixandre's unique importance for those who followed him. When the end of the Spanish Civil War scattered writers all over the world, leaving behind the powerless Aleixandre, "fragile and unbroken," he kept on writing and became "the gathering point and source of energy for Spain's spiritual life, which today we are happy to honor." On another point – the political question – both Ahnlund and Gierow maintained an eloquent silence. In all probability, Holmqvist's idea that a prize to Aleixandre alone would be construed as a tribute to the inner emigration at the cost of the resistance in exile never occurred to the committee or to the academy, or to the specialist.

Favoring the poet who stayed behind was based on the fact that Aleixandre had greater significance for the rebirth of poetry in Spain.

Holmqvist's arguments for a shared prize in 1979 have a wider implication. It was his opinion that Jannis Ritsos–whose work, powerful and headstrong but difficult to see as a whole, was of an equal quality to that of the more readily viewed Elytis–should in fact have shared the prize with Elytis. The issue had a distinctly political accent. Ritsos was on the red side in the civil war and had been treated by the Greek bourgeoisie as a leper. A shared prize, argued Holmqvist, would "have contributed to the Greek reconciliation that must come yet is so desperately hard to achieve."[5] Lundkvist adhered to the reasoning behind the implicit ranking of the poets but was not altogether averse to the idea of sharing: "Ritsos I have read thoroughly in French translation, and I find him, in his best moments, a great poet, but in his worst he can deteriorate into Stalinistic clichés or verbosity. But it is certainly not his politics that make me put him somewhat lower than Elytis. For my part I could very well have thought of letting him share with Elytis" (*Svenska Dagbladet,* 20 December 1979).

Lundkvist did not address the political motive for a shared prize that was in Holmqvist's mind. The idea of using the prize to "contribute" to some "reconciliation," national or otherwise, was not, as we have seen, in line with either the academy's wishes or its practice. The academies of the 1910s and the 1930s could air such a thought about Finnish literature; nothing in the postwar era has corresponded to that situation.

Another question of principle has greater relevance. In his discussion of Elytis and Ritsos, Holmqvist referred to the division of the 1974 prize between Eyvind Johnson and Harry Martinson. More than two or three such "mutually incomparable great figures ... are not often found active at the same time in a small country," and the academy "drew the only defensible conclusion." But this was "by no means a special Swedish case ... this happens in country after country ... Who for instance would take it upon himself to choose between the two great old poets of Hungarian literature, Gyula Illyes and Sándor Weöres? Or between the Poles Zbigniew Herbert and Tadeusz Różewicz? ... Absolutely worthy candidates, at home surrounded by passionate adherents who with hard-proven arguments give the one favorite or the other the advantage ... In the case of the other Nobel Prizes, sharing is now the rule rather than the exception. Eventually this reasonable arrangement must apply also to the literature prize."

Eventually, perhaps. In the short run, reality has contradicted Holmqvist. Indeed, the choice of Miłosz challenges his thesis; at the same time he himself found it "hard to imagine many better choices" (*Dagens Nyheter,* 10 October 1980). Nor have the subsequent choices, from Canctti to Cela, inspired any call for shared prizes. Two names could, however, very well have been gleaned in 1982 from the rich Latin American literature. Faced with a wealth of literature from an ever-widening area of responsibility, the academy's problems with shared prizes are not likely to go away.

CHAPTER 9

"Intended for the Literature of the Whole World"

The Nobel Prize in Literature seemed for a long time to be a European affair. Nobel's will indicated that the prize was to have an international aim, but in cautious wording: "It is my express wish that in awarding the prizes no consideration whatever shall be given to the nationality of the candidates, but that the most worthy shall receive the prize, whether he be a Scandinavian or not." The emphasis in the last clause on Scandinavian authors was reflected in the practice of the early Nobel Committee. In principle, however, the international scope of the prize is assured by its very conditions. A broader perspective is also implicit in Wirsén's speaking of the influential position "in world literature" available to the Swedish Academy. Yet the concept of universal literature was still to a high degree focused on European literature. Wirsén declared that if the task of administering the prize was not accepted by the academy, then "the leading men of letters throughout Europe" would be deprived of the opportunity to be recognized. Also representative of such a view was the wish expressed by the diplomat Bildt in a letter in 1904 that "to begin with we work round Europe."

A tentative move outside the European sphere was made in 1913 with the prize awarded to the Indian Rabindranath Tagore. In an important passage, to which we shall soon return, the 1922 report spoke of the danger of the Nobel Prize, "which is intended for the richly variegated literature of the whole world," being limited to "a less universal circle." Even the United States, however, had to wait until the 1930s before becoming part of the picture with the prizes to Sinclair Lewis (1930), Eugene O'Neill (1936), and Pearl Buck (1938). A further widening of the field did not occur until 1945, when Gabriela Mistral was hailed by Hjalmar Gullberg in his speech as "the spiritual queen of the entire Latin American world." The decision could have been made five years before, but the international situation prevented it. In this way both of the prizes given to writers outside Europe and North America up to that time were awarded in the margins, as it were, of the two world wars: one immediately before World War I, and the other immediately after World War II.

A further series of prizes to writers from the United States and Latin America scarcely altered this pattern. The rich culture of East Asia was first recognized in 1968 with the award to Yasunari Kawabata, for a "narrative mastery which with great sensibility expresses the essence of the Japanese mind." The wording of the prize to Australia's Patrick White in 1973 – "for an epic and psychological narrative art which has introduced a new continent into literature" – suggests how a new part of the world was incorporated into the history of the literary prize. But these occasional excursions outside European-American literature hardly fulfill the global responsibility that the academy more and more clearly faces. The vigorous literature of Africa has been neglected, like that of the Arabian countries, until very recently, and both Indian and Chinese voices have made increasingly determined claims for a more reasonable geographical distribution. At the same time, we can detect in recent years in both the Nobel Committee and the Swedish Academy a greater interest in taking this problem seriously. In an interview in the German magazine *Titel* in 1984, Lars Gyllensten said that attention to non-European writers is gradually increasing in the academy; attempts are being made "to achieve a global distribution."[1] The first fruits of this ambition were the prizes to Wole Soyinka in 1986 and to Naguib Mahfouz in 1988.

The new situation appears clearly in an exchange between the author Tsu-Yü Hwang and Gyllensten in *Göteborgs-Posten* (29 May and 24 June 1984). Tsu-Yü Hwang raised the question "whether an author writing in an 'uncommon' language has the same chance of a Nobel Prize as a Western author"; produced figures to illustrate the discrepancy between Scandinavian and English-language authors on the one side and Asian on the other ("of thousands of authors among the 800-1,000 million Chinese, not a single one has received the prize!"), and concluded that anyone who writes in an "uncommon" language and wants to be considered must "fulfill two equally important conditions: (1) He or she must have produced work showing to a high degree an idealistic tendency, and (2) He or she must find another author, preferably of the same exceptional caliber, who can translate his or her works into one of the main Western languages."

With regard to, among other things, the question of how much of the subtlety of the original text vanishes in translation, Tsu-Yü Hwang opted for the following model:

> After a certain period of time, say thirty or forty or fifty years, the academy realizes the suitability of giving the prize to an author who writes in one of those "uncommon" languages. Having thus decided, the members of the academy can take the time to consult experts from around the world in their search for suitable candidates. After reading representative works by those

authors – mostly in translation – the academy should have the last word in selecting the winner.

Gyllensten admitted that in essentials, Tsu-Yü Hwang was right. A global comparison gave "the impression that a great injustice has been done." It was "clear that Europe has been favored," but many smaller regions of Europe did not appear in the list of winners, "in spite of the fact that they have been able to demonstrate a high level of literary culture." At the same time Gyllensten stressed that the Nobel Committee had from the beginning been aware of the problem and that he saw it as "stimulating, exciting even, to come to grips with." Concerning two of the proposed methods – "the use of experts and the deliberate aim to pay due attention to 'foreign' language areas" – he confirmed that these methods were "exactly how" the work was carried out. But the academy members could not delegate their task to experts but "must in the end make up their minds independently"; thus, when it came to non-European languages – and also to "minority" languages in Europe – they had to rely on translations. But the academy was not limited to what the commercial book market could offer. The academy could commission translators, "but of course not to an unlimited extent." Gyllensten thought the best way of breaking down linguistic and cultural barriers was to "promote the translation and publication of the literature one feels enthusiastic about."

But the academy could not content itself with waiting for a flow of good translations; it had to do what it could in the circumstances:

> In the case of writers we want to take up and treat fairly it is a matter of trying to acquire some understanding of the traditions and of the literary and cultural milieu out of which they write. A great deal of background reading is needed if one is to grasp something of what a writer from a culture other than one's own feels engaged in and wants to write about. And here, too, we must assume close cooperation between external specialists and those who will in the end reach a decision.
>
> Finally, we must be able to discriminate among the specialists, to choose them properly, and to arrive at a conclusion on the reliability, impartiality and so on of their reports. That is not always so easy. Many specialists are much too patriotic; others offer highly personal judgments; others give undue attention to their countrymen's position in a hierarchy conditioned by age; others apply political criteria, explicitly or implicitly etc. Cultural differences surfaced as well – attitudes towards age and other "diplomatic" considerations may well carry a different weight in Japan or China than they do in the West.

In this highly instructive article there was one idea particularly relevant to the present discussion, and that was the challenge of learning to understand the traditions and cultural milieu of an author from a distant cultural world – and then to judge the evaluation offered by his countrymen.

The problem has been a constant, though not especially insistent, one in the earlier period. It can be glimpsed in the committee's cautious attitude toward Tagore in 1913. Among other aspects to be investigated were the connections between Tagore's poetry and that of the Vishnu cult; only then "may it be possible, for the guidance of independent evaluation, to distinguish between the original and the traditional elements in Tagore's religious mysticism and poetry." In fact, the academy was trying to judge the candidate's originality rather than attain a richer understanding of his work. Heidenstam made short business of it all with an argument that anticipated a later period's "pragmatic" line of thought; the problem of principle was not discussed further on that occasion. But it returned in 1922. In "the difficult choice" between Yeats and Benavente, the dilemma was formulated in words of great general relevance:

> In spite of a certain exclusive, aesthetically refined disposition, the Irishman, with his exceptionally highly developed English poetic culture, is more likely to master our emotions, to delight the lyrical sense that for us Swedes and for Germanic people in general plays such a large part in the enjoyment of art, than the Spaniard, representative as he is of a literature whose aims are quite otherwise. We must always reason with ourselves to maintain objectivity in our evaluation, but such objectivity is highly necessary. There is a real danger of the Nobel Prize, intended for the richly varied literature of the whole world, awarded by Nobel's countrymen, gradually being limited to a less universal circle, if our greater or lesser ease of access to the individuality of the different national spirits should affect our judgments. It is a matter of being on guard and assessing what is foreign to us not simply according to our own demands but according to its own conditions, and according to what we can gather of what it means where it has been created, and where tradition and culture facilitate comprehension of its content and form. With regard to both of the writers before us now there is reason to believe that each in his own place is a worthy representative of his people.

These words of Per Hallström's "on behalf of the committee" belong to a different epoch than Gyllensten's in 1984. For Hallström poetry reflected "the individuality of the national spirits"; Gyllensten spoke of "the traditions" and "the literary and cultural milieu" in which an author writes. But the problem is basically the same. It is still a question of trying to understand what the foreign work "means where it has been created, and where tradition and culture facilitate comprehension." One change since the 1920s, however, is that the academy's ambition to "gather" what it can has acquired wider geographical horizons; it is also more likely to resort to experts to acquire enough background understanding for it to make a reasonably empathetic assessment.

The desire apparent in 1922 to judge foreign work in accordance with its own conditions and frames of reference returned in Schück's report on the Portugese Correia de Oliveira in 1933. He found it scarcely proper "strictly to apply only our own Swedish taste to the works of one whose outlook and conception of life is remote from our own. . . . So far as it is possible for us we ought to try to understand and appreciate their way of viewing literature." The candidate in question was not "European," but appeared to base his work "on purely native traditions. . . . Several of his poems seem to *us* to be rather simple and trivial, but I suspect that the Portuguese see them with other eyes, while they in turn would not appreciate, for example, Fröding." Schück voted for Correia de Oliveira's *Job* – "even a non-Portuguese must recognize this poetic drama of ideas as a significant work of art" – and he suggested a complete translation of the work; only small parts were available in Swedish. This practical gesture, however, carried with it no solution to the problem of principle. Foreign literature, which in its own milieu was seen "with other eyes," continued to offer a difficult challenge. We note recurring expressions of the wish to "understand and appreciate" the literature of remote peoples. Bridging the distance in a real sense – that is, translating "remote" literature in a manner more thorough-going than the merely linguistic – is perhaps the most intimidating task facing those who in future will distribute the Nobel Prize in Literature.

The overall intention behind the remarks quoted above is to comply with Nobel's will in making the prize available worldwide. Early on, consideration was given to "the idea that the Nobel Prize, as far as possible, should circulate in turn between different countries." These words from 1904 refer to the possible objection to the Nobel Committee's candidate Mistral that the prize – which in 1901 went to Sully Prudhomme – "should not so soon afterwards go to France." The rightness of the argument was not denied, but reference was made to the fact that Mistral "nonetheless writes in an independent language, through the consolidation of which he has earned himself new honor." The committee had also to act with a certain haste, "in consideration of his advanced age." The principle recurred rather defensively when a majority of the committee proposed Swinburne in 1908. It had "not ignored the possible objection that last year's prize went to an Englishman and that reasons of expediency could well suggest that the prize should circulate among the different cultures." After duly recognizing the suitability of "such a circulation as a rule taking place," the committee claimed that "there is no real obstacle, when the circumstances are appropriate, to giving the prize to the same country in close, and even in immediate, succession." As it happened, the prize did not go to Swinburne and the principle was never tested on this point. Since then, two prize-winners from the same country have never been chosen in close succession. It is more significant that in 1922, "in the difficult choice" between Yeats and Benavente, the latter was given preference largely in consideration of the "omissions in the geographical distribution of the Nobel Prize." This line of reasoning recurs more recently. When in a letter in 1964 Gierow weighed Sartre and Auden against each other, one of his arguments against Sartre was "the series of French Nobel Prize winners – four Frenchmen already since the war"; it was therefore an argument in Auden's favor that "so far English literature has been remarkably little kept in mind." Another example is the prize to Böll in 1972; there was a certain pressure behind it because no literary prize had gone to Germany since 1929.[2]

Circulation of the prize, however, was for a long time restricted to Europe. The unrest noted in 1922 over the uneven distribution allowed the committee's horizon to cease immediately beyond England and Spain. The prize to Tagore in 1913 seemed like an expansive gesture, but in reality it illustrates this limitation. The proposal originated not in India but from a member of the Royal Society of Literature in Britain, and the final decision was based on Tagore's English version of Gitanjali, without the aid of Oriental experts to assess the rest of his production. (One of the committee members, Esaias Tegnér, Jr., could in fact read Tagore in Bengali, but there is no indication that use was made of his expertise in the matter.) The impression of a narrow Eurocentric discussion persisted. It was not until 1929 that the committee expressed a wish "to greet with satisfaction the opportunity, through the medium of the Nobel Prize, to draw attention to the great and vigorous literature of the South American language area." Unfortunately, Venezuela's Rufino Blanco Fombona could not meet with the committee's approval as, "in the eyes of the non-Spanish world, a sufficiently important author to fill the place of a representative of his culture."

The prize to Gabriela Mistral did mark a breakthrough. It is known that in 1940 her candidacy was enthusiastically supported by Latin American spokesmen. When Valéry, who had been destined to receive the 1945 prize, died in the summer of that year, Gabriela Mistral, in Österling's words in a letter to Hallström on 2 August, had "a new chance. . . . I have nothing against it, bearing in mind the idea of a gesture to Latin America, which we have neglected." But it was not simply an effort to extend the award itself to that part of the world for the first time. The 1940 report, written by Hallström, also extends to Latin America the committee's willingness to "understand and appreciate" a foreign literature. This intention was already clear in Hallström's attempt to view the original "through the veils of translation. . . . Even for one who does not feel sufficiently at home in Spanish to have an ear sensitive to the harmony of the language, and who can but dimly guess his way into the associations that mean so much for lyrical beauty, even for such a reader it is possible to approach a fair appreciation by comparing original and translation line by line."

But his efforts went further than dealing with translation problems and were extended to gaining an understanding of "the emotional differences" between Spaniards and Swedes, and "not the least the [Spanish] poetic tradition and the means of expression it offers. . . . One must accustom oneself to finding genuineness in foreign dress." This ambitious reader was feeling his way into "the energetic and passionate language, compressed almost to breaking point, that streams from this poetess" and toward "the human being" behind the voice, its captivating personality that with its "unchecked, open-hearted, courageous, and spontaneous poetry has appeared as a revelation in her homeland." Here again we catch a glimpse of the wish – now extended beyond the European horizon – to understand what the literary work "means where it was created."

The result was a judgment that in one important respect resembled that of Schück on Correia de Oliveira – Hallström abstained from making objections conditioned by his own tradition in order to do justice to the genuine poetry he perceived in its foreign framework: "If she does not always attain to what we strangers are accustomed to seek in poetry, if the intellectual content does not seem to us to be particularly profound or new, this ought not to be decisive for our assessment, when we are able to get as far as appreciating the emotional sincerity and purity and without difficulty seeing that we are confronting a great personality."

It was harder to reach correspondingly fair evaluations of Asian literature. In the 1930s just finding serious candidates was a problem. One of the few was Sarvepalli Radhakrishnan. On the basis of the philosopher Hans Larsson's highly positive report, the committee members in 1933 felt "lively interest" but expressed "the same doubts as usual about the suitability of awarding Nobel Prizes in the area of philosophy." Interest remained cool in the following years; occasional candidates from several Asian countries appeared in the late thirties but as a rule were promptly dismissed. The proposals, in some cases quite strange, illustrate a decisive weakness in the whole system. For areas outside the West not enough had been done to secure competent proposers. And the idea of the committee actively searching for such candidates, on its own initiative, was still a long way in the future. The process thus got no further than a state of willingness to promote, for example, new Chinese poetry, "for the appreciation of the Western world," if only a body of work could be found that was "aesthetically significant and captivating." In 1940 it was possible to consider, alongside Selma Lagerlöf, the "Chinese writer Pearl Buck recommends," Lin Yutang,[3] but the academy was not entirely convinced. A degree of help in finding one's way around this literature was available from the Asian specialist Sven Hedin. But the matter stopped there.

Nowadays, proposals come in from countries such as China, Japan, and India, as well as from various parts of the Arab world, and they are representative of their respective literatures in a manner quite different from such proposals in the 1930s. In the early 1960s the nominations from Japanese literature included Junichiro Tanizaki, first proposed by Pearl Buck in 1958; Junzaburo Nishiwaki, whose name was put forward by, among others, the Japanese Academy; Yasunari Kawabata, proposed by, among others, PEN of Japan; and Yukio Mishima, proposed by Americans.[4] In an interview with the London *Sunday Times* (23 November 1980), Artur Lundkvist revealed that there were by that time nominations from black Africa. To the question whether in the near future we might see a black prize winner, he replied, "That's possible." (A few years later he mentioned that his own candidate was Léopold Sédar Senghor, whom he also introduced and translated.)[5]

That the system for proposing candidates is not functioning as one could wish is apparent in an article in the 3 May 1985 issue of *Asiaweek;* it reported on the prevalent criticism that the Asian area has been neglected by the academy and listed the oft-named candidates Yasushi Inoue from Japan, Ba Jin from China, Pramoedya Ananta Toer of Indonesia, and R. K. Narayan of India.[6] The author of the article interviewed Gyllensten and learned that the nominations of Asian authors are not particularly numerous. Gyllensten ascribed this to special difficulties, such as a lack of consensus even among specialists, problems in developing criteria for the evaluation of authors with widely divergent cultural backgrounds and very different literary purposes, and (for nominations made from the West) a lack of translations. The journalist pointed out that in several countries those with the right to propose have neglected to make use of the right. Ba Jin, president of PEN in China, admitted that he was invited to make a proposal but did not reply. The other PEN groups in Asia have also let chances slip by. PEN of Thailand, for instance, is unfailingly contacted each year, but there has never been a response. Its president, Nilawan Pintong, is not sure if anyone from her country has ever been proposed: "Here in Thailand we have not done much in translation of literary work. We can have it submitted in our own language, but the fact is we have not found anything meritorious because we have not worked seriously to find it." This comment well illustrates the defeatism that so often prevents interesting candidates outside the West from even reaching the stage of being proposed.

The deficiencies in the system for proposing candidates have laid an extra responsibility upon the academy itself. Recently, the members of the Nobel Committee – and of the academy – have been making much greater use of their own right to submit proposals. The committee even asks for specialist reports on literatures that were simply not within sight in the earlier period. These reports locate particular works in their literary and cultural contexts and give some idea of the resonance and associative qualities of the language as it is handled in those works. These efforts to attain some kind of overview are reflected in the surveys included in the magazine *Artes* (published by the academies). That modern Arabic literature was no longer beyond the pale – as several critics had suggested – was clear from the fact that the first issue of *Artes* in 1984 was devoted to Arabic literature, with presentations and translations by, among others, Adonis (Ali Ahmed Said), Mohammed Dib, and Tahar Ben Jelloun.[7] Other issues have been devoted to Chinese and Indian literature.

How specialist knowledge is used to locate the worthiest representative of a literature that is both foreign and hard for Western readers to orientate themselves in is apparent in those parts of the Yasunari Kawabata background material that have been made public.[8] In this case, certain myths about the Nobel Prize meet reality. The myth was voiced by Irving Wallace when he said, "A Swedish official was flown to Tokyo to scout the field."[9] In reality, the process, from proposal to decision, took seven years. A preliminary investigation was entrusted in 1961 to a Swedish critic, who based his highly appreciative assessment of Kawabata on a number of works in German, French, and English translation. His evaluation was then supported by reports from three experts in the field: Professor Howard S. Hibbett of Harvard University, who regarded both Tanizaki and Kawabata as figures of world status; Professor Donald Keene of Columbia University, whose evaluation was equally high–in the choice between Kawabata and Mishima, he preferred Kawabata, the elder of the two; and the Japanese scholar Sei Ito, who concluded that after the death of Tanizaki, Kawabata was the only one really worthy of representing Japanese literature. On such a basis the academy was able–from the members' own reading of Kawabata in translation–to make a confident decision that for the first time went beyond the European linguistic horizon.[10]

Efforts have also been made, however, to ensure a significant level of linguistic and literary competence *within* the academy. English, German, and French have caused no problems. Competence in Spanish and Italian (and even in Provençal) has also been well represented. Academy members themselves have made significant translations, such as Gullberg's translations of Gabriela Mistral and Seferis, or Österling's of Quasimodo and Montale. And, of course, the academy continually obtains reports on European writers from outside sources. In the case of the Slavonic languages, this "extramural" aid has been necessary even if there has sometimes been a member with the relevant knowledge, such as Harald Hjärne. Language experts have been closely associated with the Nobel Institute from early on–first Alfred Jensen, then Anton Karlgren. Throughout the greater part of the Nobel Prize's existence the academy has also included eminent Orientalists–up to 1928, Esaias Tegnér, Jr., then from 1948 to 1974, H. S. Nyberg. When the Egyptian author Taha Hussein was proposed in 1967, the relevant specialist was at hand.[11] At an early stage recourse could also be made to a specialist in Chinese matters, Bernhard Karlgren.

None of those specialists, however, can be said to have shown a bold approach to the global task. More recently, the academy has often made use of a more active expertise with a view to the ever-widening scope of the

Nobel commission. With the election of Artur Lundkvist in 1968, the academy acquired regular access to Sweden's foremost advocate for foreign literature, especially from the Spanish-speaking areas. An idea of his role in this widening of perspective can be suggested by two small items of information. On 26 May 1962, in *Stockholms-Tidningen,* he opened the first Swedish presentation of Patrick White's work with the words: "As far as I am aware, no Swedish critic or publisher has drawn attention to Patrick White. Yet he is something that nowadays is rather rare and special – a great epic storyteller who, in addition, is an admirable psychologist and stylist." Eleven years later it was Lundkvist who made the speech to the Nobel Prize winner Patrick White.

Competence in Spanish literature was further strengthened in 1970, when Knut Ahnlund, as the holder of a professorship attached to the Nobel Committee, began to serve as a specialist adviser. He has been a member of the academy since 1983, and of the Nobel Committee since 1984. With the election in 1985 of Göran Malmqvist, a translator and professor of sinology, the academy has secured the services of one of the West's foremost experts in modern Chinese literature, one who is also in close contact with specialists in Oriental literature in general.

The support of such expertise – from close at hand or from further afield – makes it possible for the academy to acquire an overview, to find its way, and to arrive at a preliminary conception of the worth of various candidates. But this cannot, of course, replace the personal study upon which the members of the committee and the academy must base their final decisions. For such study, when it comes to the more "remote" languages, reliance on translations is unavoidable. Over the years, the significance of translation has been a recurring theme in the reports. The doubts felt by the 1920s committee over Kostis Palamas is closely related to the difficulty of assessing the language of the original works. In 1931 it was expressly confirmed that the award to Bunin "shall relate to the works as they exist in their original language." It had been difficult for the academy members to understand the "stylistic mastery" attributed to Bunin by his countrymen; they relied on "cultivated Russian opinion, both among emigrants and at home."

This problem is a constant part of the work of the Nobel Prize. An important expedient can be seen in Schück's 1933 statement commissioning a translation of a work by Correia de Oliveira. The opportunities the academy had of "itself procuring translations" was touched upon, as we have seen, in Gyllensten's 1984 article. He added: "Paradoxically, this is easier with poets than with prose writers, since a poet can be reasonably represented by a quantitatively more limited body of text than that required by a prose writer." In several cases such exclusive translations – with eighteen readers – have played an important role in the recent work of the academy.

But even in such favorable conditions the problem of finding access to a foreign culture remains. Faced with this persistent dilemma, Artur Lundkvist adopted a position that stimulated reactions from around the world. In his article "Nobelpris åt vem?" ("The Nobel Prize to Whom?") in *Svenska Dagbladet* (12 October 1977) he described the task of the Nobel Prize as one of drawing "attention to achievements that have not been sufficiently regarded and to a high degree deserve recognition." He believed "that the smaller areas of literature, defined in terms of either language or nationality, suffer particularly" from the difficulties of acquiring an overall view of the "enormous range of contemporary literature." He continued:

> Those literatures that are great yet exist in languages to which we do not have ready access present another problem. The academy is often reproached for thus neglecting the literatures of Asia and Africa and other "remote" parts. But I doubt if there is so far very much to find there. It is a question of literatures that (with a certain exception, particularly in the case of Japan) as far as can be judged have not achieved that level of development (artistic, psychological, linguistic) that can make them truly significant outside their given context.

> The Nobel Prize is after all a Western institution and cannot reasonably be distributed on the basis of other than Western evaluations. In itself this may be regrettable, and I hope, of course, that these more distant literatures will soon enough catch up on the lead so far enjoyed by Western literature, so that they can fully participate in a global cultural exchange.

Lundkvist's views, repeated in an interview in the London *Sunday Times* on 23 November 1980, naturally met with sharp criticism in the Third World, not least from official Indian quarters. Quite objectively, there is good reason to question Lundkvist's idea of a qualitative *development* in literature, with a Western "lead" that Asia and Africa must "catch up" on. Even within the context of European literature that perspective is rather peculiar – in what sense do twentieth-century authors exist on a higher "level of development" than Sophocles, Dante, Shakespeare, or Tolstoy? And from the point of view of Asian literature, how is Western tradition superior to a tradition that includes on the one hand Tang poetry and *The Dream of the Red Pavilion,* and on the other, Firdausī, Rūmī, and Hāfiz?

Lundkvist was responding to the reproaches against the Swedish Academy for its alleged neglect of Asian and African literature. The same can be said of his views in the London *Sunday Times* interview: when asked how the Nobel Committee could judge the value of literature in countries such as China or India, whose cultures are altogether foreign, he replied that they were "primitive cultures" that he did not believe capable of "developing on a global scale." Such remarks, however, are not representative; they deviate sharply from the thoughtful self-questioning that can be traced from

Hallström and Schück to Gyllensten.[12] The spirit of this tradition is perhaps best caught in Gyllensten's words, already quoted: "In the case of writers we want to take up and treat fairly, it is a matter of trying to acquire some understanding of the traditions and of the literary and cultural milieu out of which they write."

Further, Lundkvist's statement is incompatible with the modest practice that can be distinguished. The idea of a Western lead that only Japan has to a certain extent managed to close is hardly compatible with Österling's authoritative words on Kawabata. To him, Kawabata represents a cultural consciousness that *vindicates itself* against Western influence. Österling finds Kawabata capable – in his analysis of erotic episodes – of small, secretive nuances that "often put European narrative art in the shade." Those words in the speech to Kawabata well catch the spirit of the 1968 choice. They imply at the same time a criticism of the other candidate, Mishima, whose methods show a strong European inspiration.

The picture of the academy's Eurocentric policy has been significantly altered by the choices of Wole Soyinka in 1986 and Naguib Mahfouz in 1988. The awarding of two prizes so close in time to authors outside the European-American cultural sphere naturally raises the question of whether the academy radically changed course during the latter half of the 1980s. That a change is involved is abundantly clear, but it is less dramatic than may at first be thought. In 1984 Gyllensten expressed a desire – already felt by others in the academy – to achieve a global spread. But it takes time to realize such ambitions, and a few years had to pass before the first results were apparent. Obviously, even more time is required before a serious attempt to encompass – knowledgeably – the whole of the rich and variegated field of world literature will be possible.

The point ought to be made that, in the light of this more expansive policy, the procedure offered by Tsu-Yü Hwang – that we should first decide upon a neglected language area and then seek out the best candidate in it – is not being followed. Doing so would amount to a politicization of the prize. Instead, efforts are being made to extend the area under scrutiny so that in the course of the normal process of arriving at decisions it is possible to weigh sometimes a prominent Nigerian dramatist and poet, sometimes an Egyptian novelist, against candidates from parts of the linguistic atlas closer to our own – with all such evaluations continuing to be made on *literary* grounds. That more than one candidate from the same region may figure simultaneously in a choice does not detract from such a statement; the proposal of a candidate from one particular literature may, within the committee and the academy, evince a counterproposal in favor of another candidate from the same sphere.

Two of the more recent criteria that I have described do have a bearing on the final adjudication between different candidates. The matter can be illustrated by way of an indiscretion on the part of Artur Lundkvist shortly after the 1988 choice was made: in an interview in *Göteborgs-Tidningen* on 4 December, he revealed that he himself "had another Arabic author as a candidate – Adonis." The juxtaposition of the names of Mahfouz and Adonis is immediately significant to anyone at all versed in Arabic literature: the choice was between two pathfinders – more exactly, between the great pioneer of Arabic fiction and the more recent regenerator of Arabic poetry. The academy opted for the larger epic figure, while Lundkvist felt more strongly in favor of the younger, more exclusive poetic innovator. But alongside the "pioneer" criterion, applicable in both cases, the "pragmatic" aspect of the assessment had made itself felt, quite naturally. Mahfouz was admittedly no obscure genius – about ten of his works could be read in, among other languages, English and French – but his readership outside the Arabic area was greatly limited. A prize could be expected to function as a signal to a large number of potential readers, at the same time, of course, as it signified a just and overdue recognition of a rich contemporary literature. It should hardly need to be said that criteria of that kind can in the end only supplement a powerful experience of the artistic strength of the oeuvre in question.

This widening of the academy's horizons requires a constant effort to understand the cultural identity of the writing under consideration and to overcome as far as possible personal prejudices. Gyllensten's speech at the Nobel Festival in 1986 echoed his statement two years before about the importance of becoming acquainted with the environment of the writers the academy wants "to take up and treat fairly." In connection with Soyinka's description of his childhood in a small Nigerian village, he sketched a cultural background of just the kind it was necessary to try to comprehend: "We encounter a world in which tree sprites, ghosts, sorcerers, and primitive African traditions were living realities. We also come face to face with a more complicated world of myth, which has its roots far back in African culture handed down by word of mouth. This account of childhood gives a background to Soyinka's literary works – a self-experienced, close connection with a rich and complex African heritage."

Gyllensten observed that Soyinka's drama "is closely linked with the African material and with African forms of linguistic and mime creation." Of course, he also stressed that Soyinka is "familiar with Western literature, from the Greek tragedies to Beckett and Brecht" – an acknowledgment of the "wide cultural perspective" mentioned in the wording of the award. But the presentation lingered, significantly, on Soyinka's original milieu. Far from talking, like Lundkvist, of any Western "lead" that must be "caught up," Gyllensten focused on the genuine African provenance of Soyinka's drama, its roots in a "composite culture with a wealth of living and artistically inspiring traditions." His speech was a much more accurate testimony to the spirit behind the academy's recent attempts to address the prize to "the literature of the whole world."

Donald Keene has written that, through the award of the Nobel Prize to Kawabata, the Japanese novel tradition–the world's oldest–has been incorporated into "the world stream of writing."[13] It is in this wide assimilative process, rather than in any expectation that the Third World should catch up on a Western lead, that the Nobel Prize has its global future.

CHAPTER 10

"A Fairly Decent Testimonial"

This is not the place to draw up a balance sheet of the manner in which the Swedish Academy has carried out its Nobel commission – with the successes weighed against the failures. What a work of this kind can contribute is a historical perspective on the process of selection. Yet it may be worthwhile to conclude with a concise survey of the Nobel Prize in Literature's international reception, in the light of the foregoing chapters. Immediate press reactions are then of limited interest;[1] more rewarding comment is to be found in the wider ranging assessments that have been carried out in the postwar period in several quarters, but above all in the United States and in France.

The most ambitious assessment was undertaken by William F. Lamont and published in *Books Abroad* in 1951.[2] Taking as his starting point Irving Wallace's provocative article "Those Explosive Nobel Prizes" in *Collier's* in 1949, Lamont distributed a questionnaire to a selection of 350 international "experts in belles-lettres" with the aim of seeking their opinions on (1) which prize winners were not worthy of the award and (2) which writers passed over should in fact have been chosen. The result showed, among other things, that about two-thirds of the prizes were felt to be fully justified, and the rest less so – "a fairly decent testimonial," as Österling commented.[3]

In the same year Lamont's article was followed by another assessment, published in the next issue of *Books Abroad* – "What's Wrong with the Nobel Prize?" A battalion of international specialists in comparative studies were asked the same two questions. Generally the results corresponded with those of the previous survey: "I don't think that, generally speaking, [the prize] has been too badly awarded" (Constant Burniaux). Henri Perruchot found the choices of the Swedish Academy more satisfactory on the whole than those of certain national academies, adding that the former had in some cases acted as a corrective to the latter. It had thus atoned for the injustice done to Gide by the French Academy and the Goncourt Academy.

Two important French contributions to the debate followed in 1959: François Mauriac's examination in *Figaro Littéraire* (10 October 1959) of the French prize winners – his thesis was that the Swedish Academy had favored representatives of a "committed" literature – and Alain Bosquet's balance sheet in *Combat* (8 October 1959), with the title "Le Prix Nobel est démodé." Bosquet proposed the establishment of an international literary prize distributed by a group of fifteen authors "de première grandeur," a jury that would be more successful than "les inconnus de Stockholm" in ministering "la sensibilité de l'époque." Among those "incontestable" arbiters he suggested were Sartre, Sholokhov, Borges, and Lindegren, a list of names not untouched by the irony of history. A similar thought crystallized from the continued interest shown in the question by *Books Abroad,* most particularly in its Nobel Prize symposium in 1967. On the basis of a positive and comprehensive view of the literary prize and its international value, the discussion generated a number of constructive proposals to which we shall have cause to return. In this assiduous concern shown by *Books Abroad,* however, we can detect an element of impatience, and the Neustadt Prize, instituted in 1969 and distributed by a specially chosen international jury of authors, can be seen as an attempt to realize the intentions that had been found to be neglected by the Swedish Academy.

At about the same time as this symposium, Donald Fleming, in his article "Nobel's Hits and Errors" (*Atlantic Monthly,* 1966), assessed the Nobel Prizes in all their branches – and did so more harshly than the 1967 panel. One of the most biting judgments, however, came as recently as 1984, in George Steiner's "The Scandal of the Nobel Prize" (*New York Times Book Review,* 30 September); in this article, reproduced in the newspapers of many countries, Steiner maintained that the prize "has scored more misses than hits." A revision, in a more moderate tone, was undertaken in 1988 in a new symposium arranged by *World Literature Today* (as *Books Abroad* is now called); we shall return to that later. To these more ambitious critiques we may add a series of shorter reviews published in, for example, the *Washington Post, Corriere della Sera,* the London *Sunday Times,* and *Asiaweek.* Points from some of these will be taken up later, but in the present context the bulk of those shorter articles can be passed over because their essential arguments are to be found in the more comprehensive essays mentioned above.

The survey I have given in this book provides one immediate objection to these assessments: it is quite indefensible to try to generalize about the entire history of the Nobel Prize, as, for instance, Steiner did when he talked sweepingly of "the general pattern of political, aesthetic and psychological conservatism, officiousness and déjà vu." It is simply not possible to establish any such "general pattern." That criticism may apply to Wirsén's epoch but would be irrelevant to Österling's. An important conclusion of this book is that each period has had its special character and its own criteria. We ought therefore to treat the matter layer by layer and examine how the literary choices have been judged phase by phase over the nine decades.

Judgment of the first period, Wirsén's, has been consistently severe. Sully Prudhomme, Mistral, Echegaray, Eucken, and Heyse have generally been considered much too insignificant for the award. The committee's homage to Heyse has been bluntly described as one of its worst mistakes: according to Theodor Ziolkowski, the committee's verdict on Heyse "as Germany's greatest lyric poet since Goethe . . . the creator of the modern psychological novelle . . . betrays a total lack of understanding for developments in literature since Nietzsche."[4] There has also been widespread agreement that Ibsen should have been given precedence over Bjørnson and that Tolstoy, Zola, and Strindberg should have been obvious choices. As a rule, commentators have glanced over Mommsen, Carducci, and Selma Lagerlöf with neither complaint nor enthusiasm. Reservations about Mommsen, the historian in the series, have been due mainly to the fact that his brilliant achievement falls outside the field of literature.[5]

The only decision of the Wirsénian academy to have won more general approval is the prize to Kipling. Yet that name brings to light a phenomenon that tends to be neglected in these international reviews of the academy's activity – the historically conditioned fluctuations of taste. Many commentators are too willing to attribute a general validity to their own viewpoint, rooted in their own time. Indeed, the choice of Kipling met with disapproval from the 350 arbiters of 1951, while those of 1967 took note of his rising stock and believed his final status will be high, for the reason given by Auden – because of his "brilliant writing." In 1984 his name was, quite rightly, "canonic."[6] Assessing the value of a writer is a relative business and can tempt those who watch the literary market into a kind of bookkeeping, as happened in the case of Maeterlinck. On the one hand, he has been credited with initiating symbolist drama, while on the other hand he has been found to have little to say to our generation (Gene J. Barberet). In an evaluation of the wisdom of that choice, vital importance ought, of course, to be attached to the fact that the author of *L'Intruse* (The Intruder) and *Les Aveugles* (The Blind) occupies a prominent place in the history of modern drama; another critic believes, moreover, that Maeterlinck will return to favor.[7] Such a return, we may suppose, is not to be expected for Frédéric Mistral. For the historical perspective, however, it is necessary to distinguish between his generally high standing at the time when he received the prize, and the more recent judgment of *Mirèio* as "a literary monument of the Provençal revival primarily of interest to philologists and students of folklore" (Gene J. Barberet). An evaluation of the efforts of those who select Nobel Prize winners must, in other words, distinguish between those aspects of their choices that appear to be justified within the context of the time and those forward-looking aspects of their choices that are perceptible to us now in retrospect – and are becoming obsolete as we speak.

Chapter 1 was an attempt to contribute to an understanding of something that is hard to understand: that the Wirsénian interpretation of Nobel's will, in the light of conservative idealism, obstructed the most obvious choice of the decade – Tolstoy. By its very nature, that interpretation caused the academy members to prefer Bjørnson over Ibsen; the heathen and rebel Strindberg, sworn enemy of both the establishment and the academy, was, of course, beneath consideration.[8] Spencer, Zola, and Hardy in various ways fell short of the requirement of possessing an idealistic tendency, and Henry James violated the Goethean demand for restraint. When Wirsén's spectacles for once succeeded in focusing on a great figure who has since maintained (or rather regained) a position of wide renown – Kipling – his praise was for qualities in Kipling's work other than those that have shown themselves to be lasting. The meager posthumous reputation of the Wirsénian period, it turns out, is well justified. The most severe verdict, however, has come from those who, speaking out of the same historical context, could express, in the manner of Strindberg or Levertin, censure of the jury's lack of competence for the task.[9]

The next period has received a better but somewhat uneven report. It began splendidly: Gerhart Hauptmann proved in posterity to be "one of the genuinely commanding figures in twentieth-century literature." The author of *Die Weber* and *Die Versunkene Glocke* (The Sunken Bell) revolutionized German drama and, "among German writers, only Brecht had a similar impact on the international theater"; besides, in 1912 Hauptmann was still the *enfant terrible* of the German stage and "had not yet frozen into representational posing and posturing" (Theodor Ziolkowski). In certain recent evaluations of this period, Tagore has been labeled a similarly good choice. The shorter critical appraisals tend to ignore him; he has on the whole been thought of as a little pale. In the literature of his own country, however, he has kept his place, and the specialist in the 1967 symposium, Albert Howard Carter, declared that if he were compelled to choose only one prize-winner from Asia or Africa, he would opt for Tagore. The recent publication of an English selection of his poems can be seen as an attempt at rehabilitation.

With regard to the first prize winner chosen during World War I, Barbaret made an exemplary distinction between the Rolland who in 1915 could be defended as most in line with the intentions of Nobel and the executors of his will and the Rolland whose eloquent idealism and heroic exaltation is now regarded as old-fashioned (except in the Soviet Union, where Rolland has for long been the most acclaimed French author). Spitteler seemed to be more problematic: in 1967 he was perceived as a tragic dinosaur from the past (Theodor Ziolkowski), but in 1984 he had been transformed into one of the academy's few significant discoveries (George Steiner). The alleged overrepresentation of Scandinavian authors has been subjected to more thorough criticism. Heidenstam, almost without exception, is given a low score.[10] Of the Danish pair from 1917, Gjellerup has been consistently rejected as insignificant, and Pontoppidan has been labeled "classical." The latter verdict, however, reflects the opinion of a Scandinavian specialist (Richard B. Vowles); lay opinion has tended to be less kind–one can only ask if those lay critics really know the author of *De Dødes Rige* (The Kingdom of the Dead). The only Scandinavian who emerges with credit has been Hamsun, who, according to Steiner's assessment, is the only one of "this longish list" who "is an undoubtedly major figure."

The presentation so far given throws some light on this outcome. The period got off to a promising start in the thaw following the departure of Wirsén: the "Poison–Beware" labels were removed from Hauptmann's work, and Heidenstam managed to introduce his unknown kindred spirit, Tagore, to an international public. The newcomers to the academy, however, could not stretch as far as awarding a prize to Georg Brandes.[11] The more mediocre results of the succeeding years were due mainly to the policy of literary neutrality. From a diminishing number of proposals there had to be chosen a candidate who as far as possible had succeeded in avoiding any kind of compromise. The heavy representation of Scandinavian authors, which has been much criticized, can be seen as a direct result of those political conditions that affected the process of choice.

The years from 1921 to 1929 included a number of choices that have won the approval of a later age. France, Yeats, Shaw, and Mann were among those found worthy in the 1951 survey, and all four of them were included in the "canonic" list of 1984. It was only in 1967 that France was considered an out-of-date, second-class author. In return, Barberet placed Bergson among the leading figures: he and Sartre had initiated "two of the major movements that affect our modern intellectual climate" (the other two being Marxism and Freudianism). In Fleming's eyes, Yeats was the only author to be "caught while his carrier was still on the upswing."

The four other prizes–to Benavente, Reymont, Deledda, and Undset–have been judged much more coolly. The choice of Benavente has been called "less unfortunate" than that of Echegaray–a defensible investment that for various reasons failed to pay dividends (Manuel Durán and Michael Nimetz). The similarly neglected Reymont received a token of approval in 1951; in 1967 Robert Vlach credited only the work specified by the award, *Chłopi*, and added that many Poles would have preferred Stefan Żeromski. In 1951 the ranks of the approved included Sigrid Undset; in 1967 only her *Kristin Lavransdatter* was found worthy. Only one of the four, Grazia Deledda, has received altogether unfavorable treatment; in 1951 she had already been excluded from the ranks of the worthy.

These later ratings of the work devoted to choosing the winners in the 1920s as having been at least half successful seem somewhat surprising, considering the criteria governing the academy's work. The Nobel Committee that hailed "the great style" seemed poorly equipped to distinguish the significant achievements of an age whose literary orientation was essentially otherwise. The Nobel harvest was not more meager owing to the fact that the hazardous "idealistic" criterion was interpreted more generously. Schück's reading of this criterion as "broad-hearted humanity" opened the way for both France and Shaw. With Shaw an attempt was also made to extend understanding beyond the "stricter measure" of great drama in order to do justice to a fearless new art of the theater. The limits of such a capacity for reorientation were nonetheless apparent when in 1929 *Buddenbrooks* was awarded a prize and *Der Zauberberg* was passed over in silence. Later criticism has not unexpectedly understood this in terms of an "implicit lament that contemporary literature had departed from the sober paths of nineteenth-century realism and the committee's determination to do what it could to stop the insidious trend towards experimentation among young literary upstarts" (Ziolkowski). Signs of any such militant determination cannot be traced in the documentation; what we see rather is evidence of the committee's strong sense of alienation from new endeavors in artistic creation, increasingly accompanied by its demand for accessibility as a principal criterion alongside the criterion of "the great style." The criticism that the yardstick of nineteenth-century realism was applied, however, is quite correct. Ironically, the yardstick was actually Tolstoy, who had been rejected during Wirsén's tenure.

The results of the period 1930-39 are poorer. Sinclair Lewis has held his own fairly well; his novels from the 1920s have been rated as rather bound to their time but they have also been credited with an incontestable brilliance. With the benefit of time and history, however, it is clear that Lewis as the 1930 choice was wrong; Dreiser's reputation has grown with the years (Robert E. Spiller). Early on, the 1951 survey dispatched both Galsworthy and Pearl Buck.[12] Bunin and Martin du Gard have met with consistent disapproval. Nor has Sillanpää found an advocate. Scandinavian specialists have granted a little niche to Karlfeldt. The criticism of Karlfeldt's prize has been aimed not at his individual achievement but rather at the excessive Scandinavian representation on the roll of honor.

In this series of prizes, there has been universal agreement that two choices were splendid: Pirandello in 1934, and O'Neill in 1936. For decades after his death, Pirandello continued as a force to be reckoned with in modern theater – a precursor of existential drama as well as a representative *avant la lettre* of absurd theater (Olga Ragusa). O'Neill's renown as the leading figure of the new American drama dwindled somewhat in the eyes of the new criticism of the 1940s. But *Long Day's Journey into Night* survived this period, and a series of studies confirmed O'Neill's prominent position in the history of modern drama – the period 1920-50 has come to be known as "the Age of O'Neill" in American theater. Spiller, whom we are citing here, saw O'Neill and the three succeeding American prize winners, Eliot, Faulkner, and Hemingway, as "bull's-eye hits on the part of the committee."

The rather low ratings of this period must take into account the committee's principle of general accessibility; with such an objective justice could not be done to the literary creation of the time. That principle, however, could accommodate two discoveries. The theater veteran Hallström could recognize in Pirandello "a remarkable and independent attempt to renew the world of the stage." O'Neill, on the other hand, was not a "bull's-eye hit" from the committee's point of view; it was Schück, the minority voice, who succeeded in persuading the academy of the great poetic strength of the author of *Mourning Becomes Electra.*

The serious aspect of that policy is that the relatively high number of mediocre prizes conceals just as many cases of neglect. Antonio Machado or Miguel de Unamuno ought to have been rewarded instead of Benavente, Virginia Woolf instead of Pearl Buck, and so on. Generally it can be said that criticism on that score is largely justified; as we have seen, the academy of the interwar years quite simply lacked the necessary tools to evaluate one of the most dynamic periods in Western literature. On many points, though, criticism has shown a faulty grasp of history, and in several instances it has shown discreditable ignorance.

It is true that in the years between the wars a good number of great writers came to the attention of the Nobel arbiters without their greatness being duly noticed – or at least without their merits being allowed to outweigh the misgivings inspired by the preconceptions of the time: Hardy, Valéry, Claudel, George, Hofmannsthal, Unamuno, Gorky, Freud, and Hesse (who was, of course, awarded a prize later). We may also recall the omission of *Der Zauberberg* from the wording of Mann's prize.

With every new critique of the Nobel Prize in Literature, the catalogue of omissions is repeated, though with new variations.[13] On some points opinions diverge. Hofmannsthal gathered considerable support in 1951, and his total achievement as reviewed by Ziolkowski raised him above most of his contemporaries; in Steiner's 1984 list of misdemeanors, however, Hofmannsthal was ignored. Claudel, on the contrary, was "still a matter of dispute" in 1967 – "the dogmatic tone of his religious persuasion seems to dwarf all other considerations" – but in 1984 his dramas soared to the level of Aeschylus and Shakespeare (Steiner). In such cases the critics' judgment is affected by their unhistorical perspectives. For instance, there have been complaints about the absence of Joseph Conrad from the Nobel list. In fact, Conrad was never proposed; a realization of his true significance emerged so late that none of those in the English-speaking world who were entitled to nominate (and they were numerous) reacted in time.[14]

As to James Joyce–one of the most serious and most frequently mentioned omissions–we can see a change of perspective in the academy itself as a result of the continuous replacement of older members by younger members. Like Conrad, Joyce, too, was never proposed; his stature was not properly recognized even in the English-speaking world. Joyce would have been unthinkable to the 1930s academy that hailed Galsworthy and Pearl Buck. On the other hand, he would in all probability have received a Nobel Prize during the Österling period, if he had lived until then. In his speech to Eliot in 1948, Österling mentioned that *The Waste Land* "appeared in the same year as another pioneer work, which had a still more sensational effect on modern literature, the much discussed *Ulysses,* from the hand of an Irishman, James Joyce." Such an opinion would have led to a prize for Joyce in the late 1940s.

In many other cases the academy was not given enough time–or even a theoretical opportunity–to pay attention. Among the omissions of the period under discussion, the various surveys have produced, in addition to the names already mentioned, those of Proust, Kafka, Rilke, Musil, Cavafy, Lawrence, Mandelstam, García Lorca, Pessoa, and others; this list, if it had any chronological justification, would undeniably suggest serious failure. Kafka was mentioned in the 1951 survey, but without being accorded any high priority. In Steiner's 1984 account, Kafka had achieved the status of one of the most serious omissions, a figure "whose presence towers over our sense of literature and of the meaning of man." When Kafka died in 1924, however, he was not the great writer we know: *Das Schloss* (The Castle), *Der Prozess* (The Trial), and *Amerika* were, after all, published posthumously. He could scarcely, as Ziolkowski has pointed out, have been considered on the basis of the few stories that appeared in his lifetime. Likewise, the main works of both Cavafy and Pessoa were not published until after their deaths. The true dimensions of Mandelstam's poetry were revealed above all in the unpublished poems that his wife saved from extinction and gave to the world long after he had perished in his Siberian exile.[15]

In other cases there has been much too brief a period of time between publication of an author's most deserving works and the author's death for a prize to have been possible. The second part of *À la recherche du temps perdu* (Remembrance of Things Past) was published in 1919; in December of that year Proust finally achieved notoriety by winning the Goncourt Prize. But less than three years later he was dead. Rilke's *Duineser Elegien* (Duino Elegies) was published in 1923–three years before his death. García Lorca's *Bodas de Sangre* (Blood Wedding), *Yerma,* and *La Casa de Bernarda Alba* (The House of Bernarda Alba) came out between 1933 and 1936, and *Poeta en Nueva York* was first published in 1940; the poet was murdered in 1936. Österling met the accusations of neglect of Proust, García Lorca, and Synge by referring to the lack of time in each case; he added, "In such instances even the most widely distributed literary information apparatus must admit defeat."[16]

As for D.H. Lawrence and Robert Musil, the time available was not so absurdly brief. Lawrence's international breakthrough, nonetheless, occurred in the late 1920s; in 1930 he was dead. (It is another question whether the academy of the 1930s would have been capable of realizing the importance of this controversial figure.) The first parts of Musil's *Der Mann ohne Eigenschaften* (The Man without Qualities) were, admittedly, already published in the early 1930s, but it was not until the appearance of his collected works between 1952 and 1957 that Musil's significance began to be recognized outside a narrow circle of connoisseurs – and by then he had been long dead (he died in 1942). He belonged, as pointed out by Ziolkowski, to the category of authors who "on closer examination . . . exclude themselves." It should be mentioned that none of the candidates on the traditional lists of notorious omissions managed to achieve sufficient recognition among those in their respective countries who were entitled to send in proposals. In other words, the academy of the interwar years must be found not-guilty of many of the worst accusations. Nevertheless, the 1930s Nobel Committee in particular seemed tragically handicapped in dealing with the rich body of literature available to it.

The postwar academy has in a quite different manner fulfilled the expectations of serious criticism. In his survey of "hits and errors" in 1966 Donald Fleming found that the postwar Nobel Prize winners – including Gide, Eliot, Faulkner, Mauriac, Hemingway, Camus, Pasternak, and Sartre – probably make up a higher share of the foremost living authors than was the case in any earlier period. Such a verdict has in many recent commentaries been repeated. Spiller, reviewing the American winners, counted, as we have just seen, Eliot, Faulkner, and Hemingway as "bull's-eye hits." Of particular interest was his thesis that the 1949 prize provoked a rereading that "revealed an entirely new Faulkner. . . . In this case, if in no other, the Nobel Prize seems to have had an appreciable effect in helping to bring just recognition to a major writer."

The 1967 evaluation of the French prizes added the name of Perse, who inspired unusually effusive admiration among French critics and, even before his prize, was regarded in English-speaking countries as the greatest living poet of his generation. The postwar prizes contribute largely, it seems, to the general impression that as far as the French candidates are concerned the good choices have been in a majority. Similarly, Ziolkowski's evaluation of German-language authors added Hesse's name to the list of "hits"; we shall return, however, to his reservations.

The same list, covering the first twenty years of the postwar period, can also include Jiménez – "It is safe to say that some of his work will endure as long as the Spanish language" (Durán and Nimetz) – and Quasimodo, who has recently been classified among the academy's "discoveries" (Steiner).

But Fleming arrived at the sweeping verdict that "the roster is weakened by the increasingly evident determination to single out the literature of previously neglected nationalities." Those familiar with the respective literatures do not share that view. The choice of Laxness "seems very sound indeed" and has meant that an author who was previously unknown internationally is read in more than twenty-five languages (Vowles). Andrić was "an incontestable choice" (Vlach), and Agnon has been called "the greatest poet of Hasidism" (Silberschlag). Recently, Seferis has been counted among the canonic names (Steiner).

Mistakes of the order of Eucken and Heyse have not been made in this period. Several prize winners, however, have received a rather meager posthumous reputation. Jensen has been called "a genius to his own people," but that in itself "did not elevate him to international stature" (Vowles). Gabriela Mistral's international reputation has gone up and down, but it is accepted that the 1945 decision was a wise one; she still has a secure place in Spanish literature (Durán and Nimetz). Lagerkvist has met with divided opinion – on the one side, great respect from the French, on the other, American distrust of his "oracular solemnity" (Vowles). Rather low value has been placed on the prizes to Churchill – "Blenheims of prose: elaborate copies of by-gone literature" (Howarth) – and Sholokhov – "talent without stature" (Filipoff). Steinbeck's blend of contrasts was found to be not yet ripe for evaluation in 1967; in 1984 the scrutiny was severe: the Nobel Prize had gone to an emperor with almost no clothes (Thomas R. Edwards).[17] Finally, the award to Nelly Sachs – one among a dozen good poets in German but not a representative figure – should have been a Peace Prize (Ziolkowski); in such a judgment irritation at the Scandinavian overrepresentation has clearly affected a poet with Swedish connections.

It is the Österling academy's investment in the pioneers that has received due recognition in the many favorable assessments. Some, including Fleming, have drawn attention to the higher percentage of leading authors on the list; but they have not reflected on the background to those choices – the academy included younger members and had altered aims. When Ziolkowski imagined that Hesse was chosen because, like Thomas Mann, Hesse was "felt to reflect the values and styles of the past," he was generalizing quite without regard to the boundaries between the various Nobel epochs. The academy that chose Hesse was quite another academy from the one that honored Mann – and Hesse was, in fact, selected for, among other things, his bold renewal of the art of fiction. As we have seen, this new orientation was also applied to the innovators within a language area; the prize to Jiménez was one result of that principle. Taking initiatives and assessing what was new and creative were activities that were gradually taken over by the younger generation, with the appropriate adjustments. At the same time senior members like Österling tried to widen their understanding to also include regenerators of more exclusive character – like Perse, for instance, who was much admired by several of the younger members.

When this book was first published in 1986, I complained that for the latter half of the postwar period we lacked criticism of the Nobel Prize in Literature of the kind in *Books Abroad*. That journal's editor, Ivar Ivask, said he "picked up this suggestion" and arranged for the Spring 1988 issue of *World Literature Today* to be a second Nobel Prize symposium on the theme, "Choices and Omissions, 1967-1987."[18] Several of the prize winners from this period had by 1988 taken their places among the "great, canonic names," specifically, Beckett, Solzhenitsyn, and Montale, to which have been added two "valid discoveries" in Miłosz and Canetti (Steiner). Two authors had been allotted this high status even before they won their prizes: Neruda, according to Fleming and others, the greatest living poet in Spanish; and Seifert, declared by Roman Jakobson to be quite simply the best living poet of all.[19] The international reaction to Seifert's prize in 1984 was characterized by respect, but not by such superlative appreciation. García Márquez had also in many quarters been assigned a place among the classics of our age before he was chosen for a Nobel Prize.

The 1988 symposium was characterized by a slightly reserved appreciation of the choices of the two decades in question. William Pratt concluded that the academy had "done its job well" but "added no special luster to the prize" as far as English-language writing was concerned – his contribution carries the title "Missing the Masters." He looked at the practice of the last twenty years against the background of the series of prizes to Yeats, Shaw, O'Neill, Eliot, Faulkner, and Hemingway – "enough distinguished Nobel laureates in English alone to crown anyone's canon of major twentieth-century literature" – and suggested that "some might want to add more recent prize winners such as John Steinbeck, Samuel Beckett, or Saul Bellow, but these are more open to question than the first six." Rather than Beckett, White, Bellow, and Golding, Pratt would have chosen Ezra Pound, W. H. Auden, Robert Penn Warren, and Robert Lowell, or as a second choice – if "these undisputed masters" had met with strong resistance from his putative colleagues in the academy – the quartet of Katherine Anne Porter, John Crowe Ransom, Marianne Moore, and Allen Tate. He acknowledged, however, the greater geographical and ethnic range of the choices that were made – from Beckett, who had "written in French as well," to White, who "for the first time has given the continent of Australia an authentic voice." His viewpoint *was* surprisingly narrow, most of all perhaps with regard to Beckett; one recalls that, to Harold Bloom *(Ruin the Sacred*

Truths), Beckett seemed to be "certainly the strongest living Western author, the last survivor of the sequence that includes Proust, Kafka, Joyce."

John L. Brown, examining the French winners and with an eye on the whole history of the prize, thought that "the choice of a respectable majority of Francophone laureates can be legitimately defended," in spite of several "sins of omission," especially in the field of poetry. Most of the winners had, it is true, been "old men at the end of their careers," and the genuine discoveries had been "very few," Brown said, in agreement with Steiner. But he objected to Steiner's excessively harsh denunciation by pointing out that the selection of Perse, Beckett, and Simon "does testify to a desire to recognize the new and the innovative." Like Pratt, Brown also offered a view of the general reputation of the Nobel Prize in Literature in recent times. Looking not so much at the quality of the prize winners as at the large number of prizes, the even more controversial aspects of the assessments, and the reduction of literature to one form of *écriture* among others, he suggested that "even the Nobel has lost something of its former luster."

Reviewing the Spanish-language area, Manuel Durán, who took part in the 1967 symposium, followed Pratt in contrasting the earlier and later choices in his field – but with a result that is in part the opposite of Pratt's. Durán declared the prizes to Echegaray and Benavente to have been "squandered," and felt that Gabriela Mistral was given the laurel that ought to have gone to "a real pioneer, to a Vicente Huidobro or a César Vallejo." Of late, however, he believed the academy's judgment "has improved steadily." In Jiménez the academy had "for the first time . . . found a worthy Hispanic recipient," and "after this success the rest of the way seems to have been relatively easy." Among the four Hispanic winners in this period – Asturias, Neruda, Aleixandre, and García Márquez – only Neruda seemed to him an indisputable choice, "a great poet" whose "creative power and . . . influence upon other Latin American poets were at their peak." Nevertheless, Durán found it "difficult to quarrel with the choice [of Aleixandre], a major poet." Other poets of the same generation, such as Jorge Guillén, Rafael Alberti, and Dámaso Alonso, certainly deserved recognition as well, but "the prize belongs not to a man, in this case, but to a whole generation." He found the two remaining choices more questionable. Asturias had "undeniable literary quality," and "his masterpiece was both stylistically experimental . . . and socially committed"; but the prize to him also meant that candidates such as Borges and Cortázar were passed over. The commendable choice of García Márquez hid more serious omissions. The prize to this leading figure in South American writing, responsible for "the so-called Boom," was "an excellent choice" through which the Swedish Academy "was redeeming itself from past mistakes." Yet the award to this relatively young author doomed "much older Hispanic writers to die unrewarded." In 1982 the academy should have put García Márquez on a "waiting list" and chosen Borges, "the real leader ... the seminal artist, the major thinker and theoretician without whom neither García Márquez nor Cortázar (nor many other Boom writers) makes much sense."

The German prizes were surveyed by A. Leslie Willson, who had no objections to the choices of Böll in 1972 and Canetti in 1981, both "without doubt deserving of selection." What did trouble him, considering the time lapse of forty-three years between the choice of Thomas Mann and Böll was "the continuing Swedish mistrust of German authors" that he thought he could detect; his contribution concluded with an appeal:

> Given the incredible energy and variety of German-language authors, given the broad range of their vehement, exuberant, and expansive concentration on the ghosts of the past, the terrors of the present, and the specters of the future, and given the rising international attention accorded their often distinctive artistry in the production of enduring literary works, the Nobel Committee and the Swedish Academy cannot long continue to ignore the international German community, in spite of the calamitous historical events that for decades obviated the chance that the honor might have fallen on more than two of them.

In the Japanese perspective on this period, as viewed by Yoshio Iwamoto, Junichiro Tanizaki was "by far the most deserving of Nobel recognition." He died, however, in 1965; the prize going to Kawabata instead in 1968 must "be judged a felicitous choice." Iwamoto also gave an account of the questions raised by the Japanese in the midst of their rejoicing: "Why Kawabata, without a doubt the most 'Japanese' in his artistry, when there were in their estimation other writers more international in their appeal?" He supposed that "exoticism" was a decisive factor. As we have seen, that was a misunderstanding: the highly favorable evaluation of Kawabata, on the contrary, was a serious attempt to do justice to the native culture.

The prize to Soyinka in 1986 was regarded in Bernth Lindfors's African survey as much more than an honor to "one more literary giant who had produced outstanding work 'of an ideal tendency'—it also signaled to the world at large that the prize itself was no longer entirely an intramural Aryan affair, monopolized by authors from Europe and the European diaspora." What Lindfors deplored principally was that the Swedish Academy, although "adventurous enough to explore fresh literary terrain ... has not yet managed to rid itself of a pronounced preference for authors who employ familiar European tongues." He was nonetheless aware of the enormous problems attendant on any attempt to adjudicate literature in the African languages; there is a lack of authoritative experts, and "in Africa, institutions for promoting international awareness of local literatures simply do not exist."

Given the composition of the symposium, we unfortunately have no proper assessment of the prizes to Slavonic literature (nor of the prize to

Montale). The most distinct verdict comes from Ivask himself in his introduction, where he declared that the choice of Miłosz was "definitely much more justified than the crowning of Jaroslav Seifert." The prize to Milosz was "both a coronation *and* a discovery of a major poet for most"; consequent translations into various languages "have only confirmed the perspicacity of the Swedish Academy's choice." Ivask also filled in the gap where Greek literature was concerned: "Few would quarrel with the two laureates singled out from modern Greek literature, George Seferis and Odysseus Elytis. If the fame of C. P. Cavafy had not been largely posthumous, he certainly would have been a prime third candidate."

Finally, there was Roger Allen's examination, "Arabic Literature and the Nobel Prize," an essay that turned out to be prophetic. His short list contained only two names, Mahfouz and Adonis – as we have seen, the very two Arabic candidates who were being considered – and his argument concluded in a plea for the former. He fully accepted the point that the Nobel Prize has too often favored novelists but explained the specific Arabic situation: "It was in the new and largely imported field of fiction that enormous efforts had to be made by Arab litterateurs during the early decades of this century. Najib Mahfuz [*sic*] is acknowledged throughout the entire Arab world as the great pioneer in the mature Arabic novel." This reads like a justification several months in advance for a choice that, in the usual way, was prepared for over the course of several years.

The symposium gave a reasonably accurate reflection of the generally favorable international press reaction during the past two decades. Criticism was focused, as elsewhere, on a number of omissions. A thoroughgoing reproach for aesthetic conservatism was formulated by Steiner: "We look in vain in the Nobel register for the experimental, formally subversive, controversial movements and texts that distinguish modernism. No Surrealist has been rewarded, no major Expressionist, no poet or playwright out of the seminal world of Dada or absurdism (André Breton, Hugo Ball, Gertrude Stein). The boat is not to be rocked."

This kind of criticism is lopsided, as we have seen, because it tries to encompass too much history. There is a general truth here about the practice of the first four decades, even if we must ask which "major Expressionist" has been neglected; few candidates of that sort survived World War I. As for the postwar period, however, such criticism of aesthetic conservatism has little basis, for that was when a whole series of pioneers in modern literature received their prizes. That no representative of the world of absurdism has been recognized seems a peculiar claim about this particular period; the prize to Beckett is after all one of the most striking. It is certainly true that Breton is absent from the Nobel register – but it is not true that surrealism is absent. Both Aleixandre and Elytis were singled out as poets who were not only inspired by surrealism but had achieved a higher standing than the originators of the movement. The young Neruda was described in Lundkvist's presentation as a parallel to Tzara. The academy has not shunned surrealism but found its artistically most solid results among the works of its heirs.

The list of omissions in the postwar period is long, but it does not offer as troublesome reading as the earlier list, with names from Tolstoy and Ibsen to Valéry and Joyce. The great renewers were recognized to a quite different extent. Among those neglected the principal names are, in drama (in addition to the aging Claudel), Bertolt Brecht; in prose, André Malraux, Hermann Broch, Alberto Moravia, Vladimir Nabokov, Graham Greene, John Cowper Powys, and Günter Grass; and in poetry, Ezra Pound, Wallace Stevens, Nikos Kazantzakis, Anna Akhmatova, W. H. Auden, and Paul Celan. One name that recurs frequently in many upbraiding articles is that of Borges. As we have already seen, the 1988 symposium agreed on many points about the seriousness of such omissions; objections on behalf of Greene and Nabokov, however, have fallen silent. The 1988 symposium put special weight on the neglected minor European literatures – from the Baltic states, Portugal, and so on. Special attention was directed to the poetic renaissance in Hungary – with Gyula Illyés and Sándor Weöres as its foremost representatives – and Catalonia, represented by Salvador Espriu and J. V. Foix.[20]

The case of Pound has already been discussed in Chapter 7. The extent to which a candidate from the opposite political camp, Brecht, might have been encumbered by *his* tendentious luggage was never tested. He was proposed, from Switzerland, in 1956 and ought to have had a strong position in the era of pioneers; but unfortunately the process did not get as far as a discussion of the specialist report because he died in August.

The time factor had a different effect on the chances of Broch and Powys. From our later point of view, their significance is readily discernible, but at the time when they could have been considered for a prize their worth was evident only to a few. We know that Thomas Mann, who was entitled to nominate candidates, supported the idea of a prize to Broch. After the trilogy *Die Schlafwandler* (The Sleepwalkers) of 1930-32, Broch came back into view in 1946 with *Der Tod des Virgil* (The Death of Virgil). But the author died in 1951, and so far his stature had been clear to only a limited circle. Österling did not belong to that circle. His interest was certainly caught by Mann's high praise of Broch's qualities, which appealed to his appreciation of the boldly regenerative. In his review of 1946 he also recognized the grandeur in Broch's grasp of his subject matter, as well as the magnificence of his opening. But Österling did not feel at home with the new genre: he felt that Broch "attempted the impossible by stirring together narrative, poetry, philosophy, and history in an unprecedented torrent of words." His combination of respect for the grandiose aspects of the construction and criticism of the attendant excess is a fair reflection of the committee's view of Broch's work.

To an even greater degree, Powys was appreciated by only a few in his lifetime, and his legend and repute still suggest a cult following, as John Bayley has pointed out.[21] Powys may have been a suitable author according to the pragmatic principle that took shape in the 1970s; like Broch, he had something of a Canetti's position. He died early, however, in 1963.

Those complaining of neglect seldom take notice of the crowd of likely names around the prize of a specific year. (Lamont, it is true, wanted to make room for 150 authors in a fifty-year period.) We have already seen that in 1964, for example, considerable interest was expressed in Auden, but the interest in Sartre prevailed.[22] Auden's candidacy was nonetheless renewed; in 1967 Gierow advised in a letter that the main contest ought to be between Asturias and Auden or Greene – the prize went to Asturias. Two years later many expected the prize winner to be Malraux; he had then left his ministerial post and had won new currency with his *Antimémoires*.[23] But the 1969 choice was Beckett, and he was followed by Solzhenitsyn – both "canonic" names. In such an *embarras de richesses*, figures like Malraux and Auden could easily occupy a leading place several years running without actually achieving the sufficient majority of votes.

As to Moravia, the academy's foremost expert on Italian literature, Österling, gave in his successive reviews an indication of how the evaluation changed. The starting point was promising. In 1961, Moravia was "without doubt Italy's greatest fiction-writer. . . . His tireless productivity has in recent years celebrated an unforgettable triumph in the war novel *La ciociara* [Two Women]." But his works of the 1960s caused several disappointments. *L'Attenzione* (The Lie) illustrated more clearly than before the divergence between the author's "technical virtuosity and his predilection for disagreeable subjects" – it is "the erotomaniac theme" from *La Noia* (The Empty Canvas) recurring "in another light."[24] Yet there seems to be more artistic than moral scruples in the arbiter's "uncomfortable feeling that Moravia's considerable talents have been expended upon a doubtful undertaking." Great admiration for the master who wrote *La ciociara* had at any rate given way to a more careful and distant attitude.

The candidacies of writers such as Malraux and Auden should also be viewed in the light of the new pragmatic policy that was being established. What was essential in the achievements of both Malraux and Auden now belonged to an earlier period; Gierow mentioned that already in 1964 it was held to Auden's disadvantage that "the peak of his accomplishments lies fairly far back in time." Both names were very well established in the awareness of the general public. What purpose could a prize then fulfill? Without being decisive, such a question does still influence the process.

This question applies also to a certain extent to the writer whose absence from the Nobel list is perhaps most often commented upon – Graham Greene. It is well known that he had strong advocates in the academy during the 1960s and 1970s, but also determined opponents; we have just seen how in 1967 he was one of the principal candidates. Lundkvist, who in an interview in 1980 (London *Sunday Times,* 23 November) made clear his lack of support for Greene's candidacy, hinted at a possible reason: Greene's significant production had occurred far in the past, and besides, he was much too celebrated. For those involved in the discussions who, like Lundkvist, wanted to draw attention to vital but unregarded work, a prize to Greene was not exactly a priority.

Along such lines it is possible to explain why in many cases an apparently justifiable prize was not given. This is not, of course, to deny that many absences appear to be blameworthy. The list of postwar winners does not begin simply with a series of brilliant renewers; it also begins with a continued rejection of Claudel. It was his alleged "exclusiveness" that the academy of the 1930s regarded as a disqualification – and this opinion was never changed, even if Österling in a review in 1950 mentioned that Claudel had for long competed with Gide for the "role of guide and mentor for the younger generations" and in 1954 noted his position as "France's greatest living poet." Österling's later article tells us more clearly than the committee's spartan report why Claudel did not receive a prize:

> It must be said that the religiously edifying element is so dominating in Claudel's drama that more often than not it threatens to stifle the aesthetic pleasure. Supernatural powers and abstract concepts enter the stage as personifications at the same time as the thoroughgoing symbolism with its borrowings from every age and country is difficult to penetrate, in spite of the strictly didactic means of communication. The massive tirades in a sort of rhymed biblical verse cause further hindrances to the effect of the dramas, even if we do admit that now and then this strange technique creates episodes of grand, soaring poetry.

Claudel remained the "matter of dispute" that Barberet pointed out as late as 1967. With the wisdom of hindsight we can only express regret for this omission as for those of Anna Akhmatova and Paul Celan, both of whose greatness is now so much more evident than in their lifetimes.

Recent criticism has tended to focus on the limited geographical range of the choices. In 1963 the *Washington Post* cited neglect of the authors of Latin America, Asia, and Africa. The two following decades saw three prizes go to Latin America – those to Asturias, Neruda, and García Márquez – and the immediate future saw one go to Asia, that to Kawabata. The criticism, however, holds. When an American newspaper greeted Canetti in 1981 as the quintessential European, the article was headlined, "The European Prize." The limited spread was outlined: of eighty-five prize winners, seventy-three have been Europeans or Europeans in exile. The remainder consists of seven Americans, one Australian, two Chileans, and one Guatemalan, all of them writing in one or another of the major European languages. The only Asian prize winners have been the Indian Tagore and the Japanese Kawabata–but never an African, never a recognition of work in Chinese, Arabic, Parsi, Turkish, Indonesian, Hindi, Korean, Swahili, or Tagalog. If in the future the Nobel Prize in Literature is going to maintain its reputation as a *world* prize, then it "must roam the literary globe" (*Baltimore Sun,* 20 October 1981).

From all those different quarters critical voices are repeatedly raised. The *Saudi Gazette* reprimanded the academy for the disproportionate number of European prize winners and reminded its readers of the strong literary traditions in many Asian countries; the Arabic successors of the old masters "may not reach their high standards, but inspired by them, and accepted by a discerning public, they must have something in their work deserving recognition" (15 October 1984). Such Arabic viewpoints have often included a suspicion that Jewish authors have been favored. The prize to Singer was thus commented upon in the *Baghdad Observer* under the headline, " 'Zionization' of the Nobel Prize" (6 November 1978). This criticism returned in the 1988 symposium, but in a more subtle and more constructive form and with an awareness of the difficult problems to be encountered. Syed Amanuddin did not just point out cases of neglect of the various Indian literatures–such as the Hindi author Nirala and Urdu poet Faiz Ahmed Faiz–but also emphasized the need for a basis for nomination and choice in the form of standard editions and authentic translations, critical studies, historical surveys, and so on. "In other words, Third World writers, translators, scholars, editors, and publishers need to involve themselves in activities which would sustain and promote Third World writing aggressively."

In his reply (already cited) to Tsu-Yü Hwang, Gyllensten unconditionally admitted the injustice to Asian and African literature at the same time that he described the exceptional difficulties involved in coming to grips with the problem. In the previous chapter we examined the question and saw how the Swedish Academy tries to extend its competence in tackling this demanding commission. The prizes to Soyinka in 1986 and to Mahfouz in 1988, both prepared for over the course of many years of work, can be regarded as results of the ambition to give a global dimension to the area under scrutiny.

Ziolkowski formulated an interesting objection on principle in 1967 with reference to German literature, but it is relevant to world literature. He said that "anyone, certainly, who relied on the Nobel awards for an impression of twentieth-century German letters would get a grotesquely distorted view." One may well agree with his–of course, quite unhistorical–wish that Rilke, Hofmannsthal, Brecht, and Broch had taken the places of Mommsen, Eucken, Heyse, and Spitteler, but one must also question the idea that a series of literary prizes given in the nearsighted present could be so thoroughly perceptive that the result would correspond to the clearer perspective of a succeeding generation. Even the premature death of an author–for example, Proust, Kafka, Cavafy, and Mandelstam–can hinder the fulfillment of such an ambition. In addition, it is not at all certain that a choice should aim at the kind of literary "representativeness" that Ziolkowski presupposed. The "pragmatic attitude" is, in fact, one answer to that point of view.

These criticisms, particularly those in *Books Abroad,* have produced a number of constructive proposals. I shall take these up in a little more detail, since they throw light on certain problems that at approximately the same time were apparent in the work of the academy. One of the ideas proposed in 1951, a sharing of each prize between three recipients, has already been touched on in an earlier chapter; it is far from being one of the most constructive suggestions. More constructive, however, was the conclusion of the 1967 symposium as embodied in Herbert Howarth's "Petition to the Swedish Academy."[25]

The first item declared: "It is time to disregard Nobel's preference for idealism." The reasons for suggesting such a change include the difficulty in knowing just what Nobel meant by "idealistic tendency,"[26] and the belief that the best literature is also most effective in developing human consciousness: "Nobel's penitent longing for a better world will be answered whenever the academy gives the prize not to the best-*wishing* maker but the best *maker*–even if that maker appears to wish ill." In the background of this proposal there was also an awareness of not only the destructive effects of the "idealistic" criterion but of general conclusions, like Spiller's, that the prize is not a literary award in a modern sense but one branch of a program of awards intended to further world peace.

A related concept can be found in several French commentaries. Mauriac's contribution to the debate in 1959 was the claim that the academy had quite consistently favored the representatives of "committed" literature, and awarded Anatole France for his Dreyfus campaign, Rolland for his pro-German pacifism, and Gide and Camus for their ability to arouse the enthusiasm of young people in moral problems–while passing over "noncommitted" authors with purely artistic merits, such as Valéry, Claudel, and probably Perse. He attributed his own prize to his role as a moralist.

Mauriac's interpretation can be corrected in every detail. France's involvement in the Dreyfus affair had an effect only insofar as, in Schück's argument, it freed the author from the accusation of having adopted a sceptical position; the grounds *for* the prize were, as we have seen, significantly more qualified. In Valéry's case, on the contrary, it was not his lack of commitment that told against him but his exclusiveness. What is interesting here, however, is not the rightness or wrongness of particular claims but the idea that Mauriac shared with several of the participants in the

1967 symposium – that the Nobel Prize in Literature is not a literary prize but in a broad sense a kind of peace prize.

The corrective to this idea ought to be apparent in our historical survey of how prize decisions have been reached. We have seen how the interpretation of the concept "idealistic" was gradually extended after the new and more generous idea of "broad-hearted humanity" surfaced in 1921. A recent and decisive test of this change occurred shortly after the relevant critical surveys: the response to Beckett in 1969 clarified how even a vision of the utmost darkness, interpreted as a miserere from all mankind, could be reconciled with the prescriptions of Nobel's will. It has been out of the question to simply set aside Nobel's intentions on this point, but it has surely been possible to give the word *idealistic* a generous interpretation. And this is exactly what has happened in the more recent history of the prize. As early as 1950 Österling noted that "in actual practice, it has also been shown that only the loosest possible interpretation of the word can be applied with profit."[27] (The line was drawn at a case of such flagrant fascism and anti-Semitism as Pound.) In his statement on the literature prize, Gyllensten pointed out that nowadays the expression "is not taken too literally. . . . It is realized that on the whole the serious literature that is worthy of a prize furthers knowledge of man and his condition and endeavors to enrich and improve his life."

One of the contributors to the 1988 survey who – unlike many of the others – took note of the change was William Pratt: "If the suspicion of some kind of liberal humanitarian bias in the literary awards were ever justified, it has been permanently laid to rest by the award to Beckett, since no more nihilistic writer is ever likely to gain a world audience than he." Pratt also noted the pessimism of the author of *Lord of the Flies*, William Golding, and concluded, speaking of the last twenty years: "Idealism, at any rate of the patently uplifting variety . . . is no longer a requirement for the Nobel Prize in Literature."

The observation was essentially correct but requires some modification: efforts were actually made to show how Beckett's worldview was compatible with the demands of Nobel's will. A like situation recurred in 1989. The prize to Camilo José Cela was given to a writer who was certainly a great innovator, "the leading figure in Spain's literary renewal during the postwar era" (to quote the press release), but he was also a figure who needed special attention in order to reach a wider international audience. Referring to "the wealth of Latin American literature," Knut Ahnlund said in his speech to Cela that "perhaps too little attention has been paid . . . to its counterpart in the country where Spanish was first spoken." However, Cela's dark conception of the world was liable to pose the same problem to the executors of Nobel's will as Beckett's did; but it also provoked a similar solution. The prize was given "for a rich and intense prose, which with restrained compassion forms a challenging vision of man's vulnerability." Or, to quote

Ahnlund again, it was given for an oeuvre "that possesses great wildness, license, and violence, but nonetheless in no way lacks sympathy or common human feeling, unless we demand that those sentiments should be expressed in the simplest possible way." In Ahnlund's "unless" we glimpse the repudiation, implicit in recent practice, of the early narrow interpretation of the will. The Nobel Prize in Literature has gradually become a *literary* prize in a sense quite different from that possibly conceived from the vantage point of Paris in 1959 or Oklahoma in 1967. The closest the academy has adhered to applying the "idealistic tendency" criterion of an earlier age is the homage it has paid to those great artistic achievements that are characterized by uncompromising "integrity" in the depiction of the human predicament.

The second point in the petition from the 1967 symposium focused on "a new care for poetry" in the academy's choice of prize winners, in light of the earlier, overwhelming dominance of prose, and recommended that "novelists should wait their turn somewhere to the rear." It is advised that the academy be cautious, "to the point of abstinence," about nonliterary authors. As is clear from earlier parts of this book, similar assessments have been arrived at within the academy itself in the course of its work over the years. During the 1930s the academy expressed regret over the difficulties of giving due recognition to poets. Many poets then appeared in the postwar list of winners – indeed, in the period 1971-80 they outnumber the prose writers. On the whole there is a balance of quite a different kind from before. Yet the committee and the academy have never gone so far as to programmatically give first preference to a poet, second to a playwright, and only third to a novelist. The well-meaning symposium also ignored the fact that great poetry can also be found between the covers of a novel, though we can glimpse the idea when Vlach called *Dr. Zhivago* "a poet's novel."[28] But in many other prose works that have regenerated the art of fiction – from *Der Steppenwolf* to *Cien Años de Soledad* (One Hundred Years of Solitude) – it is a poet's vision that has manifested itself in the prose. Several of the postwar novelists on the Nobel Prize list are of that kind.

To turn to the question of nonliterary authors, we have noted the strong restraint on this score of the Nobel Committee of the 1920s and 1930s, which did not recommend a prize to Croce, for example. The award to Bergson was a decision of the academy's, against the recommendation of the committee. In the following years there was a certain move in favor of such prizes, as was apparent in the minority proposal for Huizinga in 1939, supported by Selma Lagerlöf, who in a letter claimed that the historians "have been much neglected." The two more recent such prizes, to Russell in 1950 and Churchill in 1953, could be seen as repairing the omission, but they are the last of their kind. For several decades the literature prize has been seen as a purely literary award, even if the academy has by no means denied itself the opportunity of also awarding "other writings which, by virtue of their form and style, possess literary value."

The next two points in the petition are really two aspects of the same pragmatic thought.[29] First:

> The academy might do more often what it has sometimes done so well: exert itself to discover writers outside the domains of the Big Powers and the current languages of diplomacy. It has been an advantage to the common reader that the judges have been immediately able to recognize a dozen Scandinavian prize men whom other regions might not have come to know without their championship. It has been an advantage that they have extended themselves to recognize the writers of Chile, Greece, Poland, Israel, and Yugoslavia.

And secondly, "Only with hesitation and restraint should the academy endorse a writer already widely recognized and rewarded."

An older master should be honored perhaps only when his lifework has not received its deserved recognition (as when he belongs to a minor language area). "If the judges miss a man in his best years, let them stay away afterward, as they stayed away from Hardy." Such a practice–abstaining from awarding the prize to some of the great names already otherwise rewarded and investing in younger authors–could result in a list that after fifty years may well "sound less magniloquent than the present record" and contain even more mistakes: "But there is such a thing as a fertile mistake. To canonize the already-canonized fertilizes no one. Whereas the mistaken election of a writer from an obscure culture, or of an innovatory young writer who eventually fades, may lead to controversy, to creative imitation, to analysis, to fresh departures and penetrations. . . . The new mistakes may be more fertile than the old."

Fleming's argument in the previous year was in the same spirit. With the exception of Yeats, and possibly also of O'Neill, Camus, and Sartre, no author has been taken up while the curve of his career was rising. Only seven have been given their recognition before the age of fifty. The academy has chosen to be sure of the prize winner's final position. "But this is quite simply a violation of Nobel's entire purpose," Fleming asserted. "He wanted to recognize the most impressive recent book, not to set the seal upon the work of a lifetime or to reward the capacity for literary and physical endurance. . . . The most profitable experiment that could be made with the prize in literature would be to go back to Nobel's express intention of honoring a recent book rather than a life's achievement." Using slightly different arguments, the commentators of 1966 and 1967 arrived at the same solution, all of them remaining aware of the increased risk of rewarding younger talents.

A pragmatic policy closely resembling the above was outlined, as we have seen, by Gyllensten a couple of years later, gained ground during the 1970s, then achieved a breakthrough in 1978. That policy revived the idea of trying to discover significant authors off the beaten track. Gyllensten made an important and well-motivated distinction, however: instead of referring to superpowers and others, he conceived the prize as supporting "an insufficiently recognized linguistic or cultural sphere" (1971), which included both Elytis and the now U.S.A.-domiciled Singer. But the second proposal also recurs in the wish to see the prize as "a kind of investment in – and as such, of course, entailing a degree of risk – the advancement of an oeuvre that still *can* be advanced" (1969). Finding support in Nobel's intentions, the idea behind it was "not simply to reward already completed achievements but equally to create propitious circumstances for *continued efforts* and *further development* of 'the promising aptitudes'" (1971).

It is undeniable that Gyllensten's proposals look like a quick and energetic reply to the critical challenges of 1966 and 1967. I have not, however, been able to find any direct connection. The objectives proposed by the critics had been held by individual members of the academy for a long time, as is clear from earlier statements from Hjärne, Heidenstam, Böök, Österling, and Siwertz; they had already been manifested in several choices. The fact that it happened to be Gyllensten who gave the well-prepared program its distinctive form is naturally explained by his early schooling in pragmatic thought and the many times he had expressed similar ideas already in his own writing.

As described in Chapter 6, this new policy in choosing prize winners was understood and appreciated widely in the international press. The response of *Le Monde* in 1979 was representative: "What is the use of breaking down doors that are already open by giving the prize to international best-sellers?" *World Literature Today* stressed in 1981 that the Nobel Prize in Literature was not intended to be only a confirmation of popularity; it could also focus attention on talents that had not yet been recognized by the majority of the world's readers and critics. "It may educate the many as it celebrates the one."[30] Both the shift in the academy's practice and the international response seem, however, to have gone unnoticed by George Steiner. The academy, he concluded unsuspectingly, ought to glory in making "discoveries. ... What great virtue is there in acclaiming that which is already of global renown?"[31]

We may nonetheless, from today's vantage point, question whether the pragmatic intentions of the Nobel Committee and the Swedish Academy have been fully realized. Several "discoveries" have undoubtedly been made. A number of internationally neglected oeuvres and regions have been brought to attention and put within reach of the "ordinary reader." One intention has proved more difficult to achieve: the "investment" in "an oeuvre that still *can* be advanced," with the "risk taking" involved. The great names caught by the searchlight have tended to be older writers, such as

Aleixandre, Singer, Canetti, and Seifert.[32] That the prize winners from the minor language areas must be such "old masters" was foreseen by those who proposed improvements in 1967. Most recently, only the choices of Soyinka and Brodsky – fifty-two and forty-seven years old, respectively – correspond to the aim of lowering the age of the recipients. There was no question, however, of "investment" or "risk taking" in either of these cases.

A basic weakness may be located in the international nominating system, which in many quarters tends to put forward not only well-established names but also the first names in the domestic ranking order and to hold back proposals that would favor strong, developing, younger talents. Consequently, the Nobel Committee should intensify its own investigations of the growth points of literature in various parts of the world. That would place great demands on a richly developed network of contacts with the capacity to report promptly. The difficulties of doing so are discouraging. Yet there would be much to gain – to a certain extent for the reputation of the prize but above all for the sake of literature. The discoveries it would be possible to make, at an earlier point in the careers of the authors concerned, could be a fitting tribute both to Nobel's spirit and to the new type of assessment that has in recent years dominated the selection process.

NOBEL LAUREATES IN LITERATURE

1901	Sully Prudhomme, France
1902	Theodor Mommsen, Germany
1903	Bjørnstjerne Bjørnson, Norway
1904	Frédéric Mistral, France
	José Echegaray, Spain
1905	Henryk Sienkiewicz, Poland
1906	Giosuè Carducci, Italy
1907	Rudyard Kipling, Great Britain
1908	Rudolf Eucken, Germany
1909	Selma Lagerlöf, Sweden
1910	Paul Heyse, Germany
1911	Maurice Maeterlinck, Belgium
1912	Gerhart Hauptmann, Germany
1913	Rabindranath Tagore, India
1914	Reserved
1915	Reserved
1916	The prize for 1915: Romain Rolland, France
	The prize for 1916: Verner von Heidenstam, Sweden
1917	Karl Gjellerup, Denmark
	Henrik Pontoppidan, Denmark
1918	Reserved
1919	Reserved
1920	The prize for 1919: Carl Spitteler, Switzerland
	The prize for 1920: Knut Hamsun, Norway
1921	Anatole France, France
1922	Jacinto Benavente, Spain
1923	William Butler Yeats, Ireland
1924	Władysław Stanisław Reymont, Poland
1925	Reserved

1926	The prize for 1925: George Bernard Shaw, Great Britain
	The prize for 1926: Reserved
1927	The prize for 1926: Grazia Deledda, Italy
	The prize for 1927: Reserved
1928	The prize for 1927: Henri Bergson, France
	The prize for 1928: Sigrid Undset, Norway
1929	Thomas Mann, Germany
1930	Sinclair Lewis, United States
1931	Erik Axel Karlfeldt (posthumously), Sweden
1932	John Galsworthy, Great Britain
1933	Ivan Bunin, stateless (domiciled in France; born in Russia)
1934	Luigi Pirandello, Italy
1935	Reserved
1936	Eugene O'Neill, United States
1937	Roger Martin du Gard, France
1938	Pearl Buck, United States
1939	Frans Eemil Sillanpää, Finland
1940-43	No award
1944	Johannes V. Jensen, Denmark
1945	Gabriela Mistral, Chile
1946	Hermann Hesse, Switzerland
1947	André Gide, France
1948	T. S. Eliot, Great Britain
1949	Reserved
1950	The prize for 1949: William Faulkner, United States
	The prize for 1950: Bertrand Russell, Great Britain
1951	Pär Lagerkvist, Sweden
1952	François Mauriac, France
1953	Winston Churchill, Great Britain
1954	Ernest Hemingway, United States
1955	Halldór Kiljan Laxness, Iceland
1956	Juan Ramón Jiménez, Spain (domiciled in Puerto Rico)
1957	Albert Camus, France
1958	Boris Pasternak, Soviet Union (accepted, later caused by the authorities of his country to decline the prize)
1959	Salvatore Quasimodo, Italy
1960	Saint-John Perse, France
1961	Ivo Andrić, Yugoslavia
1962	John Steinbeck, United States
1963	Giorgos Seferis, Greece
1964	Jean-Paul Sartre (declined the prize)
1965	Mikhail Sholokhov, Soviet Union
1966	Shmuel Yosef Agnon, Israel

	Nelly Sachs, Sweden (born in Germany)
1967	Miguel Angel Asturias, Guatemala
1968	Yasunari Kawabata, Japan
1969	Samuel Beckett, Ireland
1970	Aleksandr Solzhenitsyn, Soviet Union
1971	Pablo Neruda, Chile
1972	Heinrich Böll, Federal Republic of Germany
1973	Patrick White, Australia
1974	Eyvind Johnson, Sweden
	Harry Martinson, Sweden
1975	Eugenio Montale, Italy
1976	Saul Bellow, United States
1977	Vicente Aleixandre, Spain
1978	Isaac Bashevis Singer, United States (born in Poland)
1979	Odysseus Elytis, Greece
1980	Czesław Miłosz, United States and Poland
1981	Elias Canetti, Great Britain (born in Bulgaria)
1982	Gabriel García Márquez, Colombia
1983	William Golding, Great Britain
1984	Jaroslav Seifert, Czechoslovakia
1985	Claude Simon, France
1986	Wole Soyinka, Nigeria
1987	Joseph Brodsky, United States (born in Soviet Union)
1988	Naguib Mahfouz, Egypt
1989	Camilo José Cela, Spain

NOTES

The main sources used in this study–the reports of the Nobel Committee along with individual statements, documents supporting nominations (and lists of nominations received), and specialist reports–are to be found, with the rather spartan minutes of the committee, in the archives of the Nobel Committee of the Swedish Academy. Unless otherwise indicated, correspondence between members of the academy is in the archives of the Swedish Academy. In addition, some use has been made of the collections of letters in the Royal Library, Stockholm (KB – Kungl. biblioteket), in Uppsala University Library (UUB), and in Lund University Library (LUB).

Anders Österling's survey, "The Literary Prize," in the anthology *Nobel: The Man and His Prizes* (Stockholm, 1950), is cited from the latest edition (1972). "Strömberg" refers to Kjell Strömberg's introductions to the sections on each prize winner in various volumes of the series *Nobel Prize Library* (New York and Del Mar, Calif.).

The Nobel Festival speeches, devoted to the work of the winners, are cited from the annual volumes in the series *Les Prix Nobel* (Stockholm). Radio presentations of the winners and the more recent press announcements about the choices are cited from stencils in the academy archives. For newspaper material use has been made of the collections of cuttings in the archives of the Swedish Academy and of the Nobel Foundation, as well as of copies and microfilm in the Royal Library (KB).

The quantity of notes has been greatly reduced for this English-language edition; detailed references to material written in Swedish, and to specifically Swedish circumstances, have been omitted.

Introduction

1. *Journal of the Swedish Academy,* 6 May 1897 and 13 May 1897 (Swedish Academy archives).

2. The continuation – "Has a work which is to be rewarded been produced by two or three persons, the prize shall be awarded to them jointly" – is not relevant to the field of literature.

3. If a withheld prize cannot be given the following year either, then the amount of the prize is to be added to the capital fund.

4. To be elected to the Nobel Committee one does not, according to the regulations, need either "Swedish citizenship or membership of the adjudicating body." In reality, only members of the Swedish Academy are elected to the committee; more recently, however, one member has been co-opted from outside (Knut Ahnlund was from 1970 to 1984 special adviser in Spanish literature, without yet being a member of the academy; after his election to the academy in 1983 he became a regular member of the committee in 1984).

5. These officials and assistants "shall prepare matters referring to prizes, give reports on recently published literary works abroad, and arrange for the necessary translations of foreign publications."

6. Quoted in Elias Bredsdorff, "Vad menade Nobel med uttrycket 'i idealisk rigtning'?" ("What Did Nobel Mean by the Term 'an Ideal Tendency'?"), *BLM* 33 (1964): 353ff. A special problem, glimpsed in this title, is that Nobel actually wrote "ideal," which does not make sense; the word has been interpreted as "idealistic." Pierre Assouline, in his article "Un Francais Prix Nobel?" in *Lire,* no. 121 (October 1985), cites Sture Allén's observation that Nobel, who on occasion slightly mixed together the various languages he spoke, first wrote another word – perhaps "idealistic."

7. This idea is put forward by Robert E. Spiller, Nobel Prize Symposium, *Books Abroad* (now *World Literature Today*) 41 (1967): 32.

8. Österling in *Nobel,* 75, 78.

9. Knut Ahnlund, *Diktarliv i Norden* (Literary Life in the North) (Uppsala, 1981), 256ff.

10. Österling does, however, make occasional and sparing use of this source (which at the time of the first publication of his book, in 1950, entailed divulging confidential matters). A few quotations from the reports have also been made elsewhere.

11. The exceptions are 1912, when Hans Hildebrand acted as temporary chairman; 1913-21 when Harald Hjärne wrote the reports; and 1922-30 when Hallström was chairman. In 1931 Hallström became secretary on the death of Karlfeldt. Hallström remained chairman until 1946, while Österling was secretary from 1941. Österling filled both posts from 1947 until Gierow became secretary in 1964, and chairman in 1970. Gierow was followed by Gyllensten in both posts in 1977 and 1981, respectively. In 1986 the functions were again separated, when Sture Allén became secretary while Gyllensten remained as chairman, until 1988, when he was succeeded by Kjell Espmark.

Chapter 1. A Lofty and Sound Idealism

1. In the following text, the years in parentheses are references to the Nobel Committee's report of that year.

2. Individual memo attached to the report of 1905. Tegnér's remarks are part of his argument in favor of that year's prize being shared between Henryk Sienkiewicz and Eliza Orzeszkowa: Orzeszkowa was inferior "when it comes to narrative skill and linguistic virtuosity," but she did have something that Nobel himself "would doubtless have thought weighed more than 'the great epic touch': she has *a big, rich, loving heart.*"

3. This jibe at "naturalism" and "the natural sciences" is echoed in several contexts. In the course of a highly appreciative evaluation of the French historian Albert Sorel in 1903, the committee noted that "his view of the world is not, like Taine's, mechanistic."

4. The committee similarly remarked that Carducci's "rash" hymn to Satan ought not to be compared with Baudelaire's sickly and rancorous "satanism": Carducci's Satan was "really a Lucifer . . . a herald of freedom of thought and culture, an enemy of the asceticism that devalues or denies the right of the natural." It is interesting to note academy member Envoy Carl Bildt's plea for Carducci as one who "bears high the banner of idealism against the wicked clan of d'Annunzio and his followers" (letter to Wirsén, 12 November 1904).

5. Similarly, we can see how Paul Bourget, who in his earlier novel sequences concerned himself "too much with the physiology of love and a hairsplitting analysis of erotic deviations," acquired a "steadily more profound" view of life, characterized by "both a strict ethical seriousness and a genuine religiosity." The "idealism" that thus animated his depiction of morals "makes him worth consideration for a Nobel Prize in Literature" (1907).

6. Herbert Tingsten, *Den svenska socialdemokratins idéutveckling* (The Swedish Social Democrats: Their Ideological Development), I (Stockholm, 1941), 28f.

7. F. T. Vischer, *Aesthetik oder Wissenschaft des Schönen* (Aesthetics or the Science of the Beautiful), I (Reutlingen and Leipzig, 1846), 54, and III:2 (Stuttgart, 1857), 1, 191 ff. Cf. Hermann Glockner, *Friedrich Theodor Vischer und das neunzehnte Jahrhundert* (Theodor Vischer and the Nineteenth Century) (Berlin, 1931), 65: "Der *Idealrealismus* . . . ist der vollkommene Ausdruck dieser Synthese" ("*Ideal realism* . . . is the perfect expression of this synthesis").

8. A similar observation was made in the 1911 report. Cf. the evaluation of François Coppée in 1903: "Everything is done according to nature and thus acquires an appearance of truth."

9. This classicist idea of "plasticity," as we shall soon see in the evaluation of Mistral, was also described as "Homerian graphicness" (1901).

10. Vischer, *Aesthetik,* III:2, 1211, 1315, and 1472ff.

11. Johann Wolfgang von Goethe, *Sämtliche Werke* (Collected Works), XIII (Munich, 1977), 148ff.

12. In 1909 Emile Verhaeren's "greatest" work was deemed to be his collection *Les Héros* (1908), in which his "previous obscure, sickly, and rebellious passion and provocative defiance" were replaced by "calm heroism, clarity, and sound strength."

13. This "strange" combination helped to make the Catalan dramatist Ángel Guimerà "one of the age's most outstanding writers" (1909).

14. Vischer, *Aesthetik,* III:1 (1851), 22ff and 51ff, respectively. Nuñez de Arce otherwise showed his idealism in his implacable enmity toward the materialistic worldview. Similarly, Coppée could at times be "much too circumstantial" in his descriptions.

15. Giving the prize to Prudhomme was recommended by "such men as Gaston Boissier, Gaston Paris, Paul Bourget, André Theuriet, François Coppée, de Hérédia, J. Lemaître, Freycinet, and Paul Deschanel." There is no doubt that the weight of such names had a decisive influence.

16. Report cited by Österling, in *Nobel.* Österling does not say anything about the evaluative norms behind this judgment.

17. The matter was investigated in Karl Ragnar Gierow's illuminating article "Tolstojs Nobelpris" ("Tolstoy's Nobel Prize"), *Svenska Dagbladet,* 31 December 1965. He argues that a later letter from Tolstoy (1906) resulted in Tolstoy's deletion from the list of Nobel candidates. The evidence, though, is circumstantial.

18. The report went on to explain that, "from the point of view of the sound idealism that the will appears to call for," the academy had its doubts about writings it would "otherwise on many grounds eagerly admire." That the academy had not, "in any prejudiced manner," demanded "a certain orthodoxy" was said to be evident from the prize to "the religious doubter" Sully Prudhomme, who nevertheless "always honored the dictate of duty" and "never mocked or insulted religion." It is interesting that Tegnér, in an individual memo in 1905 about the Polish candidates, admitted that "Tolstoy's brilliant oeuvre displays certain faults of such a serious and disfiguring nature that in accordance with the laws of the Nobel Prize he should rightly not be rewarded."

19. In an unpublished account (in the archives of the Swedish Academy), Schück said the committee was here "in full agreement with Nobel, who perhaps with exactly Zola in mind wrote the will's requirement of an 'idealistic tendency' in the prize-winning work."

20. "Ibsen's Symbolism" (1910 report). See also the evaluation of Maeterlinck (1909), formulated by one of those who "entertain no special

love of symbolism in art." As already suggested, there was a significant opposition to Wirsén in favor of at least a shared prize to Ibsen (see Chapter 8). When the 1903 prize went to Bjørnson, no further evaluation of Ibsen was undertaken beyond the observation that he "is now a man whose health is broken, whose life's flame is flickering out," while Bjørnson was still "in his full strength." Wirsén's correspondence, however, gives a fuller picture: in his letter to committee member Gottfrid Billing of 10 July 1902, he said it pained him "that a Swedish bishop can recommend such a choice; I have met *Norwegian* priests who were deeply indignant over the whole of Ibsen's later activity with its desolation, negation, and bizarre mysteriousness, its manner of undermining reliance on everything substantial in existence and its secretive mockery of all of life's values. What is there of a positive nature in creations such as *Hedda Gabler* or *The Master Builder* or above all in the dreadful *When We Dead Awake,* where a man's crime consists in not having seduced a model, with whom he was not even in love?"

21. See Österling (*Nobel,* 99) on Nathan Söderblom's late (and subsequently withdrawn) proposal of Strindberg.

22. George Steiner, "The Scandal of the Nobel Prize," *New York Times Book Review,* 30 September 1984.

23. In 1903 the objection was raised that Kipling's manner of writing lacked that "nobility, that calm moderation that one loves to see in a work of art." A lack of "nobility" was barely mentioned in 1907: the report noted that the soldier slang "in certain extreme songs approaches the vulgar," which was nevertheless compensated for by the author's "fresh immediacy and ethical energy."

24. Alf Kjellen's study of Wirsén's personality, *Bakom fasaden* (Behind the Facade) (Stockholm, 1979), 167.

25. Among the other candidates reviewed in the reports of the first decade, mention ought to be made of Pierre Loti, "deserving of the Nobel Prize" for "his mastery of form and his poetic coloring." Yet the author of *Madame Chrysanthème* hardly represented the "most idealistic" in the literature of the age, and his refined charm had at times "an overlanguishing, morbid character." His work was also "more or less unsound ... because of its exotic luxuriance, its bizarre eroticism, and its basically disconsolate melancholy, which stems from an unconquerable scepticism" (1910).

Anatole France, whose prize belonged to another period, was in 1904 "a complete master" from the linguistic point of view but was disqualified by his "baffling, icy contempt" and by elements of "rather low and offensive eroticism" – objections that remained in a 1909 evaluation that otherwise seemed to open the way to a prize by seeing in France's "manly comments in the Dreyfus affair" an example of "an ethical idealism."

26. Cf. Vischer, *Aesthetik,* III:I, 37ff, and discussion of Echegaray earlier in this chapter.

27. Henrik Schück, *Några anteckningar till Svenska akademiens historia under åren 1883-1912, V: Akademien och litteraturen 1901-1912* (Some Notes on the History of the Swedish Academy 1883-1912, V: The Academy and Literature 1901-1912), (unpublished manuscript in the Swedish Academy archives), 164f.

28. Örjan Lindberger, in *Ny illustrerad svensk litteraturhistoria* (New Illustrated Swedish Literary History) (Stockholm, 1956), III:509.

Chapter 2. Literary Neutralism

1. Henrik Schück, *Några minnesanteckningar* (Some Memoranda) (unpublished manuscript in the Swedish Academy archives), 116.

2. Heidenstam's remarks are known for the most part from Österling; see *Nobel,* 101.

3. Verner von Heidenstam letters to Per Hallström, 12 April and 8 June 1913. It should be noted, however, that Heidenstam himself was more than willing to discuss sharing prizes on a country-by-country basis – in the correspondence with Hallström he aired his wish to let the prize on one occasion go to Denmark, then on the next to Finland. The apparent contradiction is explained by Heidenstam's Scandinavian leaning: "It is after all a Scandinavian prize, not a Gallic or a Spanish one." (Heidenstam to Hallström, 8 April 1913).

4. Parts of this report are cited by Österling, in *Nobel,* 102f.

5. Spitteler had been a candidate since 1912, in which year he was evaluated against Hauptmann (see Chapter 8). In the 1913 report Hallström supported Spitteler by stressing the "undeniable beauties of *Der Olympische Frühling,* which otherwise in its choice of subject and its composition presents many stumbling blocks to a modern point of view."

6. There was strong protest from certain quarters in Spain when Pérez Galdó was first proposed in 1913. This opposition seems to have died away when the proposal was renewed in the following year. In 1915 it is the committee itself that proposes him, on the assumption that his Spanish supporters have held back because of "the unrest or the uncertainty felt there, as in other places, as to the likelihood of the prize being awarded at all during the present war."

7. Österling, in *Nobel,* 105.

8. Esaias Tegnér, Jr. letter to Gottfrid Billing, 20 October 1916.

9. Grazia Deledda had already been proposed in 1913, when she was treated with appreciation but found to still "have time on her side."

Chapter 3. The Great Style

1. *Novalis's Schriften* (Works), ed. J. Minor, II (Jena, 1907), 116. *Peri Hypsos* of course acquired a special role in the greater expressiveness associated with romanticism, in which "the great style" became "the echo of a great soul" – which does not appear to have any relevance to our discussion.

2. Schück's advocacy, like that of Hjärne, is known from Österling; see *Nobel*, 105ff.

3. It is interesting to see how Karlfeldt places Hardy after George Meredith (who had been rejected by Wirsén). He did not think that Hardy would come to have the same "European standing" as Meredith: "His genius is of a coarser, less subtle variety."

4. The 1921 report, which was signed by Hjärne and characterized by the older type of evaluation, recognized Shaw's "remarkable satiric gift" but was repelled "by the often rather affected and paradoxical manner in which he makes use of that gift": his writings seemed "to lack the deeper and more serious content that in the midst of all the high-spirited joking one must still require in the work of a Nobel Prize-winner." H. G. Wells, whom Schück proposed and whom Hallström praised in his specialist report, is granted by Hjärne in the context to have "a lively imagination and great inventiveness," but Hjärne also thinks that Wells's "better things" lie fairly far back in time; there has recently been published "a most inferior history of the world." In Wells's disfavor reference is further made to the fact that he has "through composing and distributing appropriate writings actively participated in Lord Northcliff's provocative espionage propaganda behind the German front during the concluding phase of the world war." It would, says Hjärne, be compromising for the Academy "to bestow its highest honor on such a man in our days."

5. Österling in *Nobel*, 110.

6. The reference is to the tradition from Sterne's Tristram Shandy through Goethe and the Romantic variations of *Wilhelm Meister* and on to Thomas Mann and recent fiction.

7. See also Gösta Werner, *"Hugo von Hofmannsthal und der Nobelpreis"* (Hugo von Hofmannsthal and the Nobel Prize), *Hofmannsthal-Blätter*, no. 28, 1983. I cannot give much credence to the suggestion that Hallström's reservations in his four specialist reports were due to a "ihm selbst vielleicht wenig bewussten Konkurrenzsituation" ("a competitive situation that he was perhaps not very conscious of himself"). Karlfeldt – who could hardly be identified as a competitor – said he would always have to consider Hofmannsthal "a decadent, and more of an artiste than an independent creator and personality" (Karlfeldt letter to Tegnér, 5 November 1927). Werner seems to think that the Nobel Committee's discussion in 1927 put an end to the candidacy. Karlfeldt's 5 November 1927 letter shows, however, that the discussion was resumed "at the last moment"; for reasons just indicated he was "rather unhappy about the matter." On 11

November he also reported to Bildt that Hofmannsthal's candidacy came up "at the final weighing of our choices," but that no result was achieved.

Chapter 4. "Universal Interest"

1. Individual report appended to the 1932 report. Böök wished to "single out" Paul Ernst; see Chapter 6.

2. Hjalmar Hammarskjöld letter to Carl Bildt, February 1922.

3. That Claudel was proposed in 1937 was revealed by Strömberg, who thought, however, that it was the first occasion.

4. Österling argued, in vain, for a divided prize. See Chapter 8.

5. As reported by Strömberg in his introduction to the Buck volume of *Nobel Prize Library*.

6. See Strömberg's account of the press reaction, ibid.; he also mentions the proposal of *Gone with the Wind*.

7. Hallström, in his report, was prepared to "disregard the perpetually delicate question of idealism." It is clear that his colleagues on the committee had demanded sharper treatment. For him it was, in the end, decisive "that Hermann Hesse, in spite of his genuine and highly significant literary gifts, has not produced a sufficiently comprehensive and rich body of fiction to be recognized as a master of the genre, however masterful he may be purely as a stylist." Such a judgment was nonetheless given "most reluctantly . . . for his stature as a writer is more commanding, and his inspiration flows more immediately from his inner being, than we are accustomed to find in contemporary literature." *Der Steppenwolf* was "a work of genius . . . irrespective of the value of its message. . . . If we compare [this work] with the attempts, basically rather superficial and virtuosic, at a similar kind of boldness that we find in Hamsun (who is so admired in Germany), then Hesse's work has a power of emotion, a fire, an honesty, and a pathos to which nothing in the Norwegian is comparable."

Chapter 5. "Pioneers"

1. See Strömberg's introduction to the Mistral volume of *Nobel Prize Library*. The royal decree canceling the awards between 1940 and 1943 was made at the request of the selectors.

2. Anders Österling to Per Hallström, 2 August and 10 August 1945 (LUB).

3. See Strömberg.

4. Conversation with academy member Ulf Linde. It is very difficult to come to a reasonable view of the rightness of what Österling said on this point. In 1932 and 1938 – the years that saw the prize go to John Galsworthy and Pearl Buck – literary authors occupied seven of the eighteen places in the

academy, and in 1948 and 1956 – Eliot and Jiménez – they occupied eight and nine seats, respectively. More important, of course, are members' knowledge of and engagement in contemporary world literature, their affinities (often related to age), and the latitude of their critical judgment. From that point of view, the qualifications of some of the authors in the academy in the 1930s – Heidenstam, Lagerlöf, and Albert Engström – seem rather doubtful. None of them was at home in recent foreign literature, and the participation of Heidenstam and Lagerlöf in particular seemed like guest appearances; their correspondence was more often a means of receiving information than a vehicle for making contributions to decision making. None of these three, moreover, were open to the more exclusive recent literature. On the other hand, several of the postwar members from outside the literary field – such as Henry Olsson and Dag Hammarskjöld, not to mention a number of those still active – have contributed greatly to the literary side of the work. The combined variables – force of numbers, strength of engagement, affiliation to an age group, width of critical outlook – do nonetheless suggest that the literary authors had a decisive influence, which a look at the efforts of Siwertz, Hellström, and Gullberg confirms.

5. On Eliot, see Strömberg, who also cites Hallström's comment.

6. Dag Hammarskjöld to Sten Selander, 11 March and 15 October 1955 (KB). The reference is to Ezra Pound, who was an impossible choice on other grounds (see Chapter 7). Eyvind Johnson, in a radio presentation of Pasternak on 28 October 1958, was able to emphasize Pasternak's "pioneering contribution to poetry." In his letter of 11 March 1955, Hammarskjöld reviewed a series of candidates: Malraux ("the prose author I would most like to see rewarded"), Perse ("or Ungaretti!"), Frost, Pound, Edith Sitwell, Montale, Benn, O'Casey, a few prose writers whom, like Selander, he dismissed – including Feuchtwanger, Maugham, Huxley, Falkberget, Vesaas, Dinesen, Moravia, Forster ("who should have got the prize instead of, for example, Galsworthy"), Duhamel, Romains, Camus – and "the three main candidates:" "K," Laxness, and Sholokhov. Later Hammarskjöld letters to Selander added to the list Eugène Baie, who stood against two Icelandic candidates (22 September 1955) and Jiménez (15 October 1955).

7. Anders Österling letter to Bertil Malmberg, 21 October 1955 (KB).

8. Sartre had already said a few days before, in a letter of 14 October 1964, that he would not accept the prize he had heard rumored would be awarded to him.

9. The immediate cause of his exclamation was the "unnecessarily generous" selection of names under discussion, including Carossa, Benn, and Baie (who "would be a dull way of avoiding a choice between a humanist giant like Pidal and two great . . . poets").

10. Dag Hammerskjöld letter to Sten Selander, 22 September 1955.

11. Strömberg's introduction to the Perse volume of *Nobel Prize Library*.

12. Dag Hammarskjöld letter to Anders Österling (undated), copy in the Selander collection (KB). The letter comments on the choice of Jiménez, which had just been made.

13. Dag Hammarskjöld letter to Sten Selander, 22 September 1955.

14. Cf. Strömberg's account of Kjell A. Johansson's specialist report in his introduction to the Asturias volume of *Nobel Prize Library*.

15. See, however, Artur Lundkvist's remark that Borges's "political indiscretions . . . in a fascist direction" made him "unsuitable as a Nobel Prize winner on ethical and humane grounds" ("Nobelprisets vedersakare" ["The Adversaries of the Nobel Prize"], *Svenska Dagbladet*, 20 December 1979).

16. Strömberg's introduction to the Beckett volume of *Nobel Prize Library*.

17. Interviews with Artur Lundkvist in *Svenska Dagbladet* and *Dagens Nyheter*, 7 October 1983.

18. For Eyvind Johnson's views, see note 6. That Henry Olsson allowed "pioneers" and "pathfinders" a central role in his overall judgment is clear from the fact that those very words make up the title of his 1984 essay collection.

19. George Steiner's criticism on this point is taken up in Chapter 10.

20. *Die Literatur-Nobelpreisträger* (The Nobel Prize Winners in Literature), ed. G. Wilhelm (Düsseldorf, 1983), 12.

21. Dag Hammarskjöld letter to Sten Selander, 27 June 1956: "Benn does not at all convince me."

22. Evident in his letter to Erik Lindegren of 22 August 1966 (see Chapter 8).

23. Gierow was citing and agreeing with one of Aleixandre's "poetic allies," Luis Cernuda.

Chapter 6. "A Pragmatic Attitude"

1. Individual memo with reference to the report of 1913. Hallström was also sympathetic to the pragmatic line of reasoning. He wrote to Tegnér on 1 November 1913: "What Nobel in his innocence believed that we could do each year – present a new genius to the world – is something we are now free to do, for once" (LUB).

2. Dag Hammarskjöld letters to Sten Selander, 11 and 12 March 1955 (KB).

3. Karl Ragnar Geirow's speech at the Nobel Festival, 1969.

4. The previous scattered instances of efforts made in a pragmatic spirit had also been noticed in the French press. When Agnon received the prize in

1966, *Le Nouvel Observateur* (26 October 1966) illustrated how the Nobel judges chose to draw attention to works that had been previously ignored by referring to Laxness, Andrić, and Seferis.

Chapter 7. "Political Integrity"

1. Lars Gyllensten, "On Pasternak's Nobel Prize," *Rysk Kulturrevy,* no. 4 (1981). The title of this chapter is taken from his article.

2. Billing's opinion (but not Wirsén's reply) is given by Österling in *Nobel,* 94. In a letter to Billing on 10 July, Wirsén had exclaimed: "May the Nobel Prize never become a political price tag!" He added (with the proposal of a shared prize between two Norwegians in mind), "The result, besides, would be totally uncertain."

3. Ingmar Björkstén, interview with Lars Gyllensten, "Nur sehen, was man sehen will?" (Only Seeing What You Want to See?), *Titel,* no. 4 (1984).

4. Clements seemed to have inside knowledge – until one discovered that his unacknowledged source was Österling's account.

5. Girolamo Ramunni, "Prix Nobel: le poids des critères politiques," *La Recherche,* no. 148, October 1983. The prize to Bjørnson was similarly, in Ramunni's eyes, "an exceptional reward" for a last-minute political conversion in favor of the union between Sweden and Norway that was coming to a crisis. (He also believed that Ibsen never received a prize because his son, a Norwegian delegate, opposed the Swedish lack of accommodation.) The source material and correspondence confirm that this argument is nonsensical.

6. The strength of feeling against Gorky shown by several members in 1928 suggests more than literary objections. The conservative Fredrik Böök wrote to Tegnér on 25 October that for his part he was "not willing to vote for Gorky," and that it pleased him "enormously to hear that all the members from Lund [there were three] are agreed on that point" (LUB).

7. Ramunni, "Prix Nobel."

8. Instead, the Nobel Committee interpreted the Italian proposal as "a representative national opinion," something "not without significance" in comparison with other proposals originating "outside the candidate's country." It was regarded as a sign of strength if a candidate had support in his own country.

9. Björkstén, *Titel,* no. 4 (1984).

10. *Nobel,* 115. Österling's somewhat unfortunate turn of phrase was sharpened by Clements's: "The world watched a dogged little Finland fighting for its national life along the Mannerheim Line. It was a most fitting moment to award the prize to Frans Eemil Sillanpää, whose works incarnated the soul of this land resisting invasion and even genocide."

11. The result of the voting on 26 October 1939 was reported by Hallström in a letter to committee member Tor Andræ on the following day (UUB). A letter from Torsten Fogelqvist to Martin Lamm provides an interesting complement; it lacks a date, but from the context it would appear to have been written in late October or early November (Swedish Academy archives). Fogelqvist–who had "always insisted that a prize should go to *Silja* (The Maid Silja) (Sillanpää's best-known work) but had so far regarded a serious move in that direction as hopeless and had no wish to "throw away" his vote–now in spite of everything reviewed the possibilities for the 1939 prize and arrived, on the basis of a slightly different calculation, at the same result as here. Hesse could scarcely achieve a majority, and the result would then be that Sillanpää got "nine votes, but with the chance of more." In the same context Fogelqvist mentioned the "political" reasons that had been offered earlier against a (nonshared) prize to Sillanpää, that is, that it "would offend the Swedish-speaking part of Finland," and concluded that such a reason "has at present lost all its weight and relevance." One political aspect of this prize could therefore, paradoxically, lie in the possibility that the menacing situation *eliminated* a political obstacle. Fogelqvist argued that a prize to Sillanpää "should now meet with a strong response both in Finland and in Scandinavia generally," yet he was also aware of the fact that such considerations were not compatible with the integrity of the academy; this argument would be "wrong in the eyes of those who, like Brother Per [Hallström], regard unpopularity as a kind of halo and grand indifference to general opinion as the finest of the Academy's virtues."

Beyond this passage it is not possible to see any mention in the documentation of the 1939 Finnish situation. But when the prize was presented at a ceremony on 14 December, it had gained a new significance because of the Soviet attack, and Hallström's words about the prize winner and his people had acquired a distinct political accent: "At present it is something by no means insignificant that the whole world associates with the name of the Finnish people. Still as simple as you have seen them, they are now standing in the storm of the fateful powers, heroically great in their inflexible courage, their obedience to duty to the uttermost, to death, and without trembling in the face of death. In our thanks for what you have given, our thoughts go further, in admiration and high emotion, to your people."

12. Dag Hammarskjöld letter to Sten Selander, 12 May 1955 (KB).

13. See Strömberg's introduction to the Churchill volume of *Nobel Prize Library*.

14. 13 May 1948 and 2 August 1948 (KB). Strömberg gives an account of Ahnlund's report of 1948 as well as one by Hallström from two years previously.

15. In the wording of the award, however, Churchill's literary qualifications were mentioned first: "for his mastery of historical and

biographical description as well as for brilliant oratory in defending exalted human values."

16. Österling transfers the quoted words from his remarks to the committee over into his speech. His broadcast also refers to the 1952 novel as a "masterpiece."

17. According to Dag Hammarskjöld's letter to Sten Selander, 22 September 1955.

18. See also Strömberg's account of the press reception in the Laxness volume of *Nobel Prize Library*.

19. Dag Hammarskjöld letter to Sten Selander, 11 March 1955; but Hammarskjöld also had strong reservations (see the following).

20. Dag Hammarskjöld to Anders Österling, 23 December 1955. A copy sent on the same day to Sten Selander is in KB.

21. Hammarskjöld took pains to point out that he intended to speak to his contacts in the State Department not in his capacity as general secretary of the United Nations but at the request of the Swedish Academy; it was also a formal commission of this kind that Österling alluded to in his 1959 article.

22. Dag Hammarskjöld letter to Pär Lagerkvist, 24 July 1959 (KB).

23. Karl Vennberg in *Aftonbladet*, 10 December 1979, and *Svenska Dagbladet*, 31 December 1979; Artur Lundkvist in *Svenska Dagbladet*, 9 January 1980.

24. Lars Gyllensten, "Några anteckningar om Pasternaks Nobelpris 1958" ("Some Notes on Pasternak's Nobel Prize in 1958"), *Artes*, no. 1 (1983). Gyllensten revealed that Pasternak's nomination was taken up again in 1957-58.

25. We can find an account of the specialist report by Strömberg in his introduction to the Pasternak volume of *Nobel Prize Library*.

26. Cf. Gyllensten's disavowal in "Some Notes on Pasternak's Nobel Prize." Österling said in *Minnets vägar* (Paths of Memory) (Stockholm, 1967), "The decision was not accompanied by any ulterior political motives whatsoever" (p. 241).

27. Jean-Paul Sartre, press statement, 22 October 1964.

28. Karl Ragnar Gierow letters to Erik Lindegren, 9 October 1964, and Bo Bergman, 2 October 1965 (KB).

29. Gunnar Jarring, *Utan glasnost och perestrojka: Memoarer 1964-73* (Without Glasnost and Perestroika, Memoirs 1964-73) (Stockholm, 1989), 192ff. In a debate in *Svenska Dagbladet* (4 and 5 October 1989) between the journalist Per Egil Hegge (4 October) and Jarring (5 October), Hegge sharply criticized the former Swedish ambassador to Moscow for having "twice, in 1965 and in 1970, made strenuous efforts to influence the Swedish Academy's choice of the winner of the Nobel Prize in Literature – entirely with regard to relations between Sweden and the Soviet Union." The accusation in connection with the 1965 prize may deserve some comment in

the present discussion. In *Utan glasnost och perestrojka,* Jarring recounts a conversation he had with Österling in December 1964 in which he expressed reservations about Österling's idea of Konstantin Paustovsky as a candidate: "I believed that a Nobel Prize to Paustovsky, bypassing Sholokhov, would hardly meet with appreciation in the Soviet Union. It would only give rise to new bitterness at a time when people were in the process of forgetting about the affront that the prize to Pasternak had been regarded as implying" (p. 185). The Swedish ambassador, concluded Hegge, was "actively obstructing" a prize to Paustovsky. He quoted Jarring: "Österling said he would think it over again and read Sholokhov's literary works"–to which Hegge added, "In the following year, 1965, Sholokhov got the prize." Hegge further revealed the cost of the maneuver: for the Russian intellectuals who had a high regard for Paustovsky–not for Sholokhov–the matter was "a body blow to their respect for Sweden." Jarring himself was more sceptical on the question of his own influence; the academy, as he saw it, had "always been impervious to persuasion" (*Svenska Dagbladet,* 5 October 1989).

The perspective within which these comments on the 1965 choice were made is much too narrow. As we have seen, Sholokhov was a serious competitor to Pasternak as early as 1947, and after the choice of Pasternak in 1958 he simply had to bide his time. In 1964, it will be recalled, he was assessed alongside Sartre. It is therefore hardly a case of a last-minute diplomatic intervention securing the prize for Sholokhov. On the contrary, the decision was a result of many years of deliberation. The idea that it was only after the conversation with Jarring in December 1964 that Österling sat down and read Sholokhov is absurd. Hegge's quotation is also tendentious: Jarring wrote not "read" but "reread Sholokhov's literary works." But even correctly rendered the quotation is misleading. The fact is that Österling's report several months before had given evidence of thorough study. On the contrary, what Jarring in effect revealed was Österling's own uncertainty. Not that Österling ought to have argued against Sholokhov in 1965. But he has also considered Paustovsky in that context and tried to find out to what extent Paustovsky had a position as delicate as Pasternak's had once been. The not-so-reassuring response on that point was naturally a factor in Österling's evaluation. But this does not mean that Paustovsky was ever a serious competitor. In the course of the discussion over the previous years, Sholokhov's position was too well established for that to happen. Hegge's thesis that Jarring influenced the 1965 choice can be totally dismissed.

The private contacts that took place in both these cases–in the history of the prize they can be seen to be exceptions–can be questioned, however, on point of principle. Neither the Nobel Committee nor the academy should use diplomats in their investigations; the risks to the integrity of the prize are much too great. But as we have seen, the reason for such contacts being made was unease over the dangers to which a potential prize winner might be exposed. That the Swedish Academy–as Hegge insinuated–should have allowed the literature prize to become involved in diplomatic speculation is in conflict both with the facts of the case and with the spirit of all the documented evidence we have of the academy's work with the prize.

30. See Björkstén, *Titel*, no. 4 (1984).

31. Writing from the Frankfurt Book Fair, and suggesting the contrast between misinformed commercialism and the high-brow choice of winner, Bondy gives his version of the reaction from the world of publishing: "Eine politische Sache. Völlig klar" (A Political Matter. Quite Clear). Bondy found the surprise of the professionals more astonishing than the prize itself.

32. In recent practice, the reports of the committee members, with each member's preferred ranking of the final candidates, are sent out to the members of the academy in May. The committee had therefore made up its mind before the summer of 1980.

33. As quoted in *Dagens Nyheter*, 21 July 1984.

34. (The sentence, "But Seifert has never been inoffensive," was missing from the newspaper quotation.) *Le Soir* understood the press release to be "the jury's verdict," which is misleading. The report is in essentials identical to Gyllensten's speech to the prize winner, and therefore the work of the permanent secretary, yet at the same time it was presented as reflecting the opinion of the academy.

35. *Östgöta Correspondenten*, 12 October 1984.

Chapter 8. *"Shared Prizes: A Mutual Fellowship"*

1. A correction followed in the same paper on 13 June 1984.

2. Selma Lagerlöf letter to Erik Axel Karlfeldt, 2 November 1917. The words appear in a special context, a plea for Brandes instead of the two Danish writers, but the accompanying phrase "as always" makes it clear that Lagerlöf was generally opposed to divided prizes.

3. Knut Ahnlund, *Diktarliv i Norden* (Writers' Life in the North) (Uppsala, 1981), 259 ff.

4. According to Bengt Holmqvist in *Dagens Nyheter*, 23 November 1977.

5. This criticism met with the approval of both Karl Vennberg (*Aftonbladet*, 10 December 1979) and Tobias Berggren (*Expressen*, 10 December 1979).

Chapter 9. *"Intended for the Literature of the Whole World"*

1. Ingmar Björkstén, interview with Lars Gyllensten, *Titel*, no. 4 (1984) ("man versuche jedoch eine globale Verbreitung zu erreichen" ["we must still try to reach a global distribution"]). Cf. Gyllensten in *The Nobel Prize in Literature* (Stockholm, 1978), 13.

2. See also Lundkvist's statement in an interview in *Aftonbladet* (10 December 1970): "There is a kind of rotation system whereby the same country should not recur too often."

A question already apparent in connection with the strong Scandinavian representation during the neutrality policy of the 1910s is how often a Swedish or Scandinavian name may be allowed to emerge from the process. One answer is to be found in a speech by Tegnér in 1900: he thought that it would be "only as an exception" that a Scandinavian author would be worthy of the award, since "our northern nations are so small." He saw in this fact "a safeguard against partisanship," a safeguard that "the greater nations lack." Another answer was given by Heidenstam when in 1913 he recalled that the Nobel Prize was nonetheless a Scandinavian award (letter to Per Hallström, 8 April 1913).

A more recent attitude is reflected in Gyllensten's objection to the idea, raised in a newspaper debate, that Swedes should be more or less excluded:

> Oddly enough, such claims are made only concerning the literature prize. To exclude Swedes or Scandinavians, however, would be in violation of the statutes. In regard to the prizes hitherto awarded to Swedes, it can be said that in all cases the prize winners were nominated by proposers outside Sweden, most of them over a period of many years and from several quarters. Naturally, they themselves did not take part in the work of assessment when their candidacies were being dealt with (*The Nobel Prize in Literature*, 14).

A certain disagreement with such a line of thought can be detected in Lundkvist's remark in an interview that the Nobel Prize should not be given to a Swede (*Aftonbladet*, 10 December 1970; see also *Dagens Nyheter*, 30 December 1984).

3. Selma Lagerlöf to Per Hallström, 12 February 1940 (LUB). The name of Pearl Buck's candidate, first proposed in 1938, was revealed by Strömberg in the Kawabata volume of *Nobel Prize Library*. The letter also names several of the 1940 candidates in addition to "that Chinese writer"; Lagerlöf pities the secretary "for once more having to consider Jensen, Falkberget, and Palamas."

4. See Strömberg's introduction to the Kawabata volume of *Nobel Prize Library*.

5. Artur Lundkvist interview in the Czech press, cited in *Dagens Nyheter*, 30 December 1984. His other favorites for the prize were André Brink and Claude Simon.

6. Other names put forward by *Asiaweek* were Nick Joaquin and F. Sionil José from the Philippines, Kenzaburo Oë from Japan, Ding Ling from China, Kim Tong Ni from South Korea, and the deceased Faiz Ahmed Faiz from Pakistan. The unsigned article was by Isabella Wai.

7. *Artes,* no. 4 (1984) includes translations by Sabur, Bayyāti, Sayyāb, and Bachir Hadj Ali.

8. See also Strömberg's introduction to the Kawabata volume of *Nobel Prize Library.* In fact, the specialist support was greater than Strömberg suggests, a fact that unfortunately cannot at present be illustrated.

9. David Wallechinsky and Irving Wallace, *The People's Almanac* (New York, 1975), 1104.

10. Tagore was assessed, as we have seen, on the basis of his own translation of his work into English, which, it was stressed, gave the translation the character of an original work. Hebrew–Agnon's language–also belongs to a European perspective.

11. Strömberg's introduction to the Asturias volume of *Nobel Prize Library.*

12. In connection with such sensational statements by Lundkvist, it should be mentioned that the material gives no support to the widespread notion that he had a decisive influence on a line of choices and rejections in the last two decades.

13. *New York Times Book Review,* 8 December 1968.

Chapter 10. *"A Fairly Decent Testimonial"*

1. An overview of the press reception may be found in Gunnar Ahlström and Kjell Strömberg's introductions in the series *Nobel Prize Library.*

2. William F. Lamont, "The Nobel Prizes in Literature," *Books Abroad* 25 (Winter 1951).

3. Österling, "Nu gäller det nobelprisen" ("On the Subject of the Nobel Prizes"), *Stockholms-Tidningen,* 2 March 1951.

4. Theodore Ziolkowski, "German Literature and the Prize," *Books Abroad* 41 (Nobel Prize Symposium) (1967). Ziolkowski has misquoted Wirsén, as reported by Österling (*Nobel,* 99): "Germany has not had a greater literary genius since Goethe." The word used in the 1910 report was *artist.* In what follows, references to the year 1967 are to this symposium. Symposium articles in addition to Ziolkowski's include: Gene J. Barberet, "France and Belgium"; Richard B. Vowles, "Twelve Northern Authors"; Manuel Durán and Michael Nimetz, "Spain and Spanish America"; Robert Vlach and Boris Filipoff, "The Slavic Awards and Some Candidates"; Olga Ragusa, "Carducci, Deledda, Pirandello, Quasimodo"; Robert E. Spiller, "English, Anglo-Irish, and American Literature"; Albert Howard Carter, "Rabindranath Tagore"; John E. Rexine, "Seferis"; and Eisig Silberschlag, "Four Hebrew Writers." Other articles are devoted to, among other subjects, the potential of African, Arabic, Chinese, Indonesian, and Japanese literature.

5. Steiner includes Mommsen, "a great historian and epigrapher of ancient Rome," among the "illustrious recipients" whose work fell "outside normal definitions of literature." He ignores the fact that the statutes stipulate that the committee consider "not only belles-lettres, but also other writings which, by virtue of their form and style, possess literary value" (paragraph 2).

6. According to Herbert Howarth, who assisted Robert E. Spiller in his 1967 Nobel symposium article, "English, Anglo-Irish, and American Literature," and George Steiner, "The Scandal of the Nobel Prize," *New York Times Book Review,* 30 September 1984.

7. Alfred Neumeyer, as quoted in "What's Wrong with the Nobel Prize?" *Books Abroad,* Spring 1951. That Maeterlinck was also important in the development of modern poetry is something I have tried to show in *Att översätta själen, En huvudlinje i modern poesi från Baudelaire till surrealism* (To Translate the Soul: A Principal Line of Development in Modern Poetry from Baudelaire to Surrealism) (Stockholm, 1975), chap. 6.

8. See, however, the information given by Österling (*Nobel,* 99) on the proposal made (after the deadline) in 1911 by the future Archbishop Nathan Söderblom in favor of a prize to Strindberg.

9. A unique judgment was made in Lamont's 1951 survey: on the assumption that the prize was intended for contemporary authors, it dismissed candidates whose most important work was more than a decade old. The authors thus excluded automatically included Meredith, Swinburne, Strindberg, Ibsen, Tolstoy, and Zola. (The argument does not hold for Strindberg, though, for his most important output, from an international point of view, occurred during the first years of the new century.)

10. The 1951 survey, however, found him to be "worthy."

11. The absence of Brandes from the Nobel list has been noted by, among others, Constant Burniaux and Renée Lang (1951).

12. Although Spiller attempted to save the honor of Pearl Buck; *The Good Earth* was "a good novel then, it is still a good novel."

13. The 1951 survey noted the absence of them all except for Freud (and, of course, Hesse, who was rewarded in 1946). Freud also does not appear in the 1967 list of omissions. He is, on the other hand, named by Ludwig Marcuse in "What's Wrong with the Nobel Prize?" (*Books Abroad,* Spring 1951), along with Wilhelm Dilthey and Georg Simmel, as a more representative candidate in 1908, Eucken's year. To Steiner, who repeats most of the names, Freud has become a figure whose prose "honors the German language," but who was nominated "in vain, of course."

14. Spiller takes it for granted in 1967 that Conrad's "publications of 1902 and 1903 must have surely been on the early Nobel list of possibilities." In fact, not a single legitimate proposal on Conrad's behalf came from the Anglo-American world before the writer's death in 1924.

15. Steiner in particular lists omissions on the basis of these chronological impossibilities. In addition to the omissions of Kafka and Proust, he also draws attention to the academy's "dismal" record on the poets: "no Rilke," "no Cavafy," "no Mandelstam," "no García Lorca," "no Fernando Pessoa." These thinly supported accusations were repeated by some of the participants in the 1988 symposium: for instance, Durán's reprimand on behalf of Kafka, Proust, and García Lorca, and Reis's criticisms on the subject of Pessoa.

16. Österling, "Nu gäller det nobelprisen."

17. Thomas R. Edwards, "The Innocent" (review of Jackson J. Benson, *The True Adventures of John Steinbeck, Writer*), *New York Review of Books,* 16 February 1984.

18. "The Nobel Prizes in Literature, 1967-87: A Symposium," *World Literature Today,* Spring 1988. In addition to Ivar Ivask's introduction, the articles included the following: John L. Brown, "Twenty Years and Two Laureates: Francophone Nobel Prizes, 1967-87"; E. J. Czerwinski, "For Whom the Nobel Tolls: The Nationless"; Manuel Durán, "The Nobel Prize and Writers in the Hispanic World: A Continuing Story"; Yoshio Iwamoto, "The Nobel Prize in Literature, 1967-87: A Japanese View"; Bernth Lindfors, "Africa and the Nobel Prize"; William Pratt, "Missing the Masters: Nobel Literary Prizes in English, 1967-87"; Gila Ramras-Rauch, "The Nobel Prize: The Jewish/Hebraic Aspect"; George C. Schoolfield, "Might-Have-Beens: The North and the Nobel Prize, 1967-87"; A. Leslie Willson, "The German Quandary." In addition, Arabic literature in relation to the Nobel Prize was surveyed by Roger Allen, who concluded with a plea for the writer who in fact came to be chosen a few months later; and two views of "might-have-beens" are included – in Indian literatures (Syed Amanuddin) and in Luso-Brasilian writing (Ricardo Reis).

A special problem, almost ignored in previous criticism, was formulated in the 1988 symposium by E. J. Czerwinski in his plea for the "nationless." He had in mind chiefly those authors in the Soviet Union and in the Soviet bloc "whose works cannot be considered simply because, for various reasons, they cannot be published in their respective countries." The question could have wide ramifications. Those dissidents and authors belonging to minority groups who have been confined to an underground literary life undoubtedly pose an awkward problem.

19. Jakobsen in a letter to his French translator, Jean-Pierre Faye, cited by Faye in an article on Seifert in *Le Matin,* 12 October 1984.

20. In 1967 both Brecht and Broch were included among the "unforgivable omissions" in German-language literature (Ziolkowski; for Broch, see below); Malraux "is at present the highest contender in France" (Barberet), and Pound and Stevens – but not Auden – were modestly listed in a catalog of reasonable alternatives (Spiller). Kazantzakis was named

alongside Palamas, Cavafy, and Sikelianos as a worthy candidate from a neglected literature (John E. Rexine). The 1967 Nobel Prize symposium also gave us the deceased Robert Vlach's 1965 wish, speaking for all Slavonic authors, that Anna Akhmatova should have received a prize. We find no plea for Moravia or Greene in this symposium, nor any special attention to Nabokov, Powys, Grass, Celan, or Borges. In 1966 Fleming picked out from those authors previously listed only Akhmatova, Malraux, and Pound among "the nonwinners." It was not until 1984 that all of these writers appeared to be obvious winners. Celan's poetry had by then reached the point of being "the profoundest, the most innovative lyric poetry in Western literature in our time" (Steiner). Another potential candidate, Carlo Emilio Gadda, "one of the most original and inventive writers of fiction in this century" (Steiner again) was considered in 1967, rather less dramatically, alongside Ricardo Baccheli as an author who "could be proposed" but for whom the deadline was rather close (Olga Ragusa; Gadda died in 1973). The spokesmen from the 1988 symposium in *World Literature Today* were Ivar Ivask and (on the subject of Catalan writing) Manuel Durán. We may note that the unique position given to Celan by Steiner was exchanged for a less prominent position in the eyes of the 1988 judges: Celan and Peter Huchel were named as two recently deceased authors who "might have had the distinction of originality, mastery of form, and ideal, human-focused content deserving of Nobel recognition" (A. Leslie Willson).

21. *New York Review of Books,* 28 March 1985, 26. Bayley pointed out that even in 1985 it was still permissible in academic circles to be scarcely acquainted with the work of Powys.

22. Auden was supported by Lindegren (27 May 1963), who had not at that point completed his report (Erik Lindegren letter to Anders Österling [KB, Lindegren collection]); Auden was "undoubtedly the greatest English poet today," though "not fully as great as Yeats or Eliot." In another letter to Österling (7 October 1963 [KB]), Lindegren also agreed with Österling's "recommendation" in his "brilliant statement." At the same time (27 May) he said, "There are far too few translations into Swedish for him to be a serious contender for the Nobel Prize this year." He was planning a joint translation project in order to "prepare for a favorable reception of Auden's possible Nobel Prize." Auden appeared in further discussion, but Lindegren himself did not include him among his three names in 1965 (Erik Lindegren letter to Anders Österling, 9 September 1965 [copy in KB]).

23. See Strömberg's introduction to the Beckett volume of *Nobel Prize Library.* Correspondence now accessible shows support from, among others, Hammarskjöld and Selander from 1955 onward–for example, Dag Hammarskjöld letter to Sten Selander, 31 July 1956 (KB): "It would be a disturbing misjudgment to neglect Malraux in favor of Camus."

24. *Stockholms-Tidningen,* 11 January 1961, and 24 August 1965. Disappointment in Moravia's 1960 study in disgust, the "schematic and stillborn" novel *La Noia,* is apparent in *Stockholms-Tidningen* (11 January 1963). Hammarskjöld was among those with reservations: "As to Moravia, I stick to my opinion that it is only with a charitable assessment that he can come up to the standard, and in any case he ought to wait. There is in him, besides, an unpleasant feature that I have already touched on in my remarks to the academy and that Eyvind Johnson has subsequently and quite rightly characterized with the word 'voyeur'" (Dag Hammarskjöld letter to Pär Lagerkvist, 24 July 1959 [KB]).

25. Four of the five suggestions were, as we shall see, highly relevant; the fifth, which recommended a collective award in certain situations, was incompatible with the Nobel will and statutes.

26. The reference here is to Mittag-Leffler's impression (as passed on by Brandes) of Nobel's view, which is discussed in the introduction to this book.

27. *Nobel,* 80.

28. Vlach was giving a tactful polemic against the wording of Pasternak's prize: "[his achievement] in the field of the great Russian *epic* tradition" (emphasis added).

29. The reasons given in the petition for advancing poets concur with the pragmatic line of argument: the poet is not only "the purest and most sensitive and subtle commentator on life" but is also "the least rewarded. . . . The publishers help the novelists, the theaters help the dramatists, [but] the poet lacks all but an odd quixotic publisher for escort to his audience."

30. William Riggan, "The Swedish Academy and the Nobel Prize in Literature," *World Literature Today* 55 (1981), 405. In the 1988 symposium Pratt concurred with Riggan's view, especially when he cited Faulkner's new position after the prize (which we saw cited by Spiller earlier in this chapter).

31. Steiner seemed to immediately discard this idea, however, in order to argue in favor of prizes to Mailer, Borges, and other authors of "global renown."

32. Compare Milan Kundera's regretful remark in his article "A Little History Lesson" (*New York Review of Books* [22 November 1984]) to the effect that the prize reached Seifert fifteen years too late – a statement that specifically refers to 1968.

INDEX

and the assessment of Nobel
awards, 160
and Eurocentrism, 135-36
as a Nobel Academy member, 82
as Nobel Committee chairman, 82
as permanent secretary, 82
and pioneers, 78-79, 81, 83, 85
and political integrity, 101, 111,
112, 113-14, 115, 116
and the selection process, 88
and the sharing of prizes, 126, 127,
128
*See also name of specific
recipient/nominee*
Gitanjali [Tagore], 28, 136
Gjellerup, Karl, 33, 34-35, 123, 124,
125, 149
Das Glasperlenspiel [The Glass Bead
Game, Hesse], 74
Goethe, Johann W. von, 14-15, 28-29,
35, 39-40, 46, 53, 70-71, 148
The Golden Bough [Frazer], 67
Golding, William, 82, 96, 97, 155, 164
Goncourt Academy/Prize, 63, 145,
152
Gone with the Wind [Mitchell], 64-65
The Good Earth [Buck], 64
Gorky, Maxim, 50-51, 101, 151
Government. *See* Political integrity
Grace, 15, 49-50
Grass, Günter, 83, 96, 159
Great masters, 14-15, 166
"Great style"
and the assessment of Nobel
awards, 150
and the avant-garde, 53
and chance, 43-44
and clarity, 45, 46, 52-53, 54-55
and classicism, 40, 42, 49, 51, 52, 61
and completeness, 47-48, 52-53
and determinism, 42-43
emergence as a criterion of, 39-40
and eroticism/sensualism, 56
and grace, 49-50
and heroism, 47
and humanism/humanity, 40, 41-
42, 43, 44-46, 49
and idealism, 39-48, 51, 56, 150
and ideas, 44-45

and literary neutralism, 42
and materialism, 44-45, 52
and moderation, 45, 46, 49, 52-53
and morality, 40
and naturalness, 41, 49, 51, 55
and neoclassicism, 39-40, 48, 50, 53
and nobility, 41
and objectivity, 41, 49
and plasticity, 45, 46, 47-48, 52-53,
54
and poetry, 53-56, 57
and political integrity, 40, 42, 50,
51
and psychological analysis, 45, 50,
53
and realism/reality, 39, 41, 43-44,
51, 52, 53, 54, 61
and religion, 40, 42, 54-55
and repose, 45, 46, 52-53
and romanticism, 51
and simplicity, 47-48, 49, 54, 55
and symbolism, 53-56
and translations, 54
and universal interest, 48, 53, 61,
65-66, 69
See also name of specific person
Greek antiquity. *See* Classicism
Greek literature [modern], 158
Greene, Graham, 96, 159, 160-61
Gripenberg, Bertel, 37-38, 124
Guillén, Jorge, 77-78, 156
Guimerá, Angel, 38, 124
Gullberg, Hjalmar, 74, 77, 78, 131, 139
Gyllensten, Lars
and the assessment of Nobel
awards, 162, 164, 166-67
and Eurocentrism, 132, 133, 134,
138, 140, 141-42, 143-44
and humanism/humanity, 164
as a Nobel Academy member, 82
and pioneers, 82, 83-84
and political integrity, 99-100, 101,
117, 118
and a pragmatic attitude, 87, 88,
89, 94, 95, 166-67
writings of, 3

Hallström, Per

THE AUTHOR

Kjell Espmark, born in 1930, is a poet, a novelist, and a literary historian. He has published nine collections of poetry; two selections in English are to be found in his *Béla Bartók against the Third Reich* (1985) and in *Four Swedish Poets* (1990), both in Robin Fulton's translation. Espmark has also published the first two volumes of a series of novels (his "Subhuman Comedy"); the first, *Oblivion,* has recently appeared in French. His seven books of literary criticism include studies of Artur Lundkvist, Harry Martinson, Tomas Tranströmer, and the tradition from Baudelaire (*Translating the Soul*). A professor of comparative literature at Stockholm University, Espmark became a member of the Swedish Academy in 1981, and the chairman of its Nobel Committee in 1988. He is the recipient of numerous literary prizes, including the Schück Prize for literary criticism and the Bellman Prize for poetry. *The Nobel Prize in Literature* was first published in 1986 and appears in French and German translations; a Chinese translation is forthcoming.